Man Walks Into A Bar

THE ULTIMATE COLLECTION
OF JOKES AND ONE-LINERS

STEPHEN ARNOTT & MIKE HASKINS

MARKS &
SPENCER

MAN WALKS INTO A BAR

CONTENTS

'I thought today I'd start by singing one of Irving Berlin's songs. But then I thought why should I? He never sings any of mine.'

Spike Milligan

✺ ACCIDENTS

✳ A doctor examines a cowboy with back problems and asks if he's had any recent accidents. 'Nope,' replies the cowboy. 'That's odd,' says the doctor, 'I thought a cowboy's job was pretty dangerous.' 'It sure is,' replies the cowboy. 'Last week I was kicked by a mule, thrown by a mustang, and bit by a snake.' 'And you don't call those accidents?' asks the doctor. 'No, sir,' replies the cowboy, 'those varmints done it on purpose.'

✳ A man goes into a pub and admires the stuffed lion's head mounted above the bar. 'What a great trophy,' says the man to the barman. 'I wouldn't call it great,' replies the barman. 'That damn lion killed my wife.' 'My God,' says the man, 'were you on safari?' 'No,' replies the barman. 'It fell on her head.'

✳ A man is laying carpet in an old lady's home. When he's finished he looks around for his pack of cigarettes but as he does so he notices a lump in the middle of the carpet. 'Damn it,' he says to himself. 'I must have dropped my cigarettes on the floor and carpeted over them. I know, I'll whack the pack with my hammer and flatten it out.' So he gets out his hammer and beats the bump flat. Just at that moment the old lady walks in with his cigarettes in her hand. 'Here,' she says. 'You must have left these in the kitchen. Now if only I could find my pet gerbil…'

✳ A man walked into a bar and went 'Aaaagh!' It was an iron bar.

✳ A young man is trying out his new sports car on a quiet country lane. There's no traffic about so he risks taking it up to 70 mph, then 80, and then 90. He turns a corner and sees two farmers standing in the middle of the road chatting. The man wrenches the wheel sideways, the car shoots up an embankment, flies into the air, and crashes in the middle of an adjacent field. One of the farmers turns to the other and says, 'That was lucky. I reckon we got out of that field in the nick o' time.'

✳ An Essex girl is involved in a bad traffic accident. A paramedic rushes to her aid. 'Whereabouts are you bleeding from?' he asks. 'Well,' says the girl, 'since you ask, bleeding Romford.'

✳ Did you hear about the guy who lost his left arm and left leg in a car accident? He's all right now.

✳ Did you hear about the man who fell into the lens-grinding machine? He made a spectacle of himself.

✳ Harry heard that most accidents happen within two miles of home, so he moved.

✳ I lost my left hand in an accident a few years ago. It drives my girlfriend mad. She's a palm reader and wants to know what happens next.

✳ Ten per cent of all accidents on the road are caused by people who have been drinking. So ninety per cent of accidents are due to people who are stone cold sober.

✳ Most accidents happen at home – and most men have to eat them.

✳ Yesterday I saw a car parked outside a hospital with a boot dangling off the front bumper. 'Has there been a wedding?' I asked a doctor. 'No,' he replied. 'There's been some dangerous driving.'

🐦 AGE: MIDDLE

✳ 'Middle age is when your age starts to show around your middle.' *Bob Hope*

✳ 'She said she was approaching forty – I couldn't help wondering from what direction.' *Bob Hope*

✳ After forty-five your 'get up and go' gets up and goes.

✳ Maybe it's true that life begins at forty. But everything else starts to wear out, fall out, or spread out.

✳ The good news about being middle-aged is that the glass is still half-full. The bad news is that pretty soon your teeth will be floating in it.

✳ Harry has invented a bra for middle-aged women. He calls it the 'sheep dog' because it rounds them up and points them in the right direction.

✳ She's not pushing forty – she's clinging on to it for dear life.

✳ The thing about being a middle-aged woman is that when you go for a mammogram, you realise it's the only time someone's ever going to ask you to appear topless in a film.

✳ Middle age is when broadness of the mind and narrowness of the waist change places.

✳ Middle age is when you choose a cereal because of its fibre content, not the free toy.

✳ Thirty is a nice age for a woman, especially if she happens to be forty.

🍎AGE: OLD

✳ 'Everything that goes up must come down. But there comes a time when not everything that's down can come up.' *George Burns*

✳ 'How young can you die of old age?' *Steven Wright*

✳ 'If you live to the age of a hundred you have it made because very few people die past the age of a hundred.' *George Burns*

✳ 'I'm so old they've cancelled my blood type.' *Bob Hope*

✳ 'In my lifetime I saw the Berlin Wall come and I saw it go. George Burns can say the same thing about the Ice Age.' *Bob Hope*

✳ 'I've got to watch myself these days. It's too exciting watching anyone else.' *Bob Hope*

✳ Age is a very high price to pay for maturity.

'Middle age is when you go to bed at night and hope you feel better in the morning. Old age is when you go to bed at night and hope you wake up in the morning.' *Groucho Marx*

✳ 'Three things happen when you get to my age. First your memory starts to go and I've forgotten the other two.' *Denis Healey*

✳ A doctor in an old people's home is discussing an elderly resident with one of the orderlies. 'I'm worried about Mister Jones,' says the doctor. 'He claims that when he goes to the bathroom God switches on the light for him, then switches it off again when he's finished. Do you think he's going senile?' 'Nah,' says the orderly. 'He's just been peeing in the fridge again.'

✳ A group of OAPs is on a bus trip to the seaside when one of the old ladies comes up to the driver and complains she's been molested. The driver thinks she must be senile and tells her to sit down. Ten minutes later a second old woman totters to the front and makes the same complaint. He tells her to sit down too. Ten minutes later a third old lady screams she's been molested. The driver decides to investigate. He stops and walks to the back of the bus where he finds an old man on his hands and knees. 'What are you doing down there?' asks the driver. 'Looking for my toupee,' says the old man. 'Three times I thought I'd found it, but when I grabbed it, it ran away.'

✳ A husband and wife wake up one morning. The husband leans over to kiss his wife on the cheek but she says, 'Don't touch me! I'm dead!' 'What on earth are you talking about?' says the husband. 'We're both lying here talking.' The wife replies, 'I know. But I'm definitely dead.' 'You can't be dead,' replies her husband. 'What in the world makes you think you're dead?' His wife replies, 'I must be dead. I woke up this morning and nothing hurts!'

✳ A man in his nineties is watching a group of teenage girls. He turns to his friend and says, 'I wish I was 20 years older.' 'Don't you mean 20 years younger?' 'No, 20 years older. That way I wouldn't give a damn one way or another.'

✳ Even though I'm old, I've definitely still got it. Trouble is, nobody wants it.

✳ An ageing playboy visits his doctor after a lifetime of wine, women and song. 'Well,' says the doctor. 'The good news is you don't have to give up singing.'

✳ A widower and a widow have been friends for years and one day the widower decides it's time to pop the question. He takes the widow to dinner and finally gathers up the courage to say, 'Will you marry me?' The widow answers,

'Yes. Yes, I will.' The meal ends and they go to their respective homes. Next morning, the widower has a problem, he knew he asked the question but did she say yes, or no? With trepidation he calls her on the phone. 'This is kind of embarrassing,' he says. 'But when I asked if you would marry me, what did you say?' The widow answers, 'Why, I said, "Yes, yes I will" and I meant it with all my heart.' She continues, 'I'm so glad you called, because I couldn't remember who'd asked me.'

✳ An elderly couple are in a romantic mood. While sitting on their loveseat the old lady says, 'I remember when you used to kiss me every chance you had.' The old man leans over and gives her a peck on the cheek. Then she says, 'I remember when you used to hold my hand all the time.' The old man reaches over and places his hand on hers. The old lady continues, 'I can also remember when you used to nibble on my neck.' The old man sighs, stands up, and starts to shuffle out of the room. 'Where are you going?' asks the old lady. 'To find my teeth,' says the old man.

✳ An estate agent is trying to sell a very old man a new home. 'It would be a marvellous investment,' says the agent. 'You've got to be joking,' says the old man. 'At my age I don't even buy green bananas.'

✳ An old couple regularly attend church and the pastor is impressed by how harmonious they seem. One day after church, the pastor approaches them to express his admiration. 'I find it so inspirational to see how deeply in love you are,' he says. 'Even after all these years you still hold hands all through the service.' The old woman replies, 'That's not love, Pastor, I'm just keeping him from cracking his damn knuckles.'

✳ Cliff Richard goes to an old peoples' home to host a sing-a-long but is surprised to discover that none of the residents recognise him. Puzzled, he takes an old lady aside and says, 'Excuse me, but do you have any idea who I am?' 'Sorry dear,' says the old lady. 'But you ask one of the nurses, they'll tell you.'

✳ An old man hobbles up to an ice-cream van and orders a cornet. 'Crushed nuts, granddad?' asks the salesman. 'No,' replies the old man. 'Rheumatism.'

✳ Remember that age and treachery will always triumph over youth and ability.

✳ The older you get, the longer it takes you to get over a good time.

✳ The reason grandchildren and grandparents get along so well is because they have a common enemy.

✳ Three old ladies are discussing the problems of old age. One says, 'Sometimes I find myself with a loaf of bread in my hand and can't remember whether I need to put it away, or start making a sandwich.' The second lady says, 'Sometimes I find myself on the stair landing and can't remember whether I was going up or down.' The third one says, 'Well, my memory is perfect – knock on wood.' She raps her knuckles on the wooden table, then says, 'Just wait till I answer the door.'

✳ Two elderly people who have been courting for years finally decide to get married. They go for a stroll to discuss the wedding plans and go into a drug-store. The old man goes up to the sales assistant and says, 'Do you sell heart medication?' 'Of course we do,' says the assistant. 'How about medicine for the circulation?' asks the old man. The assistant replies, 'All kinds.' The old man continues, 'How about medicine for rheumatism?' 'We have that too,' says the assistant. 'How about Viagra?' asks the old man. 'We do stock that,' replies the assistant. 'Got any medicine for the memory?' says the old man. The assistant replies, 'Yes, we have a large selection of drugs to improve your mental facul-ties.' 'Okay,' says the old man. 'So what about vitamins and sleeping pills?' 'Got lots,' replies the assistant. 'Perfect!' says the old man. 'In that case we'd like to register here for our wedding gifts.'

✳ Two old ladies are playing a game of cards. One lady looks up at the other and says, 'We've known each other for so many years, but for the life of me, I just can't bring your name to mind. What was it again, dear?' There's silence for a few seconds, then the other lady replies, 'How soon do you need to know?'

✳ 'A man is only as old as the woman he feels.' *Groucho Marx*

✳ Two old men are sitting in an old people's home when one of the female residents runs past completely naked. 'What was that she was wearing?' asks the first. 'Don't know,' replies the second. 'But it sure needed ironing.'

✳ Growing old is mandatory. Growing up is optional.

✳ Three old soldiers are bragging about their ancestors. 'My great-grandfather was a drummer boy at Shiloh,' declares one. 'My great-grandfather went down with Custer at the Battle of Little Big Horn,' says another. 'Well, I'm the only soldier in my family,' confesses the third. 'But if my great-grandfather was living today he'd be the most famous man in the world.' 'What'd he do?' ask his friends. 'Nothing,' replies the old timer. 'But today he'd be a hundred and sixty-five years old.'

✳ He's so old, he lived at the Gettysburg address.

✳ He's so old, his birthday expired.

✳ He's so old, I told him to act his age and he dropped dead.

✳ She's so old, she has an autographed copy of the Bible.

✳ She's so old, she swam in the Dead Sea when it was still alive.

amish

What do you call an Amish man with his hand up a horse's backside? A mechanic.

What goes, 'Clip-clop-clip-clop-Bang!-clip-clop-clip-clop...? An Amish drive-by shooting.

🎃 APPEARANCE

✳ 'How would you like to feel the way she looks?' *Groucho Marx*

✳ 'Is it fat, bald, and Scouse in here? Or is it just me?' *Alexei Sayle*

✳ A man at the bar gave me a nasty look, I said, 'Thanks, but I've got one already.'

✳ A woman says to her husband, 'Our neighbour says I've got the skin of an eighteen-year-old girl.' 'Yeah?' says the husband. 'Well give it back You're getting it all wrinkled.'

❋ Boy, to friend, 'What do you first notice in a girl?' Friend, 'It depends which way she's facing.'

❋ Christine has such beautiful eyes, the trouble is they're so lovely they spend all their time looking at each other.

❋ Girl, to boyfriend, 'Do you think I'm vain?'
Boyfriend, 'No. Why do you ask?'
Girl, 'Because girls as good-looking as me usually are.'

❋ Is that your nose, or are you eating a banana?

❋ She was a nice girl but her legs were very thin. In fact the last time I saw a pair of legs like hers someone had tied a message to one of them.

❋ The invisible man married an invisible woman. Their kids were nothing to look at.

❋ Time is a great healer, but a lousy beautician.

❋ Why do more women pay attention to their appearance than to improving their minds? Most men are stupid but few are blind.

❋ A boy runs up to his mother and says, 'Mummy, the boys at school say I've got a big head.' 'Never mind them,' replies his mother. 'Now go to the shops and get me three cabbages, six turnips, and five pounds of potatoes.' 'Where's the shopping bag?' asks the boy. Mother replies, 'I don't know. Just stick them in your balaclava.'

❋ A man is waking up after surgery, his wife sitting by his side. His eyes flutter open and he says, 'You're beautiful,' before falling asleep again. A few minutes later his eyes flutter open again and he says, 'You're cute!' His wife is slightly taken aback and says, 'Cute? So what happened to beautiful?' The man replies, 'The drugs are wearing off.'

❋ Fred, 'I love the mole on her chin. I love the mole on her chin. I love the mole on her chin...' Harry, 'All right, you don't have to keep repeating it.' Fred, 'Yes, I do, she's got three chins.'

❋ Your teeth are like stars – they come out at night.

❋ You're dark and handsome. When it's dark, you're handsome.

❋ Harry is always going out on benders – he's not a drunk, just bow-legged.

ARGUMENTS

❋ 'I am not arguing with you – I am telling you.' *James McNeill Whistler*

❋ A woman has the last word in any argument – anything a man says after that is the beginning of a new argument.

❋ For my anniversary my wife let me do something I'd always dreamed of doing. She let me win an argument.

❋ Never argue with an idiot – they drag you down to their level then beat you with experience.

❋ Ray has just reached his 110th birthday. A reporter comes to his birthday party and says, 'Excuse me, sir, but how did you come to be so old?' Ray replies, 'It's easy. The secret is never to argue with anyone.' The reporter is not impressed. 'That's insane!' he says. 'It has to be something else – diet, meditation, or "something". Just not arguing won't keep you alive for 110 years!' Ray looks at the reporter and says, 'Y'know. Maybe you're right.'

❋ She decided to bury the hatchet – between his shoulder blades.

ART AND LITERATURE

❋ 'From the moment I picked up your book until I laid it down, I was convulsed with laughter – someday I intend reading it.' *Groucho Marx*

❋ 'Hitler! There was a painter! He could paint an entire apartment in one afternoon. Two coats!' *Mel Brooks (The Producers)*

❋ 'I'm writing a book. I've got the page numbers done, so now I just have to fill in the rest.' *Steven Wright*

✳ A chicken runs into a library, goes to the main desk and says, 'Book, bok, bok, boook.' The librarian hands the chicken a book and it tucks it under its wing and runs out. A while later, the chicken runs back in, throws the book on the desk and says, 'Book, bok, bok, bok, boook.' Again the librarian gives it a book, and the chicken runs out with it. A few minutes later the chicken is back, and returns the book saying, 'Boook, book, bok, bok, boook.' The librarian gives the chicken a third book, but this time follows it as it runs out. The chicken runs down the street, through a park and down to the river where a frog is sitting on the bank. The chicken holds up the book to the frog, saying, 'Book, bok, bok, boook'. The frog replies, 'Read-it, read-it, read-it...'

✳ A man finds an old violin and an oil painting in his attic and takes them to be valued. 'You know what you've got here,' says the antiques dealer. 'A Stradivarius and a Rembrandt.' 'Wow!' says the man. 'So they must be worth millions.' 'Unfortunately not,' replies the dealer. 'Rembrandt made the violin and Stradivarius painted the picture.'

✳ A critic is a legless man who teaches running.

✳ A man is on an operating table having his legs sawn off at the knee by a surgeon. 'Of course,' says the surgeon to the man, 'this doesn't necessarily mean you'll be able to paint like Toulouse Lautrec.'

✳ A writer dies and Saint Peter offers him the choice of Hell or Heaven. To see what he has in store Saint Peter takes him to Hell where rows of writers are chained to their desks being whipped by demons in a steaming dungeon. However, when they get to Heaven the writer is astonished to see that nothing has changed – rows of writers are chained to their desks in a steaming dungeon being whipped. 'Hey!' says the writer, 'this is just as bad as Hell!' 'No, it's not,' replies Saint Peter. 'Up here you get published.'

✳ A young man professed a desire to become a great writer. When asked to define 'great' he said, 'I want to write stuff that the whole world will read, stuff that people will react to on a truly emotional level, stuff that will make them scream, cry, howl in pain and anger!' He now works for Microsoft writing error messages.

✳ Artist, to critic, 'So what's your opinion of my painting?' Critic, 'It's worthless.' Artist, 'I know, but I'd like to hear it anyway.'

✻ Dick is introduced to an author at a party. 'My last book was terribly difficult,' the author says. 'It took me over six years to complete.' 'I can sympathise,' replies Dick. 'I'm a slow reader myself.'

✻ Of course Vincent Van Gogh was notoriously vague. Whatever you said to him just went in one ear – and straight out the same ear.

✻ My uncle's written a mystery novel. The mystery is, who's going to publish it?

✻ She asked a famous artist if he would paint her in the nude. He said that was fine, but he'd have to keep his socks on otherwise he'd have nowhere to put his brushes.

✻ The pen is mightier than the sword, but only if the sword is quite small and the pen is really, really sharp.

✻ What did the blonde say when she got a book for her birthday? 'Thanks, but I've got one already.'

astrology

'I don't believe in astrology. I'm a Sagittarian and we're sceptical.'
Arthur C Clarke

He had to fill in a form. At the bottom where it said 'Sign' he wrote 'Pisces'.

BATTLE OF THE SEXES

✻ Few women admit their age; few men act it.

✻ It's women's fault that men lie to them – they ask too many questions.

✻ Men and women should put their differences behind them – which is either physically impossible or very uncomfortable.

✳ Men are from Earth, women are from Earth. Deal with it.

✳ Nobody will ever win the battle of the sexes. There's too much fraternising with the enemy.

✳ The Five Secrets to a Great Relationship 1. It's important to find a man who works around the house, occasionally cooks and cleans and who has a job. 2. It is important to find a man who makes you laugh. 3. It is important to find a man who is dependable, respectful and doesn't lie. 4. It is important to find a man who's good in bed and who loves to have sex with you. 5. It is important that these four men never meet.

✳ To be happy with a man you must understand him a lot and love him a little. To be happy with a woman you must love her a lot, and not try to understand her at all.

✳ What's the difference between men and women? A woman wants one man to satisfy her every need. A man wants every woman to satisfy his one need.

✳ Why are women called 'birds'? Because they tend to pick up worms.

✳ 'A man's got to do what a man's got to do. A woman must do what he can't.' *Rhonda Hansome*

✿BATTLE OF THE SEXES: MEN

✳ 'Don't try to teach men how to do anything in public. They can learn in private; in public they have to know.' *Rita Rudner*

✳ 'Give a man a free hand and he'll try to put it all over you.' *Mae West*

✳ 'Men are those creatures with two legs and eight hands.' *Jayne Mansfield*

✳ 'Men do cry, but only when assembling furniture from Ikea.' *Rita Rudner*

✳ A man is talking to God, 'God, why did you make women so beautiful?' 'So you'd find them attractive,' replies God. 'But then why did you make so many of them stupid?' asks the man. 'So some of them might find you attractive,' says God.

✳ All men are animals. Some just make better pets.

✳ Give a man an inch and he thinks he's a ruler. Give him 12 inches and he is a ruler.

✳ How can you tell if a man is sexually aroused? He's breathing.

✳ How can you tell when a man is well hung? When you can just barely slip your finger in between his neck and the noose.

✳ How do men define a '50/50' relationship? We cook – they eat. We clean – they dirty. We iron – they wrinkle.

✳ How do men sort their laundry? 'Filthy' and 'Filthy but Wearable'.

✳ How do you get a man to stop biting his nails? Make him wear shoes.

✳ How do you scare a man? Sneak up behind him and start throwing rice.

✳ How does a man show he's planning for the future? He buys two cases of beer instead of one.

✳ How does a woman know her man is cheating on her? He starts bathing twice a week.

✳ How many men does it take to tile a bathroom? Two. If you slice them very thinly.

✳ Man, 'I don't know why you wear a bra – you've got nothing to put in it.' Woman, 'You wear underpants, don't you?'

✳ Man, to woman, 'Fancy a quickie?' Woman, 'As opposed to what?'

✳ Men are proof of reincarnation – you can't get that dumb in just one lifetime.

✳ Men read maps better than women because only men can understand the concept of an inch equalling a hundred miles.

✳ Research shows most men sleep on the right side of the bed. Even when they're asleep they have to be right.

✳ Scientists have just discovered something that can do the work of five men – a woman.

✳ There are a lot of words you can use to describe men; strong, caring, loving – they'd be wrong but you could still use them.

✳ What did God say after creating man? 'I'm sure I can do better than that.'

✳ What did God say after she made Eve? 'Practice makes perfect.'

✳ What do most men consider a gourmet restaurant? Any place without a drive-up window.

✳ What do you call a handcuffed man? Trustworthy.

✳ What do you call a man with 99 per cent of his brain missing? Castrated.

✳ What do you call a man with half a brain? Gifted.

✳ What do you call an intelligent, good-looking, sensitive man? A rumour.

✳ What do you do with a bachelor who thinks he's God's gift to women? Exchange him.

✳ What do you instantly know about a well-dressed man? His wife is good at picking out clothes.

✳ What does it mean when a man is in your bed gasping for breath and calling your name? You didn't hold the pillow down long enough.

✳ What has eight arms and an IQ of 60? Four guys watching a football game.

✳ What makes a man think about a candlelit dinner? A power failure.

✳ What should a woman do if she saw her ex-husband rolling around in pain on the ground? Shoot him again.

✳ What's a man's definition of a romantic evening? Sex.

✴ What should you give a man who has everything? A woman to show him how to work it.

✴ What's a man's idea of doing housework? Lifting his legs so you can vacuum.

✴ What's a man's idea of foreplay? Half an hour of begging.

✴ What's the difference between a golf ball and a G-spot? A man will spend 20 or 30 minutes looking for a golf ball.

✴ What's the difference between a man and a condom? Condoms have changed. They're no longer thick and insensitive.

✴ What's the difference between a man and Bigfoot? One is covered with matted hair and smells awful. The other has big feet.

✴ What's the difference between a man and childbirth? One can be terribly painful and sometimes almost unbearable while the other is just having a baby.

✴ What's the difference between a new husband and a new dog? A dog is always happy to see you and only takes a month to train.

✴ What's the difference between a sofa and a man watching football? The sofa doesn't keep asking for beer.

✴ What's the difference between Government bonds and men? Bonds mature.

✴ What's the one thing that all men at singles bars have in common? They're married.

✴ What's the one thing that keeps most men out of college? High school.

✴ What's the quickest way to a man's heart? Straight through the ribcage.

✴ What's the smartest thing a man can say? 'My wife says…'

✴ Why do men buy electric lawnmowers? So they can find their way back to the house.

✳ Why do men chase women they have no intention of marrying? For the same reason dogs chase cars they have no intention of driving.

✳ Why do men die before women? Who cares?

✳ Why do men like smart women? Opposites attract.

✳ Why do men snore when they lie on their backs? Because their balls fall over their butts and they vapour-lock.

✳ Why do men whistle when they're sitting on the toilet? Because it helps them remember which end they need to wipe.

✳ Why is a man like a moped? They're both fun to ride until your friends see you with one.

✳ Why is a woman different from a computer? A woman won't accept a 3-inch floppy.

✳ Why is food better than men? Because you don't have to wait an hour for seconds.

✳ Why is it difficult to find men who are sensitive, caring and good-looking? They already have boyfriends.

✳ Why is psychoanalysis quicker for men than for women? When it's time to go back to childhood, he's already there.

✳ Why is sleeping with a man like a soap opera? Just when it's getting interesting, they're finished until next time.

✳ Why would American men like to vote for a female president? Because they think they'd only have to pay her half as much.

✳ Why would women be better off if men treated them like cars? At least they'd get a little attention every six months or 50,000 miles, whichever came first.

✳ How does a man help make the bed? He gets out of it.

❀BATTLE OF THE SEXES: WOMEN

❋ 'I know I'm not gonna understand women. I will never understand how you can take boiling-hot wax, pour it on to your upper thigh, rip the hair out by the root – and still be afraid of a spider.' *Jerry Seinfeld*

❋ 'That woman speaks eighteen languages, and can't say "no" in any of them.' *Dorothy Parker*

❋ 'Women: You can't live with them, and you can't get them to dress up in a skimpy Nazi costume and beat you with a warm squash.' *Emo Phillips*

❋ Men wake up as good-looking as they went to bed. Women somehow deteriorate during the night.

❋ Adam asks God for a mate. God replies, 'You shall have the best of all companions – woman. She will be beautiful, and intelligent, and good-natured. She will cook for you, clean for you, and take care of your every need without complaint. Your life will be one of undiluted pleasure.' 'Sounds good,' says Adam. 'What do I have to do to get her?' God replies, 'You must give up an arm, a leg, a kidney, a rib, and your left eye.' Adam thinks for a second, then says 'And what do I get for just a rib?'

❋ An aeroplane is about to crash. A female passenger jumps up and shouts, 'If I'm going to die, I want to die feeling like a woman.' She strips off her clothes and says, 'Is there someone on this plane who's man enough to make me feel like a woman?' A male passenger shouts, 'Yes, me!' He stands up, tears off his shirt, and says, 'Here, iron this!'

'Men don't feel the urge to get married as quickly as women because their clothes all button and zip in the front. Women's dresses usually button and zip in the back. We need men emotionally and sexually, but we also need men to help us get dressed.' *Rita Rudner*

'Intuition: the strange instinct that tells a woman she's right, whether she is or not.' *Oscar Wilde*

✳ I haven't spoken to my wife for 18 months – I don't like to interrupt her.

✳ In an average day a man speaks 35,000 words and a woman speaks 30,000. Unfortunately, by the time I get home, I've done my 35,000 and she hasn't even started on her 30,000.

✳ In the beginning, God created the earth and rested. Then God created man and rested. Then God created woman. Since then, neither God nor man has rested.

✳ My son must get his brains from his mother – I still have mine.

✳ The geography of a woman: between the ages of 15 and 18 a woman is like China. Developing fast with a lot of potential but as yet still not free or open. Between the ages of 18 and 21 a woman is like Africa. She's half discovered, half wild and naturally beautiful. Between the ages of 21 and 30 a woman is like America. Completely discovered, very well developed and open to trade especially with countries with cash or cars. Between the ages of 30 and 40, she's like India. Very hot, relaxed and convinced of its own beauty. Between the ages of 40 and 50 she's like Iraq. She lost the war and is haunted by past mistakes. Massive reconstruction is now necessary. Between the ages of 50 and 60 she's like Canada. Very wide, quiet and the borders are practically unpatrolled but the frigid climate keeps people away. Between the ages of 60 and 70 a woman is like Mongloia. With a glorious and all-conquering past but alas no future. After 70, they become Albania. Everyone knows where it is, but no one wants to go there.

✳ The three ages of woman: at twenty-five they are attractive. At thirty-five they are attentive. At forty-five they are adhesive.

✳ There are three types of women; the intelligent, the beautiful, and the majority.

✳ Two girlfriends are on vacation when they see a five-storey store advertising men for sale. They go in and see a first-floor sign that reads 'All the men on this floor are short and ugly.' The women decide to take the elevator to the next floor. There the sign reads, 'All the men here are short and handsome.' This isn't good enough, so the women continue up. On the third floor the sign reads, 'All the men here are tall and ugly.' The women want to do better so they keep going. On the fourth floor the sign reads, 'All the men here are tall and handsome.' The women get excited but decide to see what's on the fifth floor. There they find a sign that reads, 'No men here. This floor was built to prove there's no way to please a woman.'

✳ Two men are admiring a famous actress. 'Still,' says one. 'If you take away her beautiful hair, her fantastic breasts, her eyes, her perfect features, and her stunning figure – what are you left with?' The other replies, 'My wife.'

✳ What is love? The delusion that one woman differs from another.

✳ What's the difference between a battery and a woman? A battery has a positive side.

✳ What's the difference between PMT and BSE? One's mad cow disease and the other is an agricultural problem.

✳ Why are middle-aged women like MTV? They get turned on about once a month, and you've had enough after about 15 minutes.

✳ Why did God create Adam first? So he'd have a chance to talk before Eve came along.

✳ Why did God create man before woman? He didn't want any advice.

✳ Why do men die before their wives? They want to.

✳ Why do women close their eyes while they are having sex? They can't stand to see a man having a good time.

✳ Why do women live longer than men? Because they don't have wives.

✳ Women like silent men, they think they're listening.

✳ 'Women should be obscene and not heard.' *Groucho Marx*

🍎BEAUTY TREATMENT

✳ 'Gosh. You look nice,' he said. 'It must have taken you ages.'

✳ Beauty comes from within. From within bottles, jars, tubes, compacts…

✳ Every night my wife puts a mudpack on her face and curlers in her hair. It doesn't help though. I can still tell it's her.

✳ Jill hears that milk baths will make her beautiful so she leaves a note for her milkman asking for 15 gallons of milk. When the milkman reads the note he thinks there must be a mistake so he knocks on the door. Jill answers and the milkman says, 'I found your note to leave 15 gallons of milk. Did you mean 1.5 gallons?' Jill replies, 'No. I want 15 gallons. I'm going to fill my bathtub with milk.' 'Pasteurised?' asks the milkman. 'No,' says Jill. 'Just up to my boobs.'

✳ Modern women put on wigs, fake eyelashes, false fingernails, sixteen pounds of assorted make-up/shadows/blushes/creams, living bras, various pads, have plastic surgery, then complain they cannot find a 'real' man.

✳ My wife is as beautiful today as the day I married her – it just takes her fifteen minutes longer each morning to get there.

✳ My wife tried a mudpack to make herself more attractive. It worked for a while, but then it fell off.

🍎BIRTH

✳ 'I must confess, I was born at a very early age.' *Groucho Marx*

✳ 'I was born by Caesarian. You can't usually tell but whenever I leave my house I go out by the window.' *Steven Wright*

✳ A boy is given some homework on childbirth. He goes to his mother and says, 'How was I born?' 'Well, honey,' says the embarrassed mother, 'the stork brought you to us.' 'Oh,' says the boy. 'And how did you and Daddy get born?'

'Oh, the stork brought us too,' says the mother. 'Well how were Grandpa and Grandma born?' the boy persists. 'Well darling, the stork brought them too!' says the frustrated mother. A few days later, the boy hands in his homework with the following opening sentence, 'This report has been very difficult to write due to the fact that there hasn't been a natural childbirth in my family for three generations.'

✳ A Catholic couple, trying for a baby, ask their priest to pray for them. 'I'm going to Rome for a few months,' says the priest, 'while I'm there I'll light a candle for you at the altar of Saint Peter.' The priest comes back nine months later and finds the women has given birth to quintuplets. 'Praise be to God,' says the priest, 'but where has your husband gone? I heard he left the country.' 'So he did, Father,' says the woman. 'He flew to Rome to blow your bloody candle out.'

✳ A Catholic woman has had six children in five years and is tired of being pregnant. She goes to a priest who advises her to spend every night sleeping in a chair with her feet in a ten-gallon bucket of water. The woman is puzzled by this advice but agrees to follow it. Three months later the woman comes back and tells the priest that she's pregnant again. 'And did you do as I suggested?' asks the priest. 'Yes and no,' replies the woman. 'I put my feet in water, but I couldn't find a ten-gallon bucket. I put them in two five-gallon buckets instead.'

✳ A guy phones the local hospital and yells, 'You've gotta send help! My wife's in labour!' The nurse says, 'Calm down. Is this her first child?' He replies, 'No! This is her husband!'

✳ I was born two days premature which means all my life I've been able to send post second class and it gets there the same time as if I'd gone to full term and sent it first class.

✳ Jane has a baby each year because she doesn't want the youngest one to get spoilt.

✳ My father died during childbirth. He was run over by the ambulance carrying my mother to hospital.

✳ She was a very busy woman. In fact she was too busy to attend the birth of her child.

✳ We are born naked, wet, and hungry. Then things get worse.

✳ We had our first child on the NHS. It was absolutely terrible. We had to wait nine months.

✳ When I was born the doctor came out to the waiting room and said to my father, 'I'm very sorry. We did everything we could. But he pulled through.'
Rodney Dangerfield

🐟 BLONDES: DIM

✳ A blonde is at a soda vending machine in a casino. She sticks a quarter in, pushes the button, and catches the can when it pops out. Then she puts another quarter in and does the same, then again, and again, and again. Eventually the casino manager comes over and says, 'Hey, you must be really thirsty.' 'Not really,' replies the blonde, 'but I don't want to stop while I'm winning.'

✳ A blonde sees a sign reading, 'Press bell for night watchman'. She does so, and after a few seconds she hears the watchman clomping down the stairs. He then proceeds to unlock first one gate, then another, then shut down the alarm system, and finally makes his way through the revolving door. 'Well,' he says. 'What do you want?' The blonde replies, 'I just wanted to know why you can't ring the bell yourself?'

✳ Four exuberant blondes come into a bar and order champagne. The corks are popped, the glasses are filled and they begin chanting, '51 days, 51 days, 51 days!' Three more blondes arrive, take up their drinks and the chanting grows, '51 days, 51 days, 51 days!' Two more blondes show up and join in as well, '51 days, 51 days, 51 days!' Finally, a tenth blonde comes in holding a picture. She walks over to the table, sets the picture in the middle and everyone starts dancing around it chanting, '51 days, 51 days, 51 days!' The bartender walks over to the table and sees that the picture is a framed children's jigsaw puzzle. The bartender says to one of the blondes, 'What's all the fuss about?' The blonde replies, 'Everyone thinks that blondes are dumb. So we decided to set the record straight. Ten of us got together, bought that puzzle and put it together!'

✳ How do you describe a blonde surrounded by drooling idiots? Flattered.

✳ How does a blonde commit suicide? She gathers her clothes into a pile and jumps off.

✳ What can save a dying blonde? Hair transplants.

✳ What did the blonde say when someone blew in her bra? 'Thanks for the refill.'

✳ What do bleached blondes and jumbo jets have in common? Black boxes.

✳ What's the difference between a blonde and the Panama Canal? The Panama Canal is a busy ditch.

✳ Two brunettes are riding in the front of a pick-up truck. They're giving a lift to three blondes in the back. Unfortunately the truck rolls off a cliff into the ocean. The brunettes survive, but the blondes die. Why? They couldn't get the tailgate open.

✳ What's dumber than a brunette who tries to build a house at the bottom of a lake? The blonde who tries to burn it down!

✳ Why can't you tell a blonde a knock-knock joke? Because she'll go to answer the door.

✳ Why did the blonde climb over the chainlink fence? To see what was on the other side.

✳ Why did the blonde throw away her weight-loss video? Because she noticed the people on the video weren't losing weight either.

✳ A blonde and brunette are watching an evening news story about a man about to jump off a bridge. The brunette turns to the blonde and says, 'I bet you £50 the man is going to jump.' The blonde accepts the bet and, sure enough, the man jumps. The blonde gives the brunette £50. 'I can't accept your money,' says the brunette, 'I watched the midday news and saw the man jump then.' 'I watched the midday news too,' replies the blonde, 'I didn't think he'd do it twice in one day.'

✳ A blonde comes to a river and sees another blonde on the opposite bank. 'Yoo-hoo!' she shouts. 'How can I get to the other side?' The other blonde looks around then shouts back, 'You are on the other side!'

✳ A blonde decides to kidnap a small boy and hold him for ransom. Having grabbed her victim from the playground she writes a note saying, 'I've kidnapped your boy. Tomorrow morning put £10,000 in a bag and leave it by the statue in the town square. Signed, A Blonde.' The blonde then pins the note to the boy's shirt and sends him home. The next morning the blonde checks the statue and finds the boy standing there with a bagful of money. The boy hands the blonde a note, it reads, 'How could you do this to a fellow blonde?'

✳ A blonde girl runs home from school. 'Mummy, Mummy!' she yells. 'We were counting today, and all the other kids could only count to four, but I counted to six. See. One, two, three, four, five, six!' 'Very good,' says her mother. 'Is it because I'm blonde, Mummy?' asks the girl. 'Yes, it's because you're blonde,' replies her mother. The next day, the girl runs home from school. 'Mummy, Mummy!' she yells. 'We were saying the alphabet today, and all the other kids could only say it to D, but I said it to G. See. A, B, C, D, E, F, G!' 'That's very good,' says her mother. 'Is it because I'm blonde, Mummy?' asks the girl. 'Yes, pumpkin, it's because you're blonde,' replies her mother. Next day the girl runs home from school. 'Mummy, Mummy!' she yells. 'We were in gym class today, and when we showered, all the other girls had flat chests, but I have these!' With this the blonde girl lifts up her T-shirt to reveal a pair of 38Cs. 'That's very good,' says her mother. 'Is it because I'm blonde, Mummy?' asks the girl. 'No,' says her mother, 'it's because you're 25.'

✳ A blonde has her hair dyed brown. A few days later she's out driving through the countryside when she stops her car to let a flock of sheep pass. Admiring the cute woolly creatures, she says to the shepherd, 'If I can guess how many sheep you have, can I take one?' The shepherd agrees, so the blonde thinks for a moment and says, '352.' The shepherd is amazed, 'You're right! Which sheep do you want?' The blonde picks the cutest animal. The shepherd says to her, 'Okay. How's this for a bet? If I can guess your real hair colour, can I have my dog back?'

✳ Did you hear about the blonde who sold her car to get some money for petrol?

✳ A blonde keeps checking her mail box. A neighbour notices her repeated trips to the kerb and asks if she's waiting for a special delivery. 'No,' she replies. 'But my computer keeps telling me I have mail.'

✳ A blonde on holiday in Louisiana tries to buy some alligator shoes. She goes into a shoe shop and finds a nice pair but is not prepared to pay their high price. Determined to get some she decides to catch an alligator herself and takes a club into the swamp. Curious, the owner of the shoe shop follows her and eventually tracks her down by a lake. On the lakeside is a large pile of dead alligators and the shop owner watches as the blonde beats another one to death in the water. Eventually she kills the 'gator and drags it on-shore. She looks at its feet and says, 'Damn, this one isn't wearing shoes either!'

✳ A blonde walks into a doctor's office. 'Doc, I hurt all over,' complains the blonde. She touches herself on her leg and winces. 'Ouch! I hurt there!' She touches her earlobe. 'Ouch! I hurt there too!' She touches her hair. 'Ouch! Even my hair hurts!' The doctor says, 'You've got a broken finger...'

✳ A blonde was on her way to Disneyland, but she went home when she saw a sign saying 'Disneyland Left'.

✳ A blonde, a brunette and a redhead go on holiday to a tropical island. The brunette takes a beach umbrella, the redhead takes a crate of suntan oil, and the blonde takes a car door. 'What are you doing with a car door?' asks the redhead. The blonde replies, 'If it gets too hot, we can roll the window down.'

✳ A pregnant blonde walks into a doctor's office to have an ultrasound. The doctor tells her that she is going to have a little girl. He then asks her what she'll name the baby. 'Helen,' says the blonde. 'I have five other daughters, and I named them all Helen.' 'Isn't that a little confusing?' says the doctor. 'What happens if they're all upstairs and you want to call one of them down?' 'That's easy,' replies the blonde. 'I'd just call them by their last name.'

✳ Did you hear about the blonde who was treated in the emergency room for concussion and severe head wounds? She'd tried to commit suicide by hanging herself with a bungee cord.

✳ Did you hear about the blonde who went to a library and checked out a book called *How to Hug*? She got it home and found it was volume seven of the encyclopaedia.

✳ How can you tell if a blonde sends you a fax? It has a stamp on it.

✳ How can you tell if a blonde's been using the computer? There's whiteout on the screen. How can you tell if two blondes have been using the computer? There's writing on the whiteout.

✳ How did the blonde break her leg raking leaves? She fell out of the tree.

✳ How did the blonde burn her nose? Bobbing for chips.

✳ How do blonde brain cells die? Alone!

✳ How do blondes pierce their ears? They put tacks in their shoulder pads.

✳ How do you change a blonde's mind? Blow in her ear.

✳ How do you confuse a blonde? You don't, they're born that way!

✳ How do you determine a blonde's IQ ? With a tyre gauge.

✳ How do you drown a blonde? Put a scratch 'n sniff sticker at the bottom of a pool.

✳ How do you get a one-armed blonde out of a tree? Wave to her.

✳ How do you keep a blonde busy all day? Put her in a round room and tell her to sit in the corner.

✳ How do you keep a blonde busy all day? Write 'Please turn over' on both sides of a piece of paper.

✳ How do you make a blonde laugh on Monday morning? Tell her a joke on Friday night.

✳ How do you make a blonde's eyes sparkle? Shine a torch into her ear.

✳ How many blondes does it take to make a circuit? Two. One to stand in the bathtub, and another to pass her the blow dryer!

✳ If you drop a blonde and a brunette 100ft, which hits the ground first? The brunette. The blonde has to ask directions on the way down.

✳ On a plane bound for New York, the flight attendant approaches a blonde sitting in first class and asks her to move to economy since she doesn't have a first-class ticket. The blonde replies, 'I'm blonde, I'm beautiful, I'm going to New York and I'm not moving.' The flight attendant asks the co-pilot to speak with her but again the blonde replies, 'I'm blonde, I'm beautiful, I'm going to New York and I'm not moving.' The co-pilot asks the captain what should he do. The captain says, 'I'm married to a blonde. I know how to handle this.' He goes and whispers in the blonde's ear and she immediately jumps up and runs to the economy section. 'What did you say?' asks the flight attendant. The captain replies, 'I told her the first-class section wasn't going to New York.'

✳ One day a blonde takes up ice fishing. She gets to the pond and starts to cut a hole in the ice, when she hears a loud disembodied voice say, 'There's no fish there…!' Puzzled, the blonde picks up her ice saw and cuts another hole a few feet away. Again, she hears the voice say, 'There's no fish there…!' The blonde moves another ten feet and begins to cut another ice hole. 'There's no fish there…!' says the voice. The blonde looks up and says ' Are you God?' 'No!' replies the voice. 'I'm the manager of the ice rink!'

✳ Two brunettes and a blonde work in the same office with the same female boss. They notice the boss always leaves work early so one day they decide to leave straight after she does. The two brunettes go for coffee, but the blonde decides to go home and surprise her husband. When she reaches her house she sneaks inside and hears noises from the bedroom. Peering in through the bedroom door the blonde sees her boss in bed with her husband. Horrified she creeps away. Next day in the office the brunettes suggest leaving early again. 'No way,' says the blonde. 'Yesterday I almost got caught!'

✳ What are the six worst years in a blonde's life? Third grade.

✳ What did the blonde get on her IQ test? Saliva.

✳ What did the blonde say about blonde jokes? She said they were pretty good, but might offend some Puerto Ricans.

✳ What do you call a blonde with a brain? A golden retriever.

✳ What do you call ten blondes at the bottom of the pool? Air pockets.

✳ What do you see when you look into a blonde's eyes? The back of her head.

✳ What job did the blonde have at the M&M factory? Proofreading.

✳ What's five miles long and has an IQ of forty? A blonde parade.

✳ What's the difference between Bigfoot and an intelligent blonde? There have been sightings of Bigfoot.

✳ When blondes have more fun, do they know it?

✳ Why are blondes only allowed a thirty-minute lunch break? If they took an hour it would take too long to retrain them.

✳ Why are there so few blonde pharmacists? They have a hard time getting the pill bottles into the typewriter!

✳ Why can't blondes make ice cubes? They forget the recipe.

✳ Why did the blonde ask for some burned-out light bulbs? She needed them for her darkroom.

✳ Why did the blonde have square boobs? She forgot to take the tissues out of the box.

✳ Why did the blonde keep ice cubes in the freezer? So she could keep the refrigerator cold.

✳ Why did the blonde put her finger over the nail when she was hammering? The noise gave her a headache.

✳ Why did the blonde roast a chicken for three and a half days? The instructions said 'cook it for half an hour per pound', and she weighed 125.

✳ Why did the blonde stand in front of the mirror with her eyes closed? She wanted to see what she looked like asleep.

✳ Why did the blonde throw breadcrumbs in the toilet? To feed the toilet duck!

✳ Why do blondes clean their hair in the sink? Because that's where your supposed to wash vegetables.

✳ Why do blondes take the pill? So they know what day of the week it is.

✳ Why is it good to have a blonde passenger? You can park in the handicapped spaces.

✳ Did you here about the blonde who stayed up all night to see where the sun went? It finally dawned on her.

✳ How do you know when a blonde has been making chocolate chip cookies? You find M&M shells all over the kitchen floor.

✳ Two blondes are driving through Wales when they come to a sign that tells them they are near the town of Llanfywrich. This starts an argument about how to pronounce this unusual name. They stop for lunch and one of the blondes asks the cashier to pronounce the name for them, 'Can you settle an argument for us?' asks the blonde. 'Very slowly, tell us where we are.' The cashier leans over the counter and says, 'Buuurrrrrr-Gerrrrrr Kiiiinnnnnggg.'

✳ What did the blonde say after the doctor told her she was pregnant? 'Is it mine?'

✳ What did the blonde say when she saw the banana peel on the floor? 'Oh no, I'm going to fall over again!'

✳ What do blondes and beer bottles have in common? They're both empty from the neck up.

✳ What do smart blondes and UFOs have in common? You always hear about them but never see them.

✳ What do you call it when a blonde dyes her hair brunette? Artificial intelligence.

✳ What do you call ten blondes standing ear to ear? A wind tunnel.

✳ What does a blonde think are the last two words of the national anthem? Play ball!

blondes – easy virtue

How does a blonde answer the question, 'Are you sexually active?' 'No, I just lie there.'

What does a blonde use for protection during sex? A bus shelter.

Why can't blondes pass their driving tests first time? Whenever the car stops, they hop in the back seat.

Why do blondes have more fun? They're easier to find in the dark.

BOREDOM

✻ 'When I bore people at a party, they think it's their fault.' *Henry Kissinger*

✻ Harry has a very boring hobby, he just sits in the corner and collects dust.

✻ He's so boring people throw parties just so as not to invite him.

✻ You're so boring, if you threw a boomerang it wouldn't come back to you.

BREASTS

✻ 'Who ever thought up the word 'Mammogram'? Every time I hear it, I think I'm supposed to put my breast in an envelope and send it to someone.' *Jan King*

✻ A flat-chested woman goes out shopping for a new bra. She goes into shop after shop asking if they have a size 28A but she can't find one anywhere. Eventually she tries her luck in a small lingerie shop run by an old deaf lady. 'Have you got anything in size 28A?' asks the woman. 'What was that, dear?' says the old lady. The woman lifts up her T-shirt exposing her breasts and says, 'Have you got anything for these?' The old lady peers at the woman's boobs and says, 'No, dear. Have you tried Clearasil?'

✳ What did the bra say to the hat? You go on ahead and I'll give these two a lift.

✳ What happened to the large-breasted streaker at the pop concert? She was thrown out by the bouncers.

✳ Why do men find it hard to make eye contact? Breasts don't have eyes.

🎃 CANNIBALS

✳ Did you hear about the cannibal who passed his mother in the woods?

✳ Did you hear about the cannibal who went on a diet? He only ate midgets.

✳ Hannibal Lecter is seeing someone new but she hates talking to him when he's nauseous – he keeps bringing up old girlfriends.

✳ Hear about the cannibal who ate his mother-in-law? She still didn't agree with him.

✳ I like kids, but I don't think I could eat a whole one.

✳ Some cannibals get a job in a big corporation on condition they don't eat any of the other staff. Things go very well until their boss calls them into his office one day and gives them some bad news – an office cleaner is missing in suspicious circumstances and the cannibals are under suspicion. The cannibals get together after work. Their leader says, 'Which of you idiots had the cleaner?' One of the cannibals raises his hand. 'You idiot! For weeks we've been feasting on team leaders, project managers and human resources staff, then you go and eat someone they'll actually miss!'

✳ Two cannibals are eating a clown. One says to the other, 'Does this taste funny to you?'

✳ Two cannibals are having dinner. 'Your wife makes a great roast,' says one. 'I know,' says the other. 'But I'm going to miss her.'

✳ What do cannibals like Jehovah's Witnesses? They're free delivery.

✳ Two cannibals, a father and son, walk into the jungle to look for something to eat. Before long they come across a little old man. The son says, 'Dad, how about him?' 'No,' says the father. 'There's not enough meat on him. We'll wait.' A little while later, along comes a really fat woman. The son says, 'Hey, Dad, how about her?' 'No,' says the father. 'We'd die of a heart attack if we ate her. We'll wait.' An hour later an absolutely gorgeous woman walks by. The son says, 'There's nothing wrong with this one, Dad. Let's eat her.' 'No we won't,' says the father. 'Why not?' asks the son. 'Because,' says the father, 'we're going to take her home and eat your mother.'

✳ Why aren't cannibals popular at weddings? They insist on toasting the bride and groom.

✳ Why was the cannibal student expelled from school? He kept buttering up his teacher.

✿CARS AND MOTORING

✳ 'I have a rented car, which is a flat rate 12 cents a mile. In an effort to cut down on the mileage charge, I back up every place.' *Woody Allen*

✳ A man has been driving all night. He decides to stop in the next town for a few hours and get some sleep. As luck would have it, he pulls up by a park frequented by early morning joggers. No sooner has he settled back to get some shut-eye when a jogger starts knocking on his window. 'Excuse me, sir,' says the jogger. 'Do you have the time?' The man looks at his car clock and says, '8.15.' The jogger says his thanks and leaves. The man settles back again, but just as he's dozing off there's another jogger knocking on the window. 'Excuse me, sir. Do you have the time?' asks the jogger. '8.25!' snaps the man. To prevent any more interruptions the man writes a note saying 'I do not know the time!' and sticks it to his window. He settles back but is disturbed by yet another jogger knocking on the window. 'Excuse me, sir,' says the jogger. 'It's 8.35.'

✳ A woman dents her sports car and goes to a garage to get some help. The mechanic decides to have some fun with her and tells her to take the car home and blow up the exhaust – the air pressure will make the dent spring out. She takes the car home and spends a good hour blowing up the exhaust without any success. Eventually her husband comes in and asks what she's doing. She tells him and he says, 'You idiot. That's never going to work. You've left the windows open.'

✳ A car jumper cable walks into a bar. The barman says, 'I'll serve you, but don't start anything.'

✳ A constipated elephant travelling up the motorway has shed its load. Drivers are advised to treat it as a mini-roundabout.

✳ A man comes home from work and is greeted by his wife. She tells him she has good news and bad news about their car. The man says, 'Okay, so give me the good news.' His wife replies, 'The good news is, the air bag works…'

✳ A defendant is in front of a magistrate on a speeding charge. 'I understand you were doing 60 in a 30 mile per hour zone,' says the magistrate. 'That's a lie,' replies the defendant. 'I wasn't doing 30. I wasn't even doing 10 in fact…' 'Hold it,' says the judge. 'I'm going to fine you £50 before you back into something.'

✳ A driver pulls up by a traffic warden. 'If I park on these double yellow lines and pop over the road to post a letter will you give me a ticket?' asks the driver. 'Of course I will,' replies the warden. 'But these other cars are parked on double yellow lines,' argues the driver. 'I know,' replies the warden. 'But they didn't ask me to give them a ticket.'

✳ A farmer living by a country road is increasingly concerned by speeding traffic. Worried that he and his livestock are in danger he calls the police and asks them to put up a sign. They put up a 'Slow' sign but it has no effect. They try putting up a 'Pedestrian Crossing' sign, but that has no effect either. Finally they try erecting a 'Children at Play' sign, but the traffic still keeps whizzing past. Eventually the farmer asks if he can put up his own sign and the police agree. A few days later a policeman stops by to see how things are going. He's amazed to see the traffic moving at a snail's pace, then he notices the farmer's homemade sign by the roadside, it reads, 'Nudist Colony'.

✳ A man is taking his son to school, when he inadvertently makes an illegal turn at the lights. 'Uh-oh, I just made an illegal turn!' the man says. 'It's okay, Dad,' replies his son. 'The police car behind us did the same thing!'

✳ A motorist stops at a ford and asks an old rustic sitting nearby how deep the water is. 'Couple of inches,' replies the rustic. The motorist drives into the ford and disappears in a seething mass of bubbles. 'That's funny,' said the rustic. 'It only goes halfway up on them ducks.'

✳ A police officer pulls a woman over. 'Is there a problem, Officer?' she asks. 'Ma'am, you were speeding. Could I see your licence?' 'I'm sorry,' says the woman. 'I don't have one. I lost it four times for drunk driving.' 'Okay,' says the officer. 'Can I see your vehicle registration papers.' 'Nope,' says the woman. 'Can't do that either. I stole this car, killed the owner, and put his remains in the boot.' The horrified officer calls for back-up and within minutes five police cars circle the woman. A police chief slowly approaches, clasping a gun. 'Ma'am,' he says, 'open the back of the car please.' She does so but the back of the car is empty. 'Is this your car, ma'am?' asks the chief. 'Yes,' says the woman. 'Here are the registration papers.' The chief is confused. 'The officer claimed you don't have a driver's licence.' The woman digs into her handbag and pulls out the licence. 'Ma'am, this is a puzzle,' says the chief. 'My officer told me you didn't have a licence, that you stole this car, and that you'd murdered the owner.' 'I don't believe it!' says the woman. 'Next you'll tell me the lying bastard said I was speeding too.'

✳ A policeman is investigating a crash on a railway crossing. He goes up to the injured car driver and says, 'Can you describe what you were doing at the time of the accident?' 'Well,' replies the driver. 'I got to the crossing, stopped, looked both ways, and then the train hit me.'

✳ A policeman watches as a car careers all over the road before crashing into a bollard. He runs over to help and asks the driver what happened. 'It was a nightmare,' says the driver. 'I swerved to miss a tree then another one swung in front of me so I swerved to avoid it when another one came into view. There were trees everywhere. I couldn't get away from them.' The policeman looks in the car and says, 'Those weren't trees, that was your air freshener.'

✳ A tramp knocks on the door of a large house and begs for a meal. 'Tell you what,' says the householder. 'If you go round the back and paint my porch with whitewash I'll give you all the food you can eat.' The tramp agrees. He goes round the back, finds a tin of whitewash and a brush, and gets started. Ten minutes later the tramp knocks on the door for his reward. 'That was fast work,' says the householder. 'I thought it would take hours to paint that huge porch.' 'Oh, it wasn't so big,' replies the tramp. 'And, by the way, it isn't a Porsche. It's a BMW.'

※ A truck driver looks in his rear-view mirror and sees a blonde tailgating him. The truck driver hates to be tailgated, so he stops his truck and walks back to the blonde's car. 'Lady, get out,' he says. The blonde steps out of her car, and the truck driver draws a circle on the roadside. 'Don't step out of that circle,' he says, then proceeds to tear off the car's rear-view mirrors. As he does so the blonde starts laughing. This enrages the truck driver so he rips out the seats, and bursts all the tyres. The blonde keeps laughing, so the furious driver takes a sledgehammer from his truck, and pounds the car's frame, rips out the steering wheel, and cuts the brake lines. The car is wrecked but the blonde is now laughing hysterically. The truck driver walks over to the blonde, and says, 'Lady, I just totalled your car, and you're still laughing. What's so funny?' The blonde giggles, 'Every time you turned round – I stepped out of the circle.'

※ A warning has just been issued to drivers on the M1 travelling to London on the northbound carriageway.

※ A woman is driving the wrong way up a one-way street. A cop pulls her over and says, 'Where are you going?' The woman replies, 'I don't know. But I must be late – everyone is coming back!'

※ An adult hedgehog is teaching two smaller hedgehogs how to cross the road without getting killed. 'It's easy,' it tells them. 'If you're in the middle of the road when a car comes just curl up in a ball and the vehicle's wheels will pass harmlessly on either side of you.' To illustrate this the hedgehog walks into the path of an oncoming car and curls up in a ball. The vehicle passes harmlessly over it. One of the younger hedgehogs then has a go. It walks into the middle of the road, waits until a car approaches, and curls into a ball. The car passes over, and the hedgehog it unscathed. Now it's the turn of the third hedgehog. It walks to the centre of the road, sees a car, and curls into a ball. The car passes over it and squashes the hedgehog flat. 'What did he do wrong?' asks the second hedgehog. 'Nothing,' replies the first. 'But it doesn't really work with Reliant Robins.'

※ Driver, to mechanic, 'Could you check the battery? I think it's flat.' Mechanic, 'What shape did you want it to be?'

✳ Every young woman should hang on to her youth. But not while he's driving.

✳ Harry and Bob are out in their car. They park, get out, and shut the doors when Harry realises that they've locked themselves out. Bob says, 'We can get a coat hanger and try to unlock the door.' Harry says, 'Or perhaps we could try to prise the door open.' 'Well, whatever we do, we'd better hurry,' says Bob. 'A storm's coming and the top's still down.'

✳ Harry died with his boots on – sadly one was on the accelerator at the time.

✳ Harry discovers that someone has backed into his Jaguar while it's been in the car park. He finds a note under the windscreen. It says, 'Sorry about wrecking your car. The policeman watching me from over the road thinks I'm leaving you my details. But I'm not.'

✳ Do you know why Turtle Wax is so expensive? Because turtles have really tiny ears.

✳ Harry is fiddling under the bonnet of his car. A tramp walks by, stops, and looks at him. 'Piston broke,' explains Harry. 'Ah yes,' says the tramp. 'So am I.'

✳ He got a BMW because he wanted a car he could spell.

✳ How come so many cars are named after pornographic magazines? There's the Escort, the Fiesta, the Mini Mayfair and of course the Fiat Big Jugs Monthly Popular Plus.

✳ Husband, to wife, 'I don't believe it! You just backed the car over my bike!' Wife, 'Well, you shouldn't have left it on the lawn.'

✳ I asked my wife why there were so many dinks on the driver's side of her Mercedes, she said the brakes must be bad on that side.

✳ I bought a second-hand car. It only had one previous owner. A little old lady who only used it on a Sunday – when she took it drag racing.

✳ I found a way to make my wife drive more carefully. I told her, if she ever got in an accident, the newspapers would print her real age.

✳ Policeman, to motorist, 'I'm arresting you for speeding. You were going at least 100 miles per hour.' Motorist, 'That's nonsense, officer. I've only been driving ten minutes.'

✳ Reporter, to racing driver, 'Would you say it's very dangerous taking a corner at that speed?' Driver, 'It's very dangerous taking a corner at that speed.'

✳ Somebody complimented me on my driving today. They left a note on the windscreen – it said 'Parking Fine'.

✳ The garage told me they couldn't repair my brakes, so they just made my horn louder.

✳ The journey of a thousand miles begins with a broken fan belt and a flat tyre.

✳ The Pope is visiting the USA and decides to take a turn at the wheel of his limo. The Pope gets in the driving seat, while his driver hops in the back and they shoot off at 80 mph. Not surprisingly they're pulled over by a traffic cop. The cop radios into the police station. 'We've got a VIP situation here,' says the cop. 'I just pulled over someone who's really, really important.' 'Who is it?' asks the station controller. 'I don't know,' says the cop. 'But his chauffeur is the Pope.'

✳ Three weeks ago, my wife learned how to drive. Last week she learned how to aim it.

✳ Tom and Dick are driving along when Dick goes through some red lights. 'Careful,' says Tom. 'You'll have an accident.' 'It's all right,' says Dick. 'My brother does it all the time.' At the next red light Dick again speeds through without a care in the world. 'That's really dangerous,' says Tom. 'It's okay,' replies Dick. 'My brother does it all the time.' The next set of light are green and Dick puts on the brakes. 'Why are you stopping now?' asks Tom. 'My brother might be coming the other way,' replies Dick.

✳ Tom is driving down a country lane when he slows down to let another driver pass him going the other way. The other driver shouts, 'Pig!' as he passes. Tom shouts back, 'Bastard!' then crashes into a pig.

✳ What's the difference between a Skoda and a golf ball. If you're lucky you can drive a golf ball more than 200 yards.

✻ Why do Skodas have heated rear windows? So you're hands won't get cold when you're pushing it.

✻ Why is it that when you're driving and looking for an address, you turn down the volume on the radio?

✻ A little old lady buys her first car and decides to take it on a driving holiday round the Continent. She's very excited by the trip but the day she's due to leave she rings her friend and tells her the holiday is cancelled. 'Oh dear,' says the friend. 'What made you change your mind?' 'It's all this business about driving on the left,' says the old lady. 'I thought it would be easy, but when I had a practice drive round the town I almost killed myself.'

✻ A motorist is waiting behind another car that has stalled. While the driver of the stalled car tries to get it started again, the motorist notices a 'Doctor on call' sticker on the rear window. 'Come on, Doc!' he shouts. 'Let's get quacking!'

✻ Driving Instructor, to pupil, 'When we get to the top of the hill we have to change gear.' Pupil, 'What? No one said to bring another outfit!'

✻ There are two types of pedestrians; the quick and the dead.

✻ Last week I was run over by a Sinclair C5 – the owner is now suing me for damages.

CHAT-UP LINES

✻ 'Tell me about yourself – your struggles, your dreams, your phone number.' *Peter Arno*

✻ 'Why don't we break away from all this and lodge with my fleas in the hills – I mean, flee to my lodge in the hills.' *Groucho Marx*

✻ Baby, I'm like milk, I'll do your body good.

✻ Excuse me, I just noticed you noticing me and I just wanted to give you notice that I noticed you too.

❋ Hi, I'm new in town. Can I have directions to your house?

❋ Hi. I suffer from amnesia. Do I come here often?

❋ I want to melt in your mouth, not in your hand.

❋ I'd look so good on you.

❋ Inheriting eighty million pounds doesn't mean much when you have a weak heart.

chemists

A man walks into a chemist's and asks for an anal deodorant. The chemist explains that they don't stock them. The man insists that he bought his last one from this store. The chemist asks the man to bring in his last purchase and he will try to match the product. The next day the man returns and shows the deodorant to the chemist. The words on the label read, 'To use, push up bottom.'

A Swedish man walks into a chemist's and says, 'I would like to buy some deodorant please.' 'Certainly, sir,' says the chemist. 'Ball or aerosol?' 'Neither,' says the man. 'It's for my armpits.'

🍎 CHILDREN AND CHILDHOOD

❋ 'I married your mother because I wanted children – imagine my disappointment when you came along.' *Groucho Marx*

❋ 'Men name their children after themselves, women don't. Have you ever met a Sally Junior?' *Rita Rudner*

❋ A little girl goes to her local library to take out a book called *Advice for Young Mothers*. 'Why do you want a book like that?' says the librarian. The little girl replies, 'Because I collect moths.'

✳ A little girl is pounding away on her father's word processor. She tells him she's writing a story. 'What's it about?' asks Dad. 'I don't know,' she replies. 'I can't read.'

✳ A little girl runs up to her mother and asks, 'Mummy, where do babies come from?' 'The stork, dear,' replies her mother. 'Mummy, who keeps bad people from robbing our house?' asks the girl. 'The police, dear,' answers the mother. 'Mummy,' says the girl, 'if our house was on fire, who would save us?' 'The fire department,' answers the mother. 'Mummy, where does food come from?' asks the girl. 'Farmers, dear,' says the mother. 'Mummy,' says the girl, 'what do we need Daddy for?'

✳ A man comes home from the pub pushing a baby carriage. 'You idiot!' shouts his wife, 'that's not our baby!' 'I know,' says the husband, 'but it's a nicer pram.'

✳ A mother is getting ready to go out with her small son. 'Where are you going?' asks the boy's father. 'I'm taking Billy to the zoo,' says Mum. 'Lazy buggers,' says the father. 'If they want him tell them they can pick him up themselves.'

✳ A salesman rings on the doorbell of a house. The door is answered by a young boy smoking a cigar, holding a glass of brandy, with a copy of *Playboy* tucked under his arm. 'Say, sonny,' says the salesman. 'Is your mother at home?' The boy taps the ash off his cigar and says, 'What the hell do you think?'

✳ A salesman sees a young boy siting on a porch and says, 'Hi there, sonny. Is your mummy at home?' 'She sure is,' replies the boy. The salesman rings on the bell, then again, and again, but with no answer. He turns to the boy and says, 'Hey, I thought you said your mummy was at home.' 'She is,' replies the boy. 'But I don't live here.'

✳ A six-year-old boy and his friends are looking at his family picture album. When he gets to his parents' wedding portraits he says, 'And this is the day that Mummy came to work for us.'

✳ A small boy is talking with his granddad. 'Why does it rain?' he asks. Granddad replies, 'To make the plants grow.' The boy looks puzzled and says, 'So why does it rain on the pavement?'

✳ A Sunday school teacher asks her pupils where God lives. A small girl sticks up her hand and says, 'Miss. God lives in our bathroom.' 'In your bathroom?'

says the teacher. 'Why do you think he's in there?' The girl replies, 'Because every morning my daddy bangs on the bathroom door and shouts, "God, are you still in there?"'

※ A Yorkshire couple have five children: Harry, Richard, Sally, Jane and Ho Yung. Ho Yung is an unusual name for a Yorkshireman but the couple read that every fifth baby born in the world is Chinese.

※ Daddy comes home with a big bag of sweets and says to the kids, 'I'm going to give these to the person who never answers Mummy back and always does what they're told. Now who's going to get them?' And the kids reply, 'You are.'

※ Every parent is always going on about how their baby is the most marvellous special baby in the world. It clearly can't be true – it's my baby who is the most marvellous special baby in the world.

※ Groucho Marx, to Mrs Story, a quiz show contestant, 'How many children do you have?' Mrs Story, 'Nineteen.' Groucho, 'Nineteen! Why do you have so many children? It must be a terrible responsibility and a burden.' Mrs Story, 'Well, because I love my children and I think that's our purpose here on Earth, and I love my husband.' Groucho, 'I love my cigar, too, but I take it out of my mouth once in a while!'

※ I was the kid next door's imaginary friend.

※ Little Johnny comes running into the house and says, 'Mummy, can little girls have babies?' 'No,' says his mum, 'of course not.' Little Johnny runs back outside and yells, 'It's okay, we can play that game again!'

※ Little Johnny goes to him mother and says, 'Mummy, tomorrow I have an oral exam. One question the teacher will ask me is "who made you?" What should I say?' 'Say God made you,' replies his mother. Next day Little Johnny is asked the question but forgets what his mother said. He explains, 'Teacher, until yesterday I was sure it was my father who made me. But then mother said it was someone else – and now I can't remember the guy's name.'

※ Out of the mouths of babes and sucklings comes all manner of things. Usually puke.

☜ CINEMA

✳ 'I thought *Deep Throat* was a movie about a giraffe.' *Bob Hope*

✳ 'I would have won the Academy Award if not for one thing – my pictures.' *Bob Hope*

✳ How in movies does anyone getting out of a taxi manage to pull their exact fare out of their pocket without even checking it?

✳ In movies when you're having a fight with a large group of martial arts experts, why does each of them wait patiently until you've finished with their predecessor before attacking you themself?

✳ 'One time I went to the drive-in in a cab. The movie cost me $95.' *Steven Wright*

✳ Harry got a job at the film studios to get a little extra – her name was Wendy.

✳ Hollywood movies would be improved if they shot less film and more producers.

✳ It's true that in my new film I do appear completely naked in one scene, but I felt it was artistically necessary for the story – It's about a group of Hell's Angels at a gang bang.

✳ Two goats are scavenging on some rough ground behind a Hollywood film lot when they find an old reel of celluloid film. They're munching away on the film when one goat says to the other, 'Not bad is it?' 'Mmmm,' says the other. 'It's okay, but the book was better.'

✳ Why in movies are all bombs fitted with timing devices and large read-outs so you know exactly when they're due to go off?

✳ Why in movies do they always have L-shaped duvet covers that reach up to the waist on a man and up to the shoulders of the woman lying next to him?

✳ Why in movies is it never necessary to begin or end a phone conversation with 'Hello' or 'Goodbye'?

clowns

'I had an uncle who was a circus clown. When he died, all his friends went to the funeral in one car.' *Steven Wright*

A group of clowns rent furnished apartments in a condominium but are annoyed to discover they have not been provided with ironing boards. They go to complain to their landlord saying that all the other tenants have ironing boards except the clowns. 'It's in the contract,' says the landlord. 'You clowns have to use your window sills. Every clown has a sill for ironing.'

CONSTIPATION, DIARRHOEA AND INCONTINENCE

✳ A man goes to his doctor suffering from constipation. The doctor prescribes a powerful laxative but asks the man some questions so he can calculate the right dosage. 'How long will it take you to get home from here?' asks the doctor. 'Twenty minutes,' replies the man. The doctor pours a dose of laxative into a glass. 'And how long will it take you to get from the front door of your house to your bathroom?' asks the doctor. 'I'd guess about 30 seconds,' replies the man. The doctor adds a small amount of laxative to the glass. 'And how long will it take you to drop your trousers and sit on the toilet?' asks the doctor. 'I'd say five seconds,' answers the man. The doctor adds a tiny amount of laxative to the glass and gives it to the man. 'Take that, drink it all down, and go straight home,' says the doctor. Next day the doctor calls the man to see how he's feeling. 'Not so good,' replies the man. 'Didn't the laxative work?' asks the doctor. 'It worked fine,' replies the man. 'But it was seven seconds early.'

✳ Did you hear about the constipated accountant? He couldn't budget.

✳ Did you hear about the constipated composer? He got stuck on his last movement.

✳ I go with the flow – I'm a bed-wetter.

❦COSMETIC SURGERY

✳ A 47-year-old man has a face lift for his birthday. On his way home from the clinic he pops into the newsagent to buy a paper. Before leaving he says to the newsagent, 'I hope you don't mind me asking, but how old do you think I am?' 'About 35,' is the reply. 'I'm actually 47 years old,' the man says, feeling really happy. Next he goes into the fish and chip shop and, again, before leaving he asks the same question, to which the reply is, 'Oh, you look about 29.' This makes the man feel really good. While standing at a bus stop he asks an old woman the same question. She replies, 'I'm 85 years old and my eyesight is going. But when I was young there was a sure way of telling a man's age. If I put my hand down your trousers and play with your wedding tackle for ten minutes I will be able to tell your exact age.' The man thinks 'What the hell' and lets her slip her hand down his trousers. Ten minutes later the old lady announces, 'You're 47 years old.' Stunned, the man says, 'That was brilliant. How did you do that?' The old lady replies, 'I was behind you in the chip shop.'

✳ A plastic surgeon is asked if he's ever been asked to do anything unusual. 'No,' replies the surgeon. 'But I have raised a few eyebrows.'

✳ A woman goes to a plastic surgeon and has a radical new treatment. The surgeon puts a small screw in the back of her head so she can turn it and tighten up her skin every time it shows signs of wrinkling. A month later she comes back very upset, 'Doctor your treatment is dreadful! Look at my face! The bags under my eyes are huge and so matter how much I turn the screw they won't go away!' 'They're not bags,' replies the doctor, 'those are your breasts. And if you keep turning that screw you're going to end up with a goatee.'

✳ Female patient, 'Doctor, after my bust enhancement will the scars show?' Doctor, 'Well, that's rather up to you.'

✳ I don't know anything about cosmetic surgery but a good rule of thumb is, it's time to stop when you look permanently frightened.

✳ Man, to friend, 'I'm sure that woman has had a face lift.' Friend, 'How can you tell?' Man, 'Every time she crosses her legs her mouth snaps shut.'

☻CRICKET

✳ A mother is telling a friend that her son has been selected for the school cricket team. 'That's very good,' says the friend. 'What position does he play in?' 'I'm not sure,' says the mother. 'I think his father said he was one of the drawbacks.'

✳ An expectant father rings the hospital to see how his wife is getting on. By mistake he's connected to Lord's cricket ground. 'How's it going?' he asks. 'Fine,' comes the answer, 'we've got three out and hope to have the rest out before lunch. The last one was a duck.'

✳ God and the Devil arrange a cricket match and the Devil puts a huge bet on the outcome. 'You're very confident,' says God. 'I've got the finest players ever born on my side.' 'Yes,' replies the Devil. 'But I've got all the umpires.'

☻DANCING

✳ 'I could dance with you until the cows come home – on second thoughts, I'd rather dance with the cows until you come home.' *Groucho Marx*

✳ 'I grew up with six brothers. That's how I learned to dance – waiting for the bathroom.' *Bob Hope*

✳ 'I was watching a ballet at City Center. I'm not a ballet fan at all, but they were doing the dying swan, and there was a rumour that some bookmakers had drifted into town and that they'd fixed the ballet. Apparently there was a lot of money bet on the swan to live.' *Woody Allen*

✳ 'My friend Winnie spends all of his time practising limbo. He's pretty good. He can go under a rug.' *Steven Wright*

✳ Ballet dancers are always dancing round on their toes. Why don't they just hire taller dancers?

✳ Did you hear about the overweight ballerina? She had to wear a three-three.

☻DATING

✳ 'What is a date, really, but a job interview that lasts all night? Only difference between a date and a job interview is that not many job interviews have a chance that you'll end up naked at the end of it. "Well, Bill, the boss thinks you're the man for the position, why don't you strip down and meet some of the people you'll be working with."' *Jerry Seinfeld*

✳ A bachelor asks a computer dating agency to find him the perfect mate. 'I want a companion who is small and cute,' he says. 'She must love water sports and enjoy group activities.' The computer says, 'Marry a penguin.'

✳ A college student picks up his date at her parents' home. He's scraped together every penny he has to take her to a fancy restaurant but, to his dismay, she orders everything expensive on the menu. Appetisers, lobster, champagne – everything. Finally he says, 'Does your mother feed you like this at home?' 'No,' replies his date, 'but then Mother's not looking to get laid.'

✳ A girl asks her lover, 'If we get engaged will you give me a ring?' 'Of course,' he says. 'What's your phone number?'

✳ A girl brings her boyfriend home after a night on the town. Her parents are in so she tells him to be quiet. Unfortunately the boyfriend is desperate to use the loo, but rather than send him upstairs and risk him waking the parents, she tells him to use the kitchen sink. A few minutes later he sticks his head round the corner. 'Have you finished?' she whispers. 'Yes,' he replies. 'Have you got any paper?'

✳ A young couple park in Lovers Lane. 'It's very peaceful,' says the girl. 'Listen, you can hear the crickets.' 'They're not crickets,' replies the boy. 'They're zippers.'

✳ A girl brings her boyfriend home for the first time and her father takes him aside. 'I hope you're going to respect my daughter,' he says. 'I want her to know the difference between right and wrong.' 'You've brought her up to know what's right, haven't you?' asks the boy. 'Yes, I have,' says the father. The boy replies, 'Good. Well now I'm taking care of the other side.'

✳ A kiss is an application in the top floor for a job in the basement.

❋ A little old lady sits next to an old man on a bench in Miami. The woman asks, 'Are you a stranger here?' The man replies, 'Sort of. I used to live here years ago.' 'So, where have you been?' asks the old lady. The old man replies, 'I was in prison – for murdering my wife.' 'Really?' says the old lady 'So you're single ...'

❋ A lonely frog goes to a fortune teller. 'You're going to meet a beautiful young girl who will want to know everything about you,' says the fortune teller. The frog is thrilled. 'This is great!' he croaks. 'Will I meet her at a party?' 'No,' replies the fortune teller, 'in a biology class.'

❋ A man gives his girlfriend a small diamond. 'You said I was getting an engage-ment ring,' complains the girl. 'This is just an unmounted stone.' 'Don't worry,' says the man. 'It'll be mounted the day after you are.'

❋ A man goes into a bar and sees a beautiful woman sitting at a table. After gathering up his courage he finally goes over to her and says, 'Um, would you mind if I chatted with you for a while?' She yells back, 'No! I won't sleep with you tonight!' Everyone in the bar is now staring at them and the man slinks back to his table. After a few minutes, the woman walks over to him and apologises. 'I'm sorry if I embarrassed you,' she says. 'You see, I'm a graduate student in psychology, and I'm studying how people respond to embarrassing situations.' The man shouts back, 'What do you mean £200?'

❋ A mushroom walks into a bar. He sits next to a beautiful woman and tries to pick her up. He gives her a few cheap lines, but she says, 'Get out of here, I don't want anything to do with you!' The mushroom replies, 'What's the matter? I'm a fun-gi!'

❋ Harry and Tom are discussing former girlfriends. Harry says, 'Y'know I once dumped a girl because she had an incurable speech impediment.' 'That was cruel,' replies Tom. 'What was her problem?' Harry replies, 'She couldn't say "yes".'

❋ A teenage boy is picking up his date. While she's getting ready he chats with her father. 'What are you doing tonight?' asks Dad. 'We're going to the movies,' says the boy. 'But there's not much on.' 'Then why don't you go screwing?' sug-gests Dad. 'My daughter loves screwing. She'd screw all night long if she could.' 'Wow!' says the boy. 'Thanks for the tip.' The girl then appears and the young couple go out. Five minutes later the daughter storms into the house and con-fronts her father. 'Daddy!' she shouts. 'It's called "The Twist"!'

✳ A young man takes his Chinese girlfriend on a date. After a night of drinking they go back to his place and end up in the bedroom. 'What do you fancy doing?' asks the Chinese girl. 'I'm up for anything.' 'Okay,' replies the boyfriend. 'What I'd really like is some 69.' 'Oh get stuffed!' she replies, 'I'm not cooking at this time of night!'

✳ A young woman brings her boyfriend, a theology student, home to meet her parents. 'Do you own a house?' asks her father. 'Not yet, but God will provide,' says the student. 'And how do you intend to earn a living?' asks her father. 'I don't know, but God will provide,' replies the student. 'Have you made any long-term plans?' asks her father. 'No,' says the student. 'But I trust God will provide.' Later the mother asks the father what he thought of their prospective son-in-law. 'Well, he's broke and seems fairly stupid,' replies the father. 'But on the other hand, he thinks I'm God.'

✳ A young woman is sitting in a café telling her friends her idea of the perfect mate. 'The man I marry must be a shining light among company. He must be musical. Tell jokes. Sing. Entertain. And stay home at night!' The elderly waitress overhears her and says, 'If that's all you want, get a TV!'

✳ Advice to single girls – don't look for a husband, look for a bachelor.

✳ Girl, to friend, 'I had a terrible time last night, I had to slap my boyfriend three times.' Friend, 'What, to keep him in line?' Girl, 'No, to keep him awake.'

✳ Girl, to mother, 'I've been out with dozens of boys and I haven't let one of them kiss me.' Mother, 'Really? And which one was that?'

✳ Girl, to mother, 'My boyfriend boasts to everyone that he's going to marry the most beautiful girl in the world.' Mother, 'Oh that's a shame. I thought he liked you.'

✳ Harry wants to get married but can't find a girl his mother approves of. To solve this dilemma a friend suggests that he looks for a girl just like his mother, so he does. He finds a woman who looks like her, dresses like her, and talks like her. Then he takes her home to meet his parents. 'How did it go?' asks the friend. 'Terrible,' says Harry. 'Father hated her guts.'

✳ I once met a girl who said I could fill a void in her life. It was only later I realised she'd been referring to her wardrobe.

✻ Ladies, go for younger men. You might as well – they never mature anyway.

✻ My girlfriend told me I should be more affectionate. So I got two girlfriends.

✻ On their first date, Sam asks Rosie what she'd like to do. Rosie replies, 'Get weighed!' Sam finds this a curious request but takes her to the automatic scales outside the chemist's shop. Then he suggests they go to the cinema. After seeing the film Sam again asks Rosie what she wants to do. 'Get weighed!' says Rosie. Again Sam takes her to the chemist's shop to get weighed then suggests they have a meal. After dinner he asks what she'd like to do now. 'Get weighed!' says Rosie. Sam is exasperated by these odd requests and after taking her to the chemist's for another weighing drops her home. Rosie's mother greets her at the door. 'How was your date, darling?' asks her mother. 'Wousy!' replies Rosie.

✻ Suitor, to man, 'Sir, I want your daughter for my wife.' Man, 'Well, go home and tell your wife she can't have my daughter.'

✻ Tom's very lonely. He goes to women's prisons and volunteers for conjugal visits.

✻ Tom confronts his girlfriend. 'Who were you talking to on the phone? Is there somebody else?' 'Of course not,' replies his girlfriend. 'Do you think I'd be hang-ing out with a loser like you if there was somebody else?'

✻ The date had gone well but her kisses left something to be desired – the rest of her.

✻ Tom, to Dick, 'Who was that girl I saw you with last night?' Dick, 'It was someone from school.' Tom, 'Teacher?' Dick, 'No. I didn't have to.'

✻ Two Broadway showgirls are dressing for a performance when one notices that her friend is no longer wearing a flashy engagement ring. 'What happened, Lily?' she asks. 'Is the wedding off?' 'Yeah,' replies Lilly. 'I saw him in a bathing suit last week, and he looked so different without his wallet.'

✻ What's the difference between a walrus and a fox? About seven drinks.

✻ When I was in high school, I got in trouble with my girlfriend's dad. He said, 'I want my daughter back by 8.15.' I said, 'The middle of August? Cool!'

✳ 'A woman broke up with me and sent me pictures of her and her new boyfriend in bed together. Solution? I sent them to her dad.' *Christopher Case*

✳ A teenage boy promises his girlfriend a great time on Saturday. 'I've got three tickets for the movies,' he says. 'Why do we need three?' asks the girl. He replies, 'One for your dad, one for your mum, and one for your little sister.'

✳ A young couple knock on the door of a judge's house and ask him to marry them on the spot. 'I can't do that,' says the judge, 'I am not in court and we're out of court hours. Furthermore, it's Friday and the courthouse will not be open till ten o'clock on Monday morning.' 'Oh dear,' says the young man. 'In that case, could you say a few words to tide us over the weekend?'

✳ Ad: 'Princess, having sufficient experience with princes, seeks frog.'

✳ Boy, 'Are you the girl I was kissing at the party last night?' Girl, 'I don't know. What time were you there?'

✳ Drink till she's cute, but stop before the wedding.

✳ Girl, to friend, 'My boyfriend doesn't smoke, drink, gamble, swear, or behave improperly towards me.' Friend, 'That's nice. And does he do his own dress-making?'

✳ How does a man keep his youth? By giving her money, furs and diamonds.

🍏DEATH

✳ 'Either he's dead or my watch has stopped.' *Groucho Marx*

✳ 'I always remember the last words of my grandfather – "A truck!"' *Emo Phillips*

✳ 'I'll tell you what makes my blood boil – crematoriums.' *Tim Vine*

✳ 'I'm not afraid to die. I just don't want to be there when it happens.' *Woody Allen*

✳ 'What's the death rate round here?' 'Same as everywhere else – one per person.'

'My girlfriend's weird. One day she asked me, 'If you could know how and when you were going to die, would you want to know?' I said, 'No.' She said, 'Okay, forget it.' *Steven Wright*

✳ 'When I die, I'm leaving my body to science fiction.' *Steven Wright*

✳ A doctor is speaking to his patient. 'The results of your last test are conclusive,' he says. 'You've got six months to live.' 'Oh my God,' says the patient. 'Is there any thing I can do?' 'You could try lots of mud baths,' says the doctor. 'And will that cure me?' asks the patient. 'No,' replies the doctor. 'But it will help you get used to lying in dirt.'

✳ 'I'm really worried,' says a nervous patient to his nurse. 'Last week, I read about a man who was in hospital because of heart trouble and he died of malaria.' 'Relax,' replies the nurse. 'This is a first-rate hospital. When we treat you for heart trouble, you die of heart trouble.'

✳ A father is at the beach when his four-year-old son runs up, grabs his hand, and leads him to where a seagull is lying dead in the sand. 'Daddy, what happened?' asks the little boy. 'Well, son,' says Dad. 'This seagull died and he went up to Heaven.' 'Uh huh,' says the boy. 'So why did God throw him back down?'

✳ A flabby middle-aged woman has a near-death experience on the operating table. However, she hears the voice of God telling her not to worry as he will give her another 30 years of life. When she recovers the woman decides to make the most of the time left to her. She has extensive plastic surgery and takes a long exercise programme to lose weight and get back into shape. After she's transformed herself she takes up tennis but is killed by a bolt of lightning during her first game. Standing before God the woman complains, 'So what was all that about giving me another 30 years?' God does a double-take, puts on his glasses, and says, 'Oh, sorry. I didn't recognise you.'

✳ A little boy is in his back garden filling in a hole. A neighbour looks over the fence and asks what he's doing. 'I'm burying my pet goldfish,' says the little boy. 'That's a big hole for a little goldfish, isn't it?' comments the neighbour. 'Not really,' replies the little boy. 'It's inside your damn cat.'

✳ A man goes into a library and asks where he can find books on suicide. 'First row on the left,' replied the librarian. The man replies, 'But I've already looked in that section. It's empty.' 'I'm not surprised,' says the librarian. 'They don't often bring them back.'

✳ A man goes on holiday to Jamaica. His wife is on a business trip and is planning to meet him there the next day. When the man reaches his hotel, he sends his wife a quick e-mail but mistypes the address. The next day the grieving wife of a recently dead preacher checks her e-mail, screams, and drops dead from a heart attack. Her family find a disturbing message on the screen: 'Dearest Wife, Just got checked in. Everything prepared for your arrival tomorrow. Your Loving Husband. P.S. Sure is hot down here.'

✳ A man stops by the house of his friend, Jim. Jim's wife answers the door. 'Is Jim there?' asks the friend. 'No,' replies Jim's wife. 'Jim's gone to pick cotton.' Next day the friend stops by Jim's house again. Again he knocks on the door and, again, Jim's wife answers. 'Is Jim there?' asks the friend. 'No,' replies Jim's wife. 'Jim's gone to pick cotton.' Next day the friend tries again. He knocks on the door of Jim's house and again it's opened by Jim's wife. 'Is Jim there?' asks the friend. 'No,' replies Jim's wife. 'Jim's dead. We buried him in the backyard.' Jim's friend goes round to see Jim's grave and reads the inscription on his tombstone, 'Jim. Gone. But not for cotton.'

✳ A rich businessman goes on holiday. While he's away his butler sends him a message saying 'Cat's dead'. Distraught at the death of his beloved pet the man returns home and berates the butler for being so callous. 'You should break bad news gently,' says the businessman. 'If I'd been telling you that your cat was dead I'd have written, "The cat's on the roof and can't get down." A few hours later I'd have written, "The cat's fallen off the roof and is badly hurt." A while later I would have sent another message saying, "The cat has sadly passed away."' 'Very good, sir,' says the butler, 'I'll remember that in future.' The businessman resumes his trip, books into his hotel, and finds that the butler has left another message, it says, 'Your mother is on the roof and can't get down.'

✳ Death is God's way of saying, 'Hey, you're not alive any more.'

✳ First man, 'I follow the medical profession.' Second man, 'Are you a doctor?' First man, 'No, I'm an undertaker.'

✳ George visits his solicitor to make a will. 'So what exactly do I do?' asks Harry. 'Just answer a few questions then leave it all to me,' says the solicitor. 'Well,' says George, 'I'm quite fond of you, but I was hoping to leave some of it to my wife.'

✳ Harry believed so strongly in reincarnation he wrote a will leaving everything to himself.

✳ Harry is walking down the road when he notices an unusual funeral procession approaching the local cemetery. A hearse is followed by a second hearse and behind that walks a solitary man with a pitbull on a lead. Following behind the man are 200 other men walking in single file. Curious, Harry approaches the man with the dog. 'I hope you don't mind me asking, but whose funeral is this?' The man replies, 'Well, the first hearse is for my wife. She died after my dog attacked her. And the second hearse is for my mother-in-law. She was trying to help my wife when the dog turned on her too.' A thoughtful moment of silence passes. 'Any chance I could borrow your dog?' asks Harry. 'Join the queue,' says the man.

✳ Harry's wife dies and he takes it very badly, he even collapses over her coffin at the funeral. A friend takes him aside and tries to calm him down. 'Look, Harry. It's tough right now but you'll get over it. Who knows, in five or six months you might even find yourself a new girl.' 'Five or six months?' sobs Harry. 'What am I going to do tonight?'

✳ He's not dead, he's just electroencephalographically challenged.

✳ I used to work in the membership department of the Exit Society magazine, but it was very difficult getting people to renew their subscriptions.

✳ I want to die peacefully, in my sleep, like my grandfather. Not screaming and terrified, like his passengers.

✳ I wouldn't be caught dead with a necrophiliac.

✳ If he was alive today he'd turn in his grave.

✳ If you get fed up with elderly relatives coming up to you at weddings and saying, 'You'll be next', try doing the same to them at funerals.

✳ Mary gets married and has 17 children. Her husband dies, so she remarries two weeks later and has another 12 children. Her second husband then dies, as does Mary a month later. The local priest attends her wake and looks down on her in her coffin. 'Thank God,' says the priest. 'The two of them are together at last.' 'So, Father,' says one of the mourners. 'When you say that, are you talking about her first husband, or her second husband?' 'I'm not talking about her husbands,' says the priest. 'I'm talking about her legs.'

✳ My grandmother died on her 90th birthday. It was a terrible shame. We were only halfway through giving her the bumps at the time.

✳ My grandfather worked in a whisky distillery. One night he was working late, fell in the vat and six hours later he was drowned. It shouldn't really have taken him that long to die but he'd got out three times to go to the toilet.

✳ Only the young die good.

✳ Reporter, to man, 'Is it true that you found the body of a complete stranger in your back garden?' Man, 'Well, no, he was a partial stranger – he had an arm and a leg missing.'

✳ The last funeral I went to had people in the front pew who I wouldn't have to my funeral over my dead body.

✳ The man who wrote the song 'The Hokey Cokey' was buried yesterday, but they had a lot of trouble keeping his body in the casket. They'd put his left leg in…

✳ Tom is horrified when Harry tells him he's murdered his wife and buried her in the back garden. He rushes round to Harry's house and sure enough there she is – except Harry has left her bare backside sticking up out of the ground. 'Why did you do that?' asks Tom. 'Well,' says Harry, 'I needed somewhere to park my bike.'

✳ Where there's a will, I want to be in it.

✳ Tom, Dick, and Harry are building a skyscraper. Tom falls off and is killed instantly and Harry is sent to break the news to his wife. Two hours later Harry comes back carrying a six-pack. 'Where did you get the beer?' asks Dick. 'Tom's wife gave it to me,' replies Harry. 'That's unbelievable,' says Dick. 'You told the lady her husband's dead and she gave you beer?' 'Not exactly,' replies Harry. 'When she answered the door I said to her, "You must be Tom's widow." She said, "I'm not a widow." And I said, "Wanna bet me a six-pack?"'

✳ Two men are at a friend's funeral. 'Do you know if he left his wife much?' asks one. 'Yes,' said the other. 'Almost every night.'

✳ What did the corpse say when they lowered his coffin into the wrong hole? 'You're making a grave mistake.'

✳ What do a coffin and a condom have in common? They're both full of stiffs. Why are the stiffs different? One's coming, the other's going.

✳ When her late husband's will is read out, a widow learns he's left the bulk of his fortune to another woman. Enraged, she rushes to change the inscription on her spouse's tombstone. 'Sorry, lady,' says the stone mason. 'I inscribed "Rest in Peace" on your orders. I can't change it now.' 'Okay,' she replies grimly. 'Just add, "Until We Meet Again".'

✳ Widow, to friend, 'Don't talk to me about lawyers, I had so much trouble settling his estate I sometimes wished he hadn't died at all.'

✳ Reporter, to hangman, 'Have you ever executed an innocent man?' Hangman, 'I've had no complaints.'

✳ Solicitor, to relative of deceased, 'Your grandmother has left you five hundred clocks in her will.' Relative, 'Really. How long will it take to wind up her estate?'

🍎 DEFINITIONS

'Acquaintance: a person whom we know well enough to borrow from but not well enough to lend to.' *Ambrose Bierce*

Abundance: a social event held in a farm building.

Accountant: the sort of man who'd marry Elle MacPherson for her money.

Acme: spots on the top of your head.

Alcoholic: someone who drinks as much as you do, but who you don't like.

Alimony: the screwing you get for the screwing you got.

Alimony: a mistake by two people paid for by one.

An Australian gentleman: the bloke who gets out of the bath to pee in the sink.

Anarachnophobia: the fear of spiders wearing waterproof coats.

Antibody: your uncle's wife.

Antidote: a funny story you've heard before.

Barbarian: the man who cuts your hair.

Bartender: a pharmacist with a limited inventory.

Bashful: a tired boxer.

Blunderbuss: public transport from London to Brighton, via Glasgow.

Boycott: somewhere to keep male babies.

Budget: an orderly system for living beyond your means.

Buttress: a female dairy worker.

Campers: nature's way of feeding mosquitoes.

Catacomb: hair care for a pussy.

Catastrophe: first prize at a cat show.

Claustrophobia: the fear of Santa Claus.

Cobra: a bra for conjoined twins.

Committee: a group of the unwilling, picked from the unfit, to do the unnecessary.

Conference: the confusion of one man multiplied by the number present.

Conference room: a place where everybody talks, nobody listens, and everybody disagrees later on.

Confidence: when your wife catches you in bed with another woman and you slap her on the backside saying, 'Steady tiger! You're next!'

Consciousness: that annoying time between naps.

Coward: a man who thinks with his legs.

Dancing: the perpendicular expression of a horizontal desire.

Déjà Moo: the feeling that you've heard this bullshit before.

Deliberate: to take back to prison.

Diatribe: an extinct race.

Diplomacy: the art of letting someone else get your way.

Direct: ruined by a Welshman.

Dulcet: a boring tennis match.

Duration: a long oration.

Earth: the insane asylum for the universe.

Eternity: the time between you coming and her going.

Experience: something you don't get until just after you needed it.

Factory: a set of encyclopaedias.

Faggot: a lady maggot.

Farthingale: a cheap hurricane.

Fine: a tax for doing wrong. Tax: a fine for doing well.

Flashlight: a case for holding dead batteries.

Flatulence: opulent people living in apartments.

Fortune: a singing quartet.

Germicide: when bacteria kill themselves.

Gold-digger: a girl with the gift of the grab.

Golf: a five-mile walk punctuated by disappointments.

His: pronoun, meaning hers.

Home: the place you stay while your car is being serviced.

Increment: the opposite of excrement.

Inkling: a small ballpoint pen.

Intense: a camping holiday.

Karaoke: Japanese for 'Tone Deaf'.

Lecture: the art of transferring information from the notes of the lecturer to the notes of the students without passing through the minds of either.

Lobster: a tennis champion.

Maintenance: a man's cash surrender value.

Margin: mother's ruin.

Marriage (as defined by men): an expensive way to get laundry done for nothing.

Matricide: committing suicide on a rug.

MC: a man who introduces people who need no introduction.

Middle age: when you exchange emotions for symptoms.

Monologue: woman's conservation with her husband.

Obscenity: anything that gives the judge a hard-on.

Odious: bad poetry.

Office: a place where you can relax after your strenuous home life.

Optimist: someone who allows his teenage son to borrow the car. A pessimist: one who won't. A pedestrian: one who did.

Osmosis: an early Australian prophet.

Out of bounds: an exhausted kangaroo.

Oyster: a large crane.

Palaver: a kind of jumper.

Pandemonium: a black and white musical instrument.

Pantry: a knicker cupboard.

Peace: a period of unrest and confusion between wars.

Porcupine: a yearning for bacon.

Posse: a wild west cat.

Reality: the place the pizza delivery man comes from.

Reoriented: sent back to China.

Savoury: a piggy bank.

Shamrock: imitation mineral.

Shin: a device for finding furniture in the dark.

Smattering: the act of asking 'What's the matter?'

Stabilised: an imprisoned horse.

Stalemate: old spouse.

Suburbia: where they tear out the trees and then name streets after them.

Syntax: the money collected at the church from sinners.

Tantamount: riding a French aunt.

Time: what keeps things from happening all at once.

dictionaries

'The other night I was reading the dictionary – I thought it was a poem about everything.' *Steven Wright*

I don't know if you've heard but apparently they've removed the word 'gullible' from the *Oxford English Dictionary*

DISABILITY

✳ A doctor is explaining the idea of sensory compensation to an intern. 'If a man becomes blind his sense of hearing improves to compensate,' says the doctor. 'Yes, sir,' says the intern. 'And I've noticed that if one of a man's legs is slightly short, then the other gets slightly longer.'

✳ A woman is talking with her neighbour. 'Did you know the milkman has a glass eye?' 'No,' replies the neighbour. 'How did you discover that?' 'Oh,' says the woman, 'it just came out when we were chatting.'

✳ Grandma finally figured out how to stop Grandpa chasing after other women – she let the air out of his wheelchair tyres.

✳ I tried going to the Special Olympics but I couldn't get a parking space anywhere near the place.

✳ Quasimodo comes home and finds Esmeralda holding a wok and a laundry basket. 'Great,' says Quasimodo. 'Are you cooking Chinese tonight?' 'No,' says Esmerelda. 'I'm ironing your shirt.'

✳ The Godfather, accompanied by his attorney, meets with his accountant. The Godfather says to the accountant, 'Where's the three million bucks you embezzled from me?' The accountant doesn't answer. The Godfather pulls out a gun and says, 'If you don't tell me where it is I'll shoot you in the head and splatter your brains against the wall!' The attorney interrupts, 'Sir, the man is a deaf-mute, but I can interpret for you.' The attorney, using sign language, asks the accountant where the three million dollars is. The accountant signs back, 'The money's hidden in a suitcase behind the shed in my backyard!' 'Well, what did he say?' asks the Godfather. The attorney replies, 'He says he doesn't think you have the guts to pull the trigger.'

☺ DISABILITY: BLINDNESS

✳ A blind man is at the optician's with his guide dog. Both are facing the eye test chart on the wall. The optician takes the guide dog away, replaces it with another guide dog, and asks, 'Is that better or worse?'

✳ A blind man walks into a store with his guide dog. He takes the dog's leash and starts swinging the animal round his head. The storekeeper says, 'May I help you, sir?' The blind man replies, 'No thanks. I'm just looking.'

✳ Stevie Wonder and Tiger Woods get talking in a bar. Tiger is surprised to discover that Stevie can play golf. 'How can you play golf blind?' asks Tiger. Stevie says, 'I get my caddy to stand in the middle of the fairway. Then he calls to me and I play the ball towards the sound of his voice.' 'That's fantastic,' says Tiger. 'So what's your handicap?' 'Actually I'm a scratch golfer,' says Stevie. 'Incredible,' says Tiger. 'We ought to play a round sometime.' 'I'd like that,' says Stevie. 'But I should warn you I usually play for $10,000 a hole.' 'Suits me,' says Tiger. 'When do you want to play?' 'I'm easy,' says Stevie. 'Pick a night!'

☻DISABILITY: DEAFNESS

※ A little boy is spending Christmas Eve at his grandma's house. When he goes to bed he hangs up his stocking and shouts, 'Dear Santa! Please send me a new bike!' Grandma sticks her head round the door and says 'Hush in there! Santa isn't deaf!' 'I know,' says the little boy. 'But you are.'

※ An Asian marriage broker has been given the job of finding a bride for an impoverished middle-aged groom. The broker warns the man's parents that he's not much of a catch so they'll have to make do with whatever brides are available. However, when the girl is presented the man's parents are appalled. 'Look at her,' whispers the father to the mother. 'She has knock-knees, cross-eyes, a moustache, a huge wart, and buck teeth.' 'There's no need to whisper,' says the broker. 'She's deaf too.'

※ Beethoven was so deaf he thought he was a painter.

※ If blind people wear dark glasses, why don't deaf people wear earmuffs?

☻DRINK, DRINKING AND DRUNKENNESS

※ A bus conductor asks a drunk for his ticket. He goes through all his pockets but can't find it. 'It's okay,' says the conductor. 'I'm sure you paid.' 'Never mind that,' says the drunk. 'If I can't find it how am I supposed to know where I'm going?'

※ '24 hours in a day, 24 beers in a case. Coincidence? I think not.' *Steven Wright*

※ 'Do you drink to excess?' 'I'll drink to anything.'

※ 'Here's to alcohol – the cause of, and solution to, all of life's problems.' *Homer Simpson*

※ 'It only takes one drink to get me loaded. Trouble is, I can't remember if it's the thirteenth or fourteenth.' *George Burns*

❋ 'My wife drives me to drink.' 'You're lucky. I had to walk.'

❋ 'Why is American beer served cold?' 'So you can tell it from urine.' *David Moulton*

❋ A barman offers his customers free drinks if they can name a cocktail he doesn't know how to make. Many people try to catch him out by naming the most obscure cocktails they can think of, but the barman knows them all. That is until one man names a drink called a 'Southampton'. The barman is stumped and has to admit he's never heard of it. 'So how do I make one?' he asks. 'It's easy,' says the man. 'All you need is a large port.'

❋ A biker chick is sitting at a bar drinking beer. Every time she lifts her arm to knock one back, she reveals she has an incredibly hairy armpit. A drunk at the other end of the bar watches her in fascination. Eventually he turns to the barman and says, 'Say, I'd like to buy that ballerina a drink.' 'What makes you think she's a ballerina?' replies the barman. 'Hell,' says the drunk. 'Any gal who can raise her leg that high has to be a ballerina!'

❋ A doctor is speaking to a patient after an examination, 'There are two reasons for your poor health, it's entirely due to drinking and smoking.' 'That's a relief,' replies the patient. 'I thought you were going to say it was my fault.'

❋ A drunk falls down the steps of the Hilton hotel, crawls to a waiting cab, and says to the driver, 'Hey, take me to the Hilton.' 'We're already there,' replies the cabby. 'That's great,' slurs the drunk. 'Only next time – don't drive so fast.'

❋ A drunk goes to court. The judge says, 'You've been brought here for drinking.' The drunk says, 'Great. Let's get started.'

❋ A drunk goes up to a parking meter, puts in a quarter, and watches as the dial goes to 60. 'I can't believe it,' he says. 'I just lost 100 pounds!'

❋ A drunk in a pub finishes his pint and slams the glass on the bar top. 'Piss!' he says, then asks for another. He downs this one too and, again, slams his empty glass down saying, 'Piss!' This happens again, and again until eventually the barman looks the drunk in the face and says, 'Piss off.' The drunk replies, 'Oh. In that case I'll have a vodka.'

✳ A drunk phones the offices of Alcoholics Anonymous. 'Is that AA?' asks the drunk. 'Yes,' says the switchboard operator. 'Would you like to join?' 'No,' says the drunk. 'I'd like to resign.'

✳ A drunk phones the police to report that thieves have been in his car. 'They've stolen the dashboard, the steering wheel, the brake pedal, even the accelerator,' he cries out... 'Oh hang on. I'm in the back seat.'

✳ A drunk staggers in a Catholic church late one night and collapses in the confessional. Next morning he's awoken by the sound of the priest entering the cubicle next to him. The priest addresses him through the grille. 'Good morning, my son. What can I do for you?' 'You got here just in time,' replies the drunk. 'Could you pass over some toilet paper?'

✳ A man is staggering home drunk late at night when he's stopped by a policeman. 'What are you doing out here at this time of night?' asks the officer. 'I'm going to a lecture,' replies the man. 'And who's going to give a lecture at this hour?' asks the policeman. 'My wife,' replies the man.

✳ A drunk stumbles on to a baptismal service by the river. The minister notices him and says, 'Sir, are you ready to find Jesus?' The drunk replies, 'Yesh, Your Honour, I shur am!' The minister pushes the drunk under water and pulls him up. 'Have you found Jesus?' he asks. 'No, I shur dint!' says the drunk. The preacher dunks him again and says, 'Brother, have you found Jesus yet?' 'No, I shur dint!' the drunk slurs again. The preacher holds the drunk under for half a minute and brings him up again. 'Sinner, have you still not found Jesus?' The drunk wipes his eyes and says, 'Nope. Are you sure this is where he fell in?'

✳ A hangover is the wrath of grapes.

✳ A man goes into a pub and says, 'I'd like something tall, icy and full of gin.' The barman turns and shouts into the kitchen, 'Oi, Doris! Someone to see you!'

✳ A man spends all night drinking at a pub. When it's time to go he stands up and falls flat on his face, so he decides to crawl outside in the hope the fresh air will sober him up. Once outside he stands up and falls over, so he has to crawl the half-mile to his house. When he gets home he manages to prop himself upright so he can unlock the front door, then falls on his face again and crawls up the stairs. When he reaches his bed he tries to stand one last time but collapses and falls fast asleep. The next morning he's woken by his wife's shouting, 'You've been out on the booze again, haven't you!' 'What makes you says that?' asks the man. 'Don't bother to lie about it!' shout his wife. 'The pub rang, you left your wheelchair behind again!'

✳ Did you hear about the drunk who thought Alcoholics Anonymous meant drinking under an assumed name?

✳ He doesn't drink anything stronger than pop. Mind you Pop will drink anything.

✳ A man walks into a bar and finds a drunk playing with a small ball of gloop. The drunk mutters to himself, 'It looks like plastic, but it feels like rubber.' Interested, the man looks over the drunk's shoulder and takes a peek at the strange substance. 'It's weird stuff,' says the drunk. 'It looks like plastic but it feels like rubber.' 'That's unusual,' says the man. 'I'm a chemist, perhaps I can tell what it is.' The drunk hands the man the gloop and he rolls it between his fingers. 'You're right,' he says. 'It does look like plastic but feel like rubber. Do you know where it came from?' 'Sure,' replies the drunk. 'It just fell out of my nose.'

✳ A motorcycle cop pulls over a driver. 'Have you been drinking, sir?' says the cop. 'Why?' says the driver. 'Is there a fat chick in my car?'

✳ A policeman is staking out a bar looking for drunk drivers. At closing time, he sees a man stumble out of the bar, trip on the kerb, and fumble for his keys for five minutes. When he finally gets in his car, it takes the man another five minutes to get the key in the ignition. Meanwhile, everybody else leaves the bar and drives off. When the man finally pulls away, the policeman is waiting for him. He pulls him over and gives him a breathalyser test. The test shows he has a blood alcohol level of zero. 'That can't be right,' says the policeman. 'Yes, it can,' says the man. 'Tonight I'm the designated decoy.'

✳ A woman is chatting with her friends when she points at a man in the street, 'That's my next-door neighbour. He's an alcoholic!' One of her friends asks, 'How do you know that?' The woman replies, 'Yesterday he was at the bar drinking next to me all night.'

✳ Beer: helping ugly people have sex since 3000 BC!

✳ He drank like a fish. Which would have been okay if he'd drunk what the fish drinks.

✳ He used to drink so much, Gordon's thought he was a wholesaler.

✳ He's donating his body to science. And he's preserving it in alcohol until they can use it.

✳ I feel sorry for people who don't drink. When they wake up in the morning, that's as good as they're going to feel all day.

✳ I never drink unless I'm alone or with somebody.

✳ It's night and a couple are sleeping in bed when there's a knock on the front door. The man gets out of bed and hurries downstairs. He opens the door and finds a drunk waiting outside. 'Hey,' says the drunk. 'Be a pal and give me a push.' 'No!' shouts the man. 'Do you know what time it is?' The man slams the door, goes back to bed, and explains what happened to his wife. 'You should be ashamed of yourself,' says his wife. 'That man was asking for our help and you turned him down flat. I don't care if he was drunk, go out and help him push his car.' The man gives in, puts on some clothes, and goes out to find the drunk. He opens the front door and calls out into the darkness. 'Hey!' he shouts. 'Do you still want a push!?' 'Yesh!' shouts back the drunk. 'I'm over here on your swing!'

✳ One cure for a cold consists of three shots of whisky. There are better remedies, but most people don't want to hear them.

✳ It's night and a drunk is crawling along the pavement looking for something. A passer-by offers to help and asks what's missing. The drunk replies that he's lost his watch. 'And where abouts did you lose it?' asks the passer-by. 'About half a mile up the road,' replies the drunk. 'So why are you doing down here?' asks the passer-by. The drunk replies, 'Down here the lighting is better.'

✳ My wife hates the sight of me when I'm drunk, and I hate the sight of her when I'm sober.

✳ One night Harry had been drinking so much he came home and was sick all over the cat. He looked down at it and said, 'I don't remember eating that.'

✳ Rehab is for quitters.

✳ Response to a heckle – 'Listen to him. I thought alcoholics were meant to be anonymous.'

✳ Sean gets home in the early hours of the morning after a night at the pub. He makes such a racket that he wakes up his missus. 'What on earth are you doing down there?' she yells down from the bedroom. 'Get yourself to bed and don't wake the neighbours!' 'I'm trying to get a barrel of Guinness up the stairs,' shouts Sean. 'Leave it till the morning,' she yells back. 'I can't,' he shouts. 'I've drunk it.'

✳ Sometimes too much to drink isn't enough.

✳ The Australian rugby team is being driven through Dublin. The driver shouts out, 'And if you look to your left you'll see we're going past the biggest pub in the city.' A voice from the back shouts, 'Why?'

✳ To be intoxicated is to feel sophisticated, but not be able to say it.

✳ Tom is walking home from the pub late one night when he takes a short cut across a cow field. Halfway across he drops his hat. He has to try on fifty others before he finds it again.

✳ We call my father-in-law the exorcist. Every time he visits he rids the house of spirits.

✳ Two drunks are walking down the street when they come across a dog, sitting on the kerb, licking its privates. They watch for a while before one of them says, 'I sure wish I could do that!' The other looks at him and says, 'Wouldn't you like to make friends with him first?'

✳ Why has Guinness got a white head on it? So when you're drunk you know which end to start on.

✳ A drunk goes up to a policeman and says, 'Exchuse me. But what ish the time?' The policeman says, 'One o'clock.' Then hits the drunk on the head with his truncheon. 'Christ!' exclaims the drunk. 'I'm glad I didn't ashhk an hour ago.'

✳ A man climbs in through the window of a pub, crawls up the wall, climbs across the ceiling and crawls down the other side. He then orders a pint of cider, drinks it, and leaves the same way he came in. 'That was odd,' says a customer at the bar. 'Yes,' agrees the barman. 'He usually has a Guinness.'

✳ A man staggers home after an evening at the pub and is accosted by his wife. 'What do you mean coming home half-drunk?' she yells. 'Sorry,' slurs the man. 'I ran out of money.'

✳ Harry goes through customs and has his bag searched. 'Have you got any wines or spirits in here?' asks the customs officer. 'No,' says Harry, 'just clothes.' 'And what sort of clothing is this?' asks the officer, pulling a hip flask out of Harry's case. 'That's a night-cap,' says Harry.

✳ A staggering line – the shortest distance between two pubs.

✳ Beauty is in the eye of the beer holder...

✳ Harry's bed gets burnt so he tries to claim the cost of a new one from the insurance company. The company refuses to pay up as the fire brigade report states the fire was the result of a lit cigarette dropped when Harry was drunk. Harry writes an indignant response saying that he was stone cold sober on the night of the blaze and the bed was already alight when he got in it.

✳ Magistrate, to defendant, 'How many times have you appeared before me for drunkenness?' Defendant, 'I don't know. I thought you were the one keeping score.'

✳ Man, to wife, 'Drinking makes you look beautiful.' Wife, 'But I haven't had a drink.' Man, 'No, but I have.'

✳ QC, to defendant, 'Do you drink much?' Defendant, 'That's my business.' QC, 'And do you have any other business?'

✳ The optician's daughter went to the party – it only took two glasses before she made a spectacle of herself.

✳ What do you call a man who puts people in touch with spirits? A barman.

✿DRUGS

✳ 'Why are there no recreational drugs taken in suppository form?' *George Carlin*

✳ A friend of mine confused her valium with her birth control pills. She now has 14 kids – but doesn't really care.

✳ Drugs may lead to nowhere, but at least it's the scenic route.

✳ Have you heard about the craze for Ecstasy-impregnated bubble gum that's sweeping the Yorkshire dance clubs? It's called 'E' ba gum.

✳ I said 'no' to drugs, but they just wouldn't listen.

✳ I say that if a rock star is found to have used illegal drugs, the Olympic commission should strip him of his gold discs.

✳ If you really want to get stoned, drink wet cement.

✳ In the 60s people took acid to make the world appear weird. Now the world is weird, people take Prozac to make it normal.

✳ Some people think its clever to take drugs. Most of them are customs officers.

dyslexia

A dyslexic man walks into a bra...

Did you hear about the atheist dyslexic? He didn't believe there was a dog.

Man, to job applicant, 'The spelling in your resumé is very erratic. Are you sure you don't have dyslexia?' Applicant, 'Have it? I can't even smell it.'

Why is dyslexia so hard to spell?

✎ EDUCATION

✳ 'And who can tell me the name of the Speaker of the House?' asks the fourth-form teacher. Billy's hand shoots up, 'Mummy.'

✳ 'Our bombs are smarter than the average high school student. At least they can find Kuwait.' *A Whitney Brown*

✳ 'She sends me to the principal's office. I get there and sit down, and he looks at me and says, "Emo, Emo, Emo…" I said, "I'm the one in the middle, you drunken slob."' *Emo Phillips*

✳ A boy is doing badly in mathematics so his parents send him to a strict Catholic boarding school. To his parents' delight his grades rocket. On their next visit they ask him what his new school does that the old one didn't. 'They're much tougher here,' he says. 'As soon as I saw that guy nailed to the giant plus-sign I knew they meant business.'

✳ A class has been photographed and teacher is trying to persuade them to buy a copy of the group picture. 'Just think how nice it will be to look at it when you are all grown up and say "There's Jennifer – she's a lawyer" or "That's Michael – he's a doctor".' A small voice calls out, 'And there's teacher – she's dead!'

✳ A couple send their dim son to a special tutor to help him catch up on his schoolwork. After a month they ask for a progress report. 'He's getting straight As,' says the tutor. 'That's fantastic,' say the parents. 'Yes, they're great,' says the tutor. 'But his Bs are still a little wonky.'

✳ A public school raises its fees but sends out letters mistakenly saying that the new fees will be paid 'per anum' rather than the correct 'per annum'. One parent writes back to say that he agrees to the new fees but would rather continue paying through the nose.

✳ Father, to son, 'Let me see your report card.' Son, 'You can't. My friend just borrowed it. He wants to scare his parents.'

✳ I never learned to spell at school, the teachers kept changing the words.

✳ A small boy is being tested on the Kings and Queens of England. 'And who followed Edward the Sixth?' asks the teacher. 'Mary,' replies the boy. 'And who followed her?' asks the teacher. The boy replies, 'Her little lamb.'

✳ A small boy is walking slowly to school. 'Hurry up! You'll be late!' shouts out his mother. 'There's no rush,' he replies. 'They're open till three-thirty.'

✳ A teacher is trying to explain addition to a young boy. 'Johnny, if I laid two eggs over there and two eggs over here, how many would I have?' 'I don't know,' says Johnny. 'Let's see you do it first.'

✳ An English teacher says to her pupils, 'There are two words I don't allow in my class. One is gross and the other is cool.' From the back of the room a voice calls out, 'So, what are the words?'

✳ An English teacher spots a boy staring out of the window and calls out a question, 'You, boy! Give me two pronouns.' The boy looks round and says, 'Who? Me?'

✳ Dolly Parton tried working as a schoolteacher for a while but it was no good. Every time she turned round she wiped everything off the blackboard.

✳ Father, to son, 'How do you like going to school?' Son, 'The going bit and the coming home bit are fine, but I'm not keen on the time in between.'

✳ I remember my first day at school. Some kids came up and said, 'Let's play tick.' Then they infested me with ticks.

✳ I woke up and realised I didn't have to go to school today. I was so happy – then I remembered I'm an unemployed 43-year-old.

✳ I've got qualifications in biology and metalwork. So if you need someone to weld your budgie, I'm your man.

✳ Little Johnny's second-grade teacher is quizzing them on the alphabet. 'Johnny,' she says, 'what comes after "O"?' Johnny says, 'Yeah?'

✳ Mother, to daughter, 'What was the first thing you learned in class?' Daughter, 'How to talk without moving my lips!'

✻ Make little things count. Teach arithmetic to dwarves.

✻ Man, to friend, 'My uncle was the only truant at his correspondence school.' Friend, 'How can you be a correspondence school truant?' Man, 'Easy, you send back empty envelopes.'

✻ Mother, to son, 'What did you learn in school today, dear?' Son, 'How to write.' Mother, 'And what did you write?' Son, 'I don't know, they haven't taught us to read yet.'

✻ Professor, to medical student, 'What happens when the human body is immersed in water?' Student, 'The telephone rings.'

✻ Teacher asks her class to come up with a story that has a moral. Little Billy stands up and says, 'Last week we were driving back from the market with a basket of eggs. We hit a bump in the road and some of the eggs got broke. The moral is – don't put all your eggs in one basket.' Little Susie then stands up and says, 'My grandma had five chicken eggs. She put them in an incubator but only three hatched. The moral is – don't count your chicken before they're hatched.' Little Johnny stands up and says, 'My Uncle Jim was in Vietnam. One day his helicopter crashed behind enemy lines and all he had was a machine gun, a knife and a crate of beer. He drank all the beer then killed 30 Vietcong with his gun. Then he ran out of bullets so he stabbed another 20 Vietcong with his knife. Then he lost the knife and strangled another 10 with his bare hands. Then he got home.' 'I see,' says teacher. 'And what's the moral of that?' Little Johnny replies, 'Don't mess with Uncle Jim when he's drunk.'

✻ Teacher is giving one of her pupils, Patty, a maths lesson. 'Patty, If I give you two rabbits and two rabbits and another two rabbits, how many rabbits have you got?' Patty replies, 'Seven!' 'No,' says teacher. 'Listen carefully. If I give you two rabbits and two rabbits and another two rabbits, how many rabbits have you got?' 'Seven!' replies Patty. 'Let's try this another way,' says teacher. 'If I give you two apples and two apples and another two apples, how many apples have you got?' 'Six,' says Patty. 'Good,' says teacher. 'Now if I give you two rabbits and two rabbits and another two rabbits, how many rabbits have you got?' Patty replies, 'Seven!' Teacher is getting cross, 'How on earth do you work out that three lots of two rabbits is seven?' Patty replies, 'Because that's six rabbits plus the one I've already got at home!'

✳ Teacher is playing a guessing game with her class. 'What have I got behind my back?' says teacher. 'I'll give you a clue – it's round, red and juicy.' 'A tomato?' asks Little Jenny. 'No,' says teacher. 'It's an apple, but I like the way you're thinking. Who can guess what I've got behind my back now? The clue is, it's small, green and hairy.' 'Is it a gooseberry?' asks Little Simon. 'No,' says teacher. 'It's a kiwi fruit, but I like the way you're thinking.' Little Johnny sticks up his hand. 'Miss can you guess what I'm holding in my pocket?' 'Give me a clue,' says teacher. Johnny replies, 'Well it's round, hard and has a head on it.' 'That's disgusting,' says teacher. 'No,' replies Johnny. 'It's a coin, but I like the way you're thinking.'

✳ Teacher, 'Can anyone tell me how many seconds there are in a year?' Pupil, 'Twelve. The second of January, the second of February…!'

✳ Teacher, 'Class, we'll have only half a day of school this morning…' Class, 'Hooray!' Teacher, 'We'll have the other half this afternoon!'

✳ Teacher, 'Jimmy, how do you manage to get so many things wrong in a day?' Jimmy, 'I start early.'

✳ Teacher, 'Tommy, this letter from your father looks like it was written by you.' Tommy, 'That's because he borrowed my pen to write it.'

✳ Teacher, 'What does the 1286BC inscribed on the mummy's tomb indicate?' Pupil, 'Is it the registration number of the car that ran him over?'

✳ Teacher, 'When was Rome built?' Pupil, 'At night.' Teacher, 'Why did you say that?' Pupil, 'Because my dad always says that Rome wasn't built in a day!'

✳ Teacher, 'Who can tell me where Hadrian's Wall is?' Pupil, 'I expect it's around Hadrian's garden!'

✳ Teacher, 'Why can't you ever answer any of my questions?' Pupil, 'Well, if I could there wouldn't be much point in me being here!'

✳ Teacher, 'How much is half of eight?' Pupil, 'Up and down or across?' Teacher, 'What do you mean?' Pupil, 'Well, up and down makes three and across the middle leaves a zero.'

✳ Teacher, to class, 'Can someone tell me what happens to a car when it gets old and starts to rust?' Pupil, 'My dad buys it.'

✳ Teacher, to pupil, 'When you yawn, you're supposed to put your hand to your mouth!' Pupil, 'What? And get bitten!'

✳ Teacher, 'Johnny, give me a sentence starting with "I".' Little Johnny replies, 'I is...' Teacher interrupts, 'No, Johnny. Always say "I am".' Johnny replies, 'Okay. I am the ninth letter of the alphabet.'

✳ Teacher, 'Didn't you hear me call you?' Pupil, 'You said not to answer you back!'

✳ Teacher, to pupil, 'Can you name an animal that lives in Lapland?' Pupil, 'A reindeer.' Teacher, 'Can you name another?' Pupil, 'Another reindeer.'

✳ Teacher, to pupil, 'Where's the English Channel?' Pupil, 'I don't know, my TV doesn't pick it up.'

✳ The headmistress of a girls' school asks the local vicar to give her pupils a talk on Christianity and sex. The vicar is happy to do so but doesn't want to upset his prudish wife so he tells her he'll be giving the girls a talk about sailing. A week later the headmistress meets the vicar's wife in the street and tells her what a good talk her husband gave. 'I can't imagine it was that good,' says the wife. 'He's only ever done it twice. The first time he was sick, and the second time his hat blew off.'

✳ They did a raffle at my daughter's school. First prize was a place at a better school.

✳ He was a slow starter. At kindergarten he was different from all the other five-year-olds – he was eleven.

✳ What does a maths graduate say to a sociology graduate? 'I'll have the burger and fries, please.'

✳ A boy enters a spelling competition and is asked to spell Mississippi. 'Which one?' he replies. 'The river or the state?'

✳ What's the difference between a university and a polytechnic? At university they tell you to wash your hands after visiting the toilet. At a polytechnic they teach you not to pee over your fingers.

✏ EDUCATION:
DUMB EXAM ANSWERS

✳ Descibe the functions of the human spine: 'The spinal column is a long bunch of bones. The head sits on the top and you sit on the bottom.'

✳ Explain one of the processes by which water can be made safe to drink: 'Flirtation makes water safe to drink because it removes large pollutants like grit, sand, dead sheep and canoeists.'

✳ Give the meaning of the term 'Caesarian Section': 'The caesarian section is a district in Rome.'

✳ How are the main parts of the body categorised?: 'The body is consisted into three parts, the brainium, the borax, and the abdominal cavity. The branium contains the brain, the borax contains the heart and lungs, and the abdominal cavity contains the five bowels A, E, I, O and U.'

✳ How can you delay milk turning sour?: 'Keep it in the cow.'

✳ In a democratic society, how important are elections?: 'Very important. Sex can only happen when a male gets an election.'

✳ Name the four seasons: 'Salt, pepper, mustard and vinegar.'

✳ Use the word 'diploma' in a sentence: 'Our pipes were leaking so my dad called diploma.'

✳ Use the word 'information' in a sentence: 'Geese sometimes fly information.'

✳ Use the word 'judicious' in a sentence: 'Hands that judicious can be as soft as your face.'

✳ What are steroids?: 'Things for keeping carpets still on the stairs.'

✳ What is a seizure?: 'A Roman emperor.'

✳ What is a terminal illness?: 'When you are sick at the airport.'

✳ What is a turbine?: 'Something an Arab wears on his head.'

✳ What is artificial insemination?: 'When the farmer does it to the bull instead of the cow.'

✳ What is the fibula?: 'A small lie.'

✳ Where was the Magna Carta signed?: 'At the bottom.'

✳ Which English King invented the fireplace?: 'Alfred the Grate.'

✳ Who invented fractions?: 'Henry the ⅛.'

✳ Who invented King Arthur's round table?: 'Sir Circumference.'

✳ Who succeeded the first president of the USA?: 'The second one.'

✳ Who was the Black Prince?: 'The son of Old King Cole.'

✳ Why does history keep repeating itself?: 'Because we weren't listening the first time.'

✳ Why was George Washington buried at Mount Vernon?: 'Because he was dead.'

✳ Why were the early days of history called the Dark Ages?: 'Because there were so many knights.'

✦ELECTRICIANS AND ELECTRICAL ITEMS

✳ My wife has an electric blender, an electric toaster and an electric bread maker. Then she says, 'There are too many gadgets, and no place to sit down!' So I bought her an electric chair.

✳ 'I bought some batteries but they weren't included. So I had to buy them again.' *Steven Wright*

✳ 'There was a power outage at a department store yesterday. Twenty people were trapped on the escalators.' *Steven Wright*

✳ A bricklayer, a carpenter, and an electrician are arguing about which has the oldest profession. 'We built the Pyramids,' says the bricklayer. 'We must have been the first.' 'We built Noah's Ark before the Pyramids,' says the carpenter. 'We were first.' The electrician says, 'You're both wrong. When God said, "Let there be light", it came on straight away. We must have been there to put in the wiring.'

ethnic – cockney

What do you call a cockney in a detached house? A burglar.

ethnic – french

What do you call 100,000 Frenchmen with their hands up? The Army.

☻ ETHNIC: IRISH

✳ A mine collapses near a small town. An engineer survives the disaster and goes to the local bar. The bar is empty except for one other customer. 'Hey bartender,' says the engineer. 'I'll have a beer and pour another one for my friend over there.' The bartender replies, 'I'm sorry, sir, but that guy's Irish and we don't serve his kind here.' 'Well, you'd better because if it weren't for that guy, I wouldn't be here,' says the engineer. 'You know the mine that caved in, well I was in that mine and so was that guy. When the last of us were escaping, he held the roof of the mine up with his head! So get him a beer. If you don't believe me, look at the top of his head. You'll see it's flat from holding the roof up.' The bartender serves the Irishman his beer then comes back to talk to the engineer, 'I saw the flat spot on his head but I also noticed some bruising under his chin. What's that all about?' The engineer replies, 'Oh, that's where we put the jack.'

✳ A pregnant Irish woman falls into a coma after a car crash. After a year she wakes up to find she's given birth to twins, a boy and a girl. 'Where are they?' she asks. 'It's all right,' says the doctor, 'your brother came and took them. He's had them baptised and everything.' 'Oh God, not my brother,' says the woman, 'He's such an idiot. What did he call them?' 'Well, he named your daughter Denise...' says the doctor. 'Oh, that's nice,' says the mother. '...and he called your son Denephew.'

✳ How can you spot the Irish Jew at the Wailing Wall? He's the one with the harpoon.

✳ How do you confuse an Irishman? Give him two spades and tell him to take his pick.

✳ How do you get an Irishman to burn his ear? Phone him while he's doing the ironing.

✳ How do you spot an Irishman at a car wash? He's the one on the bike.

✳ I was telling some Irish jokes in a pub the other day when a big Irishman comes up to me and shouts, 'You bastard! You should be ashamed making fun of the Irish like that! I'm going to teach you a lesson you'll never forget!' With that he went for me with a razor. Things could have got sticky, but luckily he couldn't find a place to plug it in.

✳ Paddy is going through customs in Dublin airport when he's asked to identify a bottle in his luggage. 'That's holy water I've brought back from Lourdes,' says Paddy. The customs officer opens it and sniffs it and says, 'This smells more like whisky.' 'Isn't that fantastic!' says Paddy. 'Another bloody miracle!'

✳ Patrick is walking past Michael's farm when he sees a sign saying 'Boat for sale'. 'What's all that about?' asks Patrick. 'You've got no boat. All you have is a tractor and a caravan.' 'I know,' says Michael. 'And they're boat for sale.'

✳ The Irish are famous for 'the gift of the gab' – but these days you can clear that up with antibiotics.

✳ Where did they find the Irish woodworm? Dead in a brick.

ETHNIC: SCOTTISH

✳ A 12th-century sixpence was recently uncovered at an archaeological dig in Aberdeen. Gathered around it were four skeletons on their hands and knees.

✳ A Scotsman gets a cab to take him and his girlfriend home. She's so beautiful he can barely keep his eyes on the meter.

✳ A Scotsman takes a huge jar of urine to a clinic and pays to have it tested. When the results come back he discovers that there is absolutely no sign of any illness. He gets on the phone and says, 'It's me, Willie. Tell your Aunty Mary that there's nothing wrong with you, her, me, Grandpa, or the dog.'

✳ A Scotsman, an Englishman and Claudia Schiffer are sitting together in a train carriage. Suddenly the train enters a tunnel and it goes dark. There's a kissing noise and the sound of a loud slap. When the train comes out of the tunnel, Claudia Schiffer and the Scotsman are sitting as if nothing has happened and the Englishman is nursing a sore face. The Englishman is thinking, 'The Scottish fella must have kissed Claudia Schiffer, she slapped him but missed and got me instead.' Claudia Schiffer is thinking, 'My God that English fella must have tried to kiss me, kissed the Scotsman instead, and got slapped for it.' The Scotsman is thinking, 'This is great. The next time the train goes through a tunnel I'll make that kissing noise and slap the Englishman again.'

✳ A tourist in Aberdeen saves a young boy from drowning. That evening the boy's father tracks down the tourist at his hotel. 'Are you the man that pulled my wee laddie from the river?' asks the Scotsman. 'I am,' replies the tourist. The Scotsman says, 'Where's his hat?'

✳ An Englishman, an Irishman and a Scotsman walk into a pub and buy beers. Just as they raise their drinks to their lips, three flies land in each of their pints. The Englishman pushes his beer away in disgust. The Irishman fishes the fly out of his beer and carries on drinking. The Scotsman picks the fly out of his drink and starts shaking it, 'Spit it oot, ye thieving wee bastard! Spit it oot..!'

✳ Did you hear the story about the Scotsman who gave an Irishman, an Englishman, and a Welshman fifty pounds each? No, no one has.

✳ Hamish buys a cheap vase for his sister's birthday but accidentally smashes it before he can give it to her. He has a brainwave. He wraps the vase in gift paper, puts it in a box and posts it to her – this way he'll be able to blame the breakage on the postal service. His sister rings the next day, thanks him for the vase but tells him it arrived broken. 'Oh dear,' says Hamish. 'That's a pity.' 'Yes, it is,' replies his sister. 'But it was kind of you to wrap each piece individually.'

✳ How do you spot a Scottish ship? It's the one not being followed by seagulls.

✳ How do you tell if a Scotsman is a Macdonald? Lift his kilt and see if he has a quarter-pounder.

✳ Sign outside a Scottish cinema, 'Free admission for old-age pensioners, if accompanied by both parents'.

✳ Two female tourists visiting the Scottish Isles have hitched a ride on a local fishing boat. A storm brews up and it threatens to rain. The women don't have any wet-weather gear so the skipper calls down into the bilges of the boat, 'Is there a macintosh down there big enough to cover two ladies?' A voice shouts back, 'No, but there's a small McDougal willing to try!'

✳ What's the difference between a Scotsman and a coconut? You can get a drink out of a coconut.

✳ Two Scotsmen, Jimmy and Willie, go to an expensive restaurant. When they've finished a hearty meal they call the waiter over to get the bill. Willie says, 'Don't worry about the tab, Jimmy. I'm paying for everything.' The next day Jimmy is found dead in an alley. The newspaper headline reads, 'Horrible Murder of Scottish Ventriloquist'.

✳ What's the difference between a Scotsman and a canoe? A canoe tips occasionally.

✳ Why do bagpipers walk when they play? They're trying to get away from the noise.

✳ Why don't Scotsmen buy fridges? They don't believe the light goes out when you close the door.

ethnic – scouse

What do you call a Scouser in a suit? The accused.

🍎 EXERCISE

✳ 'If God had intended Jewish women to exercise, he would have put diamonds on the floor.' *Joan Rivers*

✳ 'I ran three miles today, finally I said, "Lady, take your purse."' *Emo Phillips*

✳ 'I'm not into working out. My philosophy is no pain, no pain.' *Carol Leifer*

✳ 'You have to stay in shape. My grandmother started walking five miles a day when she was 60. She's 97 today and we don't know where the hell she is.' *George Carlin*

✳ An old woman goes to a leisure centre and asks if she can join an aerobic class. 'I'm not sure if that's a good idea,' says the instructor. 'How flexible are you?' 'Oh, very,' replies the old woman. 'But I can't make Tuesdays.'

✳ How do men exercise on the beach? By sucking in their stomachs every time they see a bikini.

✳ I have to exercise early in the morning – before my brain figures out what I'm doing.

✳ I joined a health club last year, spent about 400 bucks. Haven't lost a pound. Turns out you have to show up.

✳ I like long walks, especially when they're taken by people who annoy me.

✳ If a jogger runs at the speed of sound, can he still hear his Walkman?

✳ If God meant us to touch our toes, he would have put them further up our body.

✳ If you jog backwards, will you gain weight?

✳ My doctor told me if I took up jogging it could add ten years to my life. And he was right. I now feel ten years older.

✳ One day as I came home early from work I saw a guy jogging naked. I said to the guy, 'Hey buddy, why are you doing that?' He said, 'Because you came home early.' *Rodney Dangerfield*

✳ Running feels awful, but it will let you live longer – so, life will feel awful, but at least it will last longer.

✳ The advantage of exercising every day is that you'll die healthier.

✳ The only reason I would take up jogging is so that I could hear heavy breathing again.

✳ The other night, I went for a walk. My girlfriend asked me how long I was going to be gone, and I said, 'The whole time.' *Steven Wright*

✳ Tom was advised by his doctor to go to a health club and lose some weight. He lost 20 pounds in one day – the jogging machine tore his leg off.

✳ Two old women are sitting on a bench talking. One says to the other, 'How's your husband holding up in bed these days?' The second replies, 'He makes me feel like an exercise bike. Each day he climbs on and starts pumping away, but we never seem to get anywhere.'

✳ Why did the aerobics instructor cross the road? Some people on the other side could still walk.

fairy tales

'I used to be Snow White, but I drifted.' *Mae West*

Did you hear about the giant who threw up? It's all over town.

❦ FAMILIES

✳ 'Happiness is having a large, loving, caring close-knit family – in another city.'
George Burns

✳ Families are like fudge – mostly sweet, with a few nuts.

✳ My mother was a ventriloquist. She was always throwing her voice. For ten years I thought the dog was telling me to kill my father.

✳ This advice has been passed down from generation to generation. Okay, it's never been used.

❦ FAMILIES: PARENTING

✳ A young couple bring their new baby home and the wife suggests that her husband tries his hand at changing a nappy. 'I'm busy,' he says. 'I'll do the next one.' Next time the baby's nappy needs changing she asks him again. The husband says, 'I didn't mean the next nappy. I meant the next baby.'

✳ 'My father told me all about the birds and the bees, the liar – I went steady with a woodpecker till I was twenty-one.' *Bob Hope*

✳ 'When I was ten, my pa told me never to talk to strangers. We haven't spoken since.' *Steven Wright*

✳ A father and son are out fishing. The boy says, 'Dad, how do boats float?' 'I don't know,' replies Dad. The boy then asks, 'How do fish breathe?' 'I don't know,' replies Dad. 'Why is the sky blue?' asks the boy. 'I don't know,' replies Dad. 'Dad,' says the boy. 'I hope you don't mind me asking you all these questions?' 'Of course not,' replies Dad. 'If you don't ask questions how will you ever learn anything?'

✳ I remember Dad coming home, telling Mam the pit was closing, and there'd be no more work. Then he sat down in his chair and wailed at the top of his voice – it was possibly the wrong moment to have played the drawing pin on the seat gag.

✳ A man is helping one of his cows give birth, when he notices his four-year-old son watching from the fence. The man thinks, 'Great. He's four and I'm gonna have to start explaining the birds and bees. No need to jump the gun. I'll just let him ask, and I'll answer.' After everything is over, the man walks over to his son and says, 'Well, son, do you have any questions?' 'Just one,' gasps the wide-eyed lad. 'How fast was that calf going when he hit the cow?'

✳ A small boy is sent to bed by his father. Five minutes later the boy cries out, 'Da-ad!' 'What?' shouts back his father. 'I'm thirsty,' says the boy. 'Can you bring me a drink of water?' 'No,' says Dad. 'You had your chance. Lights out!' Five minutes pass. 'Da-aaaad!' shouts the boy. 'What?' says Dad. 'I'm thirsty,' says the boy. 'Can I have drink of water?' 'I said no!' shouts back the father. 'And if you ask again, I'll smack your bottom!' Five minutes later. 'Daaaa-aaaa!' shouts the boy. 'What?' yells his father. 'When you come in to smack me, can you bring a drink of water?'

✳ A vest is something a boy wears when his mother feels cold.

✳ A woman goes to her psychiatrist. 'I can't sleep at night,' she says. 'When I'm in the next room, I have this dreadful fear I won't hear the baby if he falls out of the crib. What can I do?' 'Easy,' replies the doctor. 'Take the carpet off the floor.'

✳ If you have any advice to pass on to your children, do it while they're still young enough to think you know what you're talking about.

✳ Mothers of teenagers know why some animals eat their young.

✳ Bubba and Becky are delighted when the adoption centre tells them they have a wonderful Russian baby. On the way home from the adoption centre they stop by the local college and enrol in night courses to learn Russian. 'You going to Russia on holiday?' asks the registration clerk. 'No,' replies Bubba. 'We just adopted a Russian baby. When he starts talking we'll want to know what he's saying.'

✳ My mother never saw the irony in calling me a son of a bitch.

✳ Never raise a hand to your children – it leaves your groin unprotected.

✳ There are three ways to get something done: do it yourself, hire someone, or forbid your kids to do it.

✳ Two little girls are in the lunchroom of the Beverly Hills Elementary School. 'Guess what?' says one. 'My mummy's getting married again and I'm going to have a new daddy.' 'Really?' says the other. 'Who's she marrying?' 'Winston James,' says the first girl. 'He's a famous director.' The second girl smiles. 'Oh, you'll like him. He was my daddy last year.'

✳ What did the girl band member's mother say to her before she went out? 'If you're not in bed by midnight you have to come home.'

✳ What never made much sense to me is why people without any children and those with children both feel sorry for each other.

✳ Why do parents always take their children to supermarkets to smack them?

fancy dress

A man goes to a fancy dress party with a woman draped over his shoulders and says he's come as a tortoise. 'Who's that on your back?' asks the host. 'That?' he says. 'That's Michelle.'

When he met her at the fancy dress party she said she'd come as an old witch. Unfortunately when he woke up beside her the next morning he discovered she hadn't been wearing a costume.

🍅FAT

✳ A man is standing on the bathroom scales desperately sucking in his stomach. 'That's not going to help,' says his wife. 'Yes, it will,' replies the man. 'It's the only way I can see the numbers.'

✳ Do you want to know how to prevent sagging as you get older? Keep eating till the wrinkles fill out.

✳ A fat man goes to a weight-loss clinic and is offered three weight-loss plans, one for £100, one for £200, and a third for £500. The man chooses the £100 plan, has a shower, then is shown into a sauna. There, sitting naked on a chair, is a young woman with a sign over her head saying, 'If you catch me you can have sex with me!' The man needs no more encouragement and starts chasing the woman round the room. His time runs out before he catches her, but he's delighted when he learns he's lost ten pounds of fat. The next day the man returns and buys the £200 plan. Again he has a shower, and again he's shown into the sauna. Here a gorgeous naked young woman in high heels is sitting under the sign saying, 'If you catch me you can have sex with me!' The fat man chases the woman round the room but even in her high heels she's able to evade him until his time is up. The next day the man returns and decides on the £500 weight-loss plan. The man has his shower and is shown into the sauna but finds it's empty. He hears a sound and looks round as a huge male gorilla is pushed into the room. Round the gorilla's neck is a sign saying, 'If I catch you, I get to have sex with you!'

✳ A woman sits opposite a fat man on a bus and can't help making a comment. 'If that stomach was on a woman I'd think she was pregnant.' The fat man replies, 'It was. She is.'

✳ An obese woman goes to a doctor to be put on a drastic weight-loss programme. The doctor tells her that she can eat anything she likes but that any food must be inserted up the anus. The woman agrees and four weeks later comes back for a check-up. The doctor is very pleased with the woman's progress but is concerned that the woman's hips keep twitching constantly. 'When did that hip twitching start?' asks the doctor. 'I ain't twitching,' replies the woman. 'I'm chewing gum.'

✳ Brain cells come and brain cells go, but fat cells live for ever.

✳ He has the body of a twenty-year-old. A twenty-year-old Volvo.

✳ I wouldn't say he was fat, but the other day he stood up on a bus and offered his seat to three women.

✳ I wouldn't say he was fat, but it takes him two trips to get through a revolving door.

✳ I wouldn't say she was fat, but she had to move off the beach to let the tide in.

✳ I'm not saying my husband is fat, but we've been married six years and I still haven't seen all of him.

✳ It's just been announced on the news that Bernard Manning, the comedian who was told by his doctors that he must lose three stone or die, has tonight sadly lost three stone.

✳ Lord, if you can't make me skinny, please make all my friends fat.

✳ Mrs Brown used to have a firm chin, sadly it has now taken on a couple of partners.

✳ My mother-in-law is a big woman. She fell asleep in the bath last week – if her mouth hadn't been open she would have drowned.

✳ My wife is so fat, last night she hung one of her dresses on the washing line and a troop of Boy Scouts moved in.

✳ She's got a million-dollar figure. Unfortunately it's all in loose change.

✳ The best way to lose weight is to stuff your face while standing naked in front of a mirror – the restaurant will sling you out before you can swallow too much.

✳ They say that travel broadens one. You must have been around the world.

✳ A fat lady fell over the other day but rocked herself to sleep before she could get up again.

✳ Why did God invent alcohol? So fat chicks can get laid too.

✳ You'd be the right weight for your height, if you were eight foot six.

✳ I may be fat, but you're ugly and I can lose weight.

✳ My mother-in-law has got so many chins it looks like she's staring at you over a sliced loaf.

feminists

A feminist gets on a bus and is disgusted when a little old man stands up to give her his seat. 'Patronising old fool,' she mutters as she pushes him back down. A minute later another woman gets on and the old man rises to his feet once more. 'Male chauvinist pig,' seethes the feminist as she pushes him back down again. The bus stops again, more women get on, and once more the little old man attempts to stand up. 'You're living in the Stone Age,' hisses the feminist as she pushes him down. 'For God's sake!' wails the little old man. 'Will you let me get off? I've missed three stops already!'

I don't know what feminists are going on about when they say television never shows any positive, dynamic female role models. I mean, what was Lassie all about?

FLATULENCE

✳ 'How dare you break wind before my wife,' says the host to his dinner guest. 'I'm sorry,' replies the guest. 'I didn't realise it was her turn.'

✳ A man walks into a doctor's. 'Doctor, I'm suffering from silent gas emissions. All day at work, I have these silent gas emissions. Last night during a movie, I had ten silent gas emissions. On the way to your office I had five silent gas emissions. And while sitting in your waiting room I had three silent gas emissions. As a matter of fact, I've just had two more.' The doctor replies, 'Well, the first thing we're going to do is check your hearing.'

✳ How does a man take a bubble bath? He eats beans for dinner.

✳ Ted goes to the doctor's suffering from continual flatulence. The doctor asks him to take off his trousers and lie down on the couch. Then, to Ted's horror, he produces a six-foot pole. 'What are you going to do with that?' asks Ted. 'I'm going to open a window,' says the doctor.

FOOD AND DRINK

✳ 'I have a nut allergy. When I was at school the other children used to make me play Russian roulette by force-feeding me a packet of Revels.' *Milton Jones*

✳ 'The remarkable thing about my mother is that for thirty years she served us nothing but leftovers. The original meal has never been found.' *Calvin Trillin*

✳ 'We've got a new toaster,' said a little boy to his friend. 'It's really clever. When the toast is done a bell rings.' 'Ours is better,' says his friend. 'When the toast's done it sends out smoke signals.'

✳ A lady is picking through the frozen turkeys at the grocery store, but can't find one big enough for her family. She calls over the shopkeeper and says, 'Do these turkeys get any bigger?' The shopkeeper replies, 'No, they're dead.'

✳ A hungry termite walks into a pub and says, 'Is the bar tender here?'

✳ A little old lady orders a burger in a café. She then watches as the cook grabs a hunk of chopped meat, stuffs it in his bare armpit, pumps his arm a few times, then tosses it on the grill. The old lady says, 'That's the most disgusting thing I've ever seen!' The waitress replies, 'Yeah? You should see him making the doughnuts!'

✳ A lord dines with an elderly duchess one evening. Next day a friend asks him if he enjoyed himself. 'Well,' says the lord. 'If the melon had been as cold as the soup, and the soup had been as warm as the wine, and the wine had been as old as the chicken, and if the chicken had been as young as the maid, and the maid had been as willing as the duchess then, yes, I would have had a very good time indeed.'

✳ A man comes home from work. 'How were your sandwiches today, dear?' asks his wife. 'They were fine,' he replies. 'Are you sure they were okay?' asks the wife. 'Yes, they weren't bad at all,' replies the husband. 'You're not feeling ill are you?' asks the wife. 'No. Why should I be?' says the husband. 'No reason,' replies the wife. 'It's just that tomorrow you're going to have to clean your shoes with fish paste.'

✳ A man goes into a restaurant and orders a starter. The waitress brings him a bowl of soup but the man notices she has her thumb stuck in it. When the soup is finished the waitress suggests beef stew as a main course. The man agrees but when she brings the stew to the table he notices she has her thumb stuck it that too. Once the stew is finished the waitress suggests hot apple pie as a dessert. The man agrees, but again, the waitress brings him his plate with her thumb stuck in his food. 'Look!' says the man. 'I wasn't going to mention it, but every time you bring food to my table you've got your thumb stuck it in it.' 'Sorry,' says the waitress. 'But my thumb's got an infection. My doctor says I have to keep it in a warm, moist place.' 'Well, why not stick it up your ass!' says the man. The waitress replies, 'Where d'you think I've been putting it when I'm in the kitchen?'

✳ A man goes into a restaurant and says, 'How do you prepare the chicken?' 'We don't,' replies the waiter. 'We just tell it straight that it's going to die.'

✳ A man orders a pizza and the clerk asks if he should cut into six pieces, or twelve. 'Make it six,' says the man. 'I could never eat twelve.'

✳ A man orders steak at a restaurant but notices that the waiter bringing it to his table is pressing the steak to the plate with his thumb. 'That's very unhygienic,' complains the man. 'It'll be more unhygienic if I drop it again,' replies the waiter.

✳ A man visiting his wife's 'organic' vegetarian parents is sent out to buy some food. 'These are for my mother-in-law,' he says to the greengrocer. 'Are you sure they haven't been sprayed with dangerous pesticides?' 'Quite sure,' replies the greengrocer. 'You'll have to do that yourself.'

✳ A man walks into a Bangkok bar and sees a sign reading, 'Cheese Sandwich: $1.50. Chicken Sandwich: $2.50. Hand Job: $10.00'. The man beckons to one of the barmaids. 'I was wondering,' he says. 'Are you the one who gives the hand jobs?' 'Yes,' she purrs. 'That's me.' 'Then go wash your hands,' says the man. 'I want a cheese sandwich.'

✳ A wife hears a noise in the kitchen one morning. She goes downstairs and finds her husband slumped at the table stinking of booze and with lipstick stains all over his shirt. 'I hope you've got a good reason for being here at seven in the morning,' she glowers. 'I certainly do,' replies her husband. 'Breakfast.'

❋ A wife is nagging her husband at the company picnic. 'Doesn't it embarrass you that people have seen you go up to the buffet table five times!' 'Not a bit,' replies the husband. 'I just tell them I'm filling up the plate for you!'

❋ A woman is preparing a French dinner for her parents and sends her husband out to buy some fresh snails. The husband buys the snails then pops into the pub for a quick drink. One thing leads to another and he stays for a few rounds, so many in fact, that by the time he leaves it's nine in the evening. Realising he's extremely late the husband runs home, pours the snails over the path leading to his house, then rings the bell. His furious wife opens the door. 'Where the hell have you been?' she screams. The husband waves back to the snails, 'Come on, lads!' he shouts. 'We're nearly there!'

❋ Did you hear about the snobby chef with an attitude problem? He had a French fried potato on his shoulder!

❋ Eating prunes gives you a good run for your money.

❋ A sandwich walks into a bar. The barman says, 'Sorry, we don't serve food in here.'

❋ Did you hear about the sword swallower who went on a diet? He had pins and needles for months.

❋ Good King Wenceslas rings up his local pizza parlour, 'The usual please. Deep pan, crisp and even.'

❋ Harry is a very noisy eater, when he started drinking soup in the restaurant six couples got up and started to dance.

❋ He attended the karate school of cookery. He could kill with just one chop.

❋ He had an accident boiling an egg this morning. He held the egg in his hand and boiled his watch.

❋ I feel great because I eat nothing but organic food these days. The only thing is, when I die my entire body will apparently decompose completely in under 24 hours.

✳ I love defenceless animals, especially in a good gravy.

✳ I found this marvellous stuff recently. It's sugar free, low in fat, and you can have as much as you want without putting weight on. I don't know why crack isn't more popular.

✳ I love cooking with wine. Sometimes I even put it in the food.

✳ I saw a café serving an all-day breakfast. But I didn't really have that much time.

✳ I think the chef here does a marvellous job. For a man with his skin condition.

✳ I went into McDonald's yesterday and said, 'I'd like some fries.' The girl at the counter said, 'Would you like some fries with that?'

✳ I wouldn't say it was a bad restaurant, but they've only just started a same-day service.

✳ I wouldn't say she's unhygienic, but the only time she washes her ears is when she eats a slice of watermelon.

✳ If they don't have chocolate in heaven, I'm not going.

✳ If white wine goes with fish, do white grapes go with sushi?

✳ If you ate pasta and antipasta, would you still be hungry?

✳ Man, to friend, 'Hot milk makes me sleepy but cold milk keeps me awake.' Friend, 'How come?' Man, 'Our milkman comes round at 4.30 in the morning.'

✳ Pierre Gaston the famous chef was cremated yesterday. The service lasted for 30 minutes at gas mark 6.

✳ Sign in a baker's window: 'Cakes like your mum used to make – £2. Cakes like she thought she used to make – £5.'

✳ There's not much Harry doesn't know about horses, he spent five years working in a French restaurant.

✳ Thank you for the magnificent dinner – it will always have a place in my heartburn.

✳ The chicken we had for dinner last night was so old they had to bring it to our table in a wheelchair.

✳ The King of Jordan visits London and is invited to dinner with the Queen. The servants bring out the first course and start dishing it out. 'No soup for me,' says the King of Jordan. 'It makes me fart.' Silence falls over the room. Everyone is horrified. 'What's the matter with you all?' asks the King patting his belly. 'Don't you think I'm fart enough already?'

✳ There once was man who was half-French and half-pygmy. He was very sad. He was a fantastic cook, but he couldn't reach the grill.

✳ Two bachelors are talking about cooking. 'I got a cookbook once,' says one. 'But I could never do anything with it.' 'Were the recipes too hard?' asks the other. 'No,' he replies. 'But each of the recipes began the same way – take a clean dish...'

✳ Two crisps were walking down the road. One was assaulted.

✳ Two foreign tourists arrive in the USA and are astonished to see a man selling hot dogs. 'I never realised Americans ate dogs,' says one. 'But since we're here we might as well try some.' The pair order a couple of 'dogs' then sit down to see what they've got. The first tourist opens his bun and looks inside. He pulls a face then turns to his friend and says, 'Well I'm not eating mine. What part of the dog did you get?'

✳ Two old ladies are swapping news. One old lady says, 'The other day my Harold went into the vegetable patch to pull up a cabbage, and he dropped dead of a heart attack.' 'Oh dear,' says her friend. 'Whatever did you do?' The old lady replies, 'I had to defrost some peas.'

'McDonald's "Breakfast for under a dollar" actually costs much more than that. You have to factor in the cost of coronary bypass surgery.'
George Carlin

✳ What did the apple say to the orange? Nothing, apples don't talk.

✳ What do you call it when you pass out after eating too much curry? A korma!

✳ What do you get if you cross a door knocker with some courgettes, onions, tomatoes and garlic? Rat-a-tat-a-touille.

✳ What food will decrease a woman's sex drive by 70 per cent? Wedding cake.

✳ What's the best way to open a jar with a stuck lid? Put it on the table and tell the kids to leave it alone.

✳ When I came home last night the wife complained that the cat had upset her – but she really shouldn't have eaten it in the first place.

✳ When I wake up in the morning, I just can't get started until I've had that first, piping hot pot of coffee. Oh, I've tried other enemas…

✳ Where there's smoke, there's dinner.

✳ Who is the most popular man in a nudist colony? The one who can carry two large coffees and a dozen doughnuts. Who is the most popular woman in a nudist colony? The one who can eat the last two doughnuts.

✳ Why shouldn't you try to swim on a full stomach? Because it's easier to swim on a full swimming pool!

✳ 'I'm not a vegetarian because I love animals. I'm a vegetarian because I hate plants.' *A Whitney Brown*

✳ A health inspector catches a baker crimping the edges of his Cornish pasties with a pair of false teeth. 'That's disgusting,' says the inspector. 'You need to have a tool for that sort of thing.' 'I have got a tool,' says the baker. 'I use it to make the holes in the doughnuts.'

✳ At the dinner table a boy makes a face at his father. 'Mum's making enthusiasm soup for dinner again.' 'Why do you call it that?' asks his father. The boy replies, 'Because she puts everything she has into it.'

✳ A man goes into a sleazy café and orders two hamburgers and a hot dog. The cook takes two hamburgers out of a freezer and sticks them under his arms. 'What are you doing?' says the man. 'Sorry, mate,' says the cook. 'The micorwave's bust. This is the only way of thawing them out.' 'Well, okay,' says the man. 'But cancel the hot dog.'

✳ A man goes to a dinner party but finds that the host's dog won't leave him alone. It keeps trying to climb on to his lap and get its head above the table. The guest turns to his host and says, 'It's funny, I always seem to have this effect on dogs. Animals just seem to love me.' 'I wouldn't be so sure about that,' says the host. 'We were short of crockery – you're eating off his plate.'

✳ A restaurant in Texas serves steaks so big you can milk them.

✳ A young man takes his girlfriend to an Italian restaurant and tries to impress her by ordering the most exotic dish on the menu. 'I'll have a luigi vercotti spamacelli,' he says to the waiter. 'I'm sorry, sir,' he replies. 'But that is impossible.' 'Have you run out?' asks the man, 'No,' says the waiter. 'It's the name of the chef.'

✳ Doris eats like a bird – a pelican.

✳ Start a movement – eat a prune.

✳ Stressed spelled backwards is desserts.

✳ The hardness of the butter is inversely proportional to the softness of the bread.

✳ The other day I saw a kitchen gadget that said it would cut my housework in half – so I bought two.

✳ They told me eating spinach would put colour in my cheeks. It did. Now I've got a green face.

✳ This year Harry didn't bother hiding any Easter eggs for the children. Why should he? They never found the ones he hid last year.

✳ What does the manager of the nuclear power station like for his dinner? Fission chips.

food and drink – convenience food

'I bought some powdered water. But I don't know what to add.'
Steven Wright

'I once put instant coffee in a microwave and almost went back in time.' *Steven Wright*

🐷FOOD AND DRINK: DIETING

✳ 'I'm not feeling well,' says a patient to his doctor. 'Do you think it might be my diet?' 'What have you been eating?' asks the doctor. 'Snooker balls,' replies the patient. 'I have two reds for breakfast, three blues for lunch. And five browns, and a pink for dinner.' 'I think I see what the problem is,' replies the doctor. 'You're not eating enough greens.'

✳ A balanced diet is chocolate in each hand.

✳ My doctor's put me on a stable diet – hay and oats three times a day.

✳ She's a light eater. When it gets light, she starts eating.

✳ My wife is on a new diet. Coconuts and bananas. She hasn't lost weight, but can she climb a tree!

✳ A dietician is lecturing an audience. 'The food we eat is enough to have killed most of us years ago,' he says. 'Red meat is dangerous. Vegetables are often sprayed with pesticides, and our drinking water is frequently polluted. However, there is one foodstuff far more dangerous than all of them combined. Who can tell me what it is?' There's a long pause, then a man in the front row sticks his hand up and says, 'Wedding cake?'

✳ Have you heard about the new Chinese diet? You're allowed to eat whatever you want but you're only allowed one chopstick.

🍏FOOTBALL

✻ A football player is walking down the street when he sees a fire in a block of flats. He runs over to help and hears a woman calling from the top of the building. 'Will someone save my baby!' she yells. 'The stairwell is blocked! There's no way down! If I throw down my baby can somebody catch him?' The footballer shouts back, 'Fear not. I'm a professional goalkeeper! Throw down your baby and I promise I won't drop him!' So the mother throws down the baby and the goalkeeper makes a perfect catch – before bouncing it twice and kicking it 30 yards down the road.

✻ A junior soccer team is playing a match one Sunday. Just before the kick-off the team coach approaches one of his young players. 'Do you understand that you mustn't swear at the ref if he gives you a card and you mustn't attack an opponent if he fouls you?' 'Yes,' replies the boy. 'Good,' says the coach. 'Now go and explain that to your mother.'

✻ A man arrives at a football match midway through the second half. 'What's the score?' he asks. 'Nil nil,' is the reply. 'Oh,' says the man. 'And what was the score at half-time?'

✻ After England draws Scotland in the Euro 2000 play-offs, Kev and the England team are chatting in the dressing room before the match. 'Look guys, I know they're crap,' says Kev. 'But we have to play them to keep UEFA happy.' 'Tell you what,' pipes up Owen. 'You guys go down to the pub and I'll play Scotland on my own.' 'Sounds good,' replies Kev and he and the rest of the team go for a drink. After an hour Kev turns on the pub TV and finds that the score is one-nil to England. The team go back to their beer and darts for an hour then switch on the TV again. The final score is a one-all draw. Horrified, they all run back to the dressing room. There they find Owen sitting with his head in his hands. 'What the hell happened?' shouts Kev. 'Sorry,' replies Owen. 'The ref sent me off in the 11th minute.'

✻ For a minute the team were in with a good chance. But then the game started.

✻ One evening Alex Ferguson's phone rings. It's the fire brigade telling him that Old Trafford is on fire. 'The cups!' shouts Ferguson. 'Save the cups!' 'Don't worry, sir,' says the fireman. 'The flames haven't got to the canteen yet.'

gangs

'Our neighbourhood was tough. We had the typical gang. You know, Shorty, Fats, Skinny, Stinky. Then there were the boys.' *Bob Hope*

🌰 GARDENING

✳ A husband and wife are standing at the window admiring their garden. 'Sooner or later you're going to have to make a proper scarecrow to keep the birds off the flower beds,' says the wife. 'What's wrong with the one we've got?' asks the husband. 'Nothing,' replies the wife. 'But Mother's arms are getting tired.'

✳ A little boy goes up to Old Ned the gardener and says, 'What do you put on your rhubarb?' 'Well, usually rotted horse manure,' replies Old Ned. 'We have custard.' says the little boy.

✳ A parson is congratulating a parishioner on his success at transforming an abandoned plot of land into a beautiful garden. 'It's wonderful what man can achieve with the help of the Almighty,' says the parson. 'Yes,' replies the parishioner. 'Mind you, you should have seen the state it was in when He had it all to Himself.'

✳ Did you hear about the successful bonsai tree grower? He got so good he ended up looking for a house with a smaller garden.

✳ Gardens need a lot of water – most of it sweat.

✳ The good thing about snow is it makes my garden look as good as my neighbour's.

✳ A woman is discussing her husband with a friend. 'My husband is an invertebrate gardener,' says the woman. 'Don't you mean "inveterate"?' says her friend. 'No,' replies the woman. 'When it comes to digging and weeding it turns out he hasn't got a backbone.'

✳ Why is the soil in my garden always dry? Because you have leeks.

GENIES AND WISHES

✳ A man finds an odd-looking bottle and rubs it. Much to his surprise, a genie appears. 'For releasing me from the bottle, I will grant you three wishes,' says the genie. 'But there's a catch. For each of your wishes, every lawyer in the world will receive double what you ask for.' First the man wishes for a Ferrari. Poof! A Ferrari appears in front of him. 'Now, every lawyer in the world has been given two Ferraris,' says the genie. 'What is your next wish?' 'I could really use a million pounds,' replies the man. Poof! One million pounds appears at his feet. 'Now, every lawyer in the world is two million pounds richer,' the genie reminds him. 'What is your third wish?' The man thinks and says, 'Well, I've always wanted to donate a kidney…'

✳ A man finds an old bottle. He rubs it and is astonished to see a pixie emerge from the bottle's mouth. 'You look tense,' says the pixie. 'Would you like a back rub?' 'Well, I'd prefer a million pounds,' says the man. 'I can't give you any money,' says the pixie. 'But how about I rub your back?' 'Well, how about you fix me a date with a *Playboy* centrefold?' asks the man. 'Sorry,' says the pixie. 'But why don't I work on those shoulders of yours?' 'Can't you make me taller?' asks the man, 'I'd prefer to be six foot six.' The pixie replies, 'Lie down and I'll get started on your clavicles.' 'Hang on a minute,' says the man. 'What's with the back rubs? I thought genies were meant to grant three wishes?' 'Who said I was a genie?' replies the pixie. 'I'm a massage in a bottle.'

✳ A man goes into a bar with a lamp. After he's had a few drinks the man says to the barman, 'This lamp is magic y'know. If you rub it a genie comes out and grants you a wish.' 'Oh yes?' replies the barman. 'Let's have a go then.' He rubs the lamp with a bar cloth and out pops a genie. 'Fantastic,' says the barman. 'It works. Er, let's see. Can I have a million bucks, please.' 'As you wish,' replies the genie and the bar is suddenly full of ducks. 'I forgot to mention,' says the man. 'He's a little deaf.'

✳ A man is sitting at home when a genie pops up out of a bottle. 'And what will your third wish be?' asks the genie. The man replies, 'What? How can I be getting a third wish when I haven't had a first or second wish?' 'You've had two wishes already,' replies the genie. 'But your second wish was for me to put everything back the way it was before you made your first wish. 'Okay,' says the man. 'I don't believe any of this, but what the hell. I wish I were irresistible to women.' 'That's funny,' says the genie as it fades from sight. 'That was your first wish too.'

* A man is walking along a beach when he comes across a lamp. He picks it up, rubs it, and a genie pops out. As is customary the genie grants him three wishes. The guy says, 'I'd like a million pounds.' Poof! A million pounds appear at his feet. 'I'd like a new Mercedes,' says the guy. Poof! A Mercedes appears in front of him. Finally the guy says, 'I want to be irresistible to women.' Poof! He turns into a box of chocolates.

* A Scotsman and an Englishman are strolling along the beach when they find a lamp. They clean it up and out pops a genie. 'I'll give you each one wish for freeing me,' says the genie. The Englishman says, 'I'm sick and tired of Scots coming into England. I wish there was a huge wall around England to keep them out.' Poof! And it's done. The Scotsman says, 'So tell me about this wall, genie.' 'Well,' says the genie. 'It's 500 feet high and a third of a mile thick. Nothing can get in, and nothing can get out.' 'Right,' says the Scotsman. 'Fill it with water.'

* An Englishman, a Scotsman and an Irishman have been stuck on a desert island for years when they find a bottle with a genie inside it. The genie gives them each a wish. 'I wish I was back home in London,' says the Englishman and in a flash he's gone. 'I wish I was back home in Glasgow,' says the Scotsman and in a flash he's gone. 'Oh it's a lonely here now,' says the Irishman. 'I wish my two mates were still here with me.'

* Harry and Tom are adrift in a lifeboat. Harry finds a lamp and, giving it the customary rub, is not surprised when a genie appears. The genie apologises to Harry and Tom and says that, due to cut-backs, it can only grant them one wish. Harry doesn't think, he just knows he thirsty so he blurts out, 'Turn the entire ocean into beer!' The genie claps its hands, the salt water changes to beer, and the genie vanishes. There's a pregnant pause as Harry and Tom consider their new circumstances. Tom looks at Harry with disgust, 'Well isn't that great,' he says. 'Now we're going to have to pee in the boat.'

* Harry is walking down the street when he sees a man who has an orange for a head. 'What happened to you?' asks Harry. The man replies, 'I released a genie from a magic lamp and it gave me three wishes. My first wish was that I wanted to be incredibly rich, and my second wish was that I would be irresistible to women.' 'Okay,' say Harry. 'But what was your third wish?' 'Isn't it obvious?' says the man. 'I wished I had an orange for a head.'

✳ Paddy finds an old lamp and starts to polish it. Poof! A genie appears and grants Paddy three wishes. 'Well now,' says Paddy. 'I've always liked my Guinness in bottles, so I'd like a bottle of Guinness that will never be empty.' Poof! There it is. Paddy opens the bottle and takes a drink. 'Oh that's grand,' says Paddy. 'Did you say I get three of these wishes?' 'Yes indeed,' says the genie. 'Great,' says Paddy. 'I'll take two more of these then.'

🍎 GOLF

✳ A female physiotherapist tees off on the golf course but she slices her shot and hits a man standing on the next green. The man collapses with his hand between his legs. The physiotherapist runs over and says, 'Don't worry, I have medical training. I can help reduce the pain.' So saying she opens his trousers and massages his privates. After a minute she says, 'Does that feel better?' The man replies, 'Yes, thank you. But I think you broke my thumb.'

✳ A golfer drives his new Honda into a petrol station. An attendant comes over and the golfer asks him to fill up the tank. As he fills up, the attendant sees a couple of tees on the passenger seat. 'What are those things for?' asks the attendant. 'They're called tees,' replies the golfer. 'What are they for?' asks the attendant. The golfer replies, 'They're for resting my balls on when I drive.' 'Blimey,' says the attendant. 'Those Japanese have thought of everything.'

✳ A golfer is being given a lesson by a pro but on his first swing he hits the ball in the path of a bus. The ball smashes the windscreen of the bus and knocks out the driver. The bus hurtles off the road into a reservoir and disappears in a seething mass of bubbles. 'Oh my God,' says the golfer. 'What am I going to do?' The pro replies, 'Well, I'd loosen your grip and keep your back straighter.'

✳ A golfing coach puts his finger on his pupil's main failing. 'The problem is that you're standing too close to the ball – after you've hit it.'

✳ A group of businessmen are playing a round of golf when a funeral cortege drives slowly alongside the green. One of the men takes off his cap and bows his head. 'It's nice to see someone showing some respect for the dead,' comments one of the players. 'It's only proper,' replies the man. 'After all we were married for twenty-five years.'

✳ A husband and wife are playing a round of golf when one of the husband's shots lands the ball into the doorway of a greenhouse. The wife holds the greenhouse door open for her husband but he misjudges the swing, hits her on the head, and kills her. A couple of years later the husband returns to the same golf course with his new wife. He slices the same shot and, again, puts the ball in the doorway of the greenhouse. 'Shall I hold the door open for you, dear?' asks his wife. 'No way,' replies the man. 'I tried that shot two years ago and I ended up taking a triple bogie.'

✳ A man and a priest are playing golf. The man takes his first shot, misses and says, 'Jesus dammit, I missed.' The priest is shocked, 'Don't use that kind of language or God will punish you.' The man takes his second shot but misses again. Under his breath he says, 'Jesus effing Christ...' The priest overhears him and says, 'My son, please refrain from blasphemy or God will surely punish you.' The man takes a third shot and misses again. He can't help himself and mutters, 'Jesus H Christ I missed again...' Suddenly a bolt of lightning strikes down and kills the priest. From the clouds a booming voice mutters, 'Ahh, Jesus, missed again...'

✳ A man has been drinking at the golf club. On his way home his car is pulled over by the police who tell him he's too drunk to drive. 'Too drunk to drive?' responds the drunk. 'I can barely putt.'

✳ A man comes across four golfers in a bunker. One of the golfers is lying on the sand and the other three are arguing. 'What's the matter?' asks the man. One of the golfers turns to him and says, 'These swine will do anything to win a game. My partner's just had a stroke and they want to add it to our score.'

✳ A terrible golfer hits his ball into a large bunker. 'Which club should I use for this one?' he asks his caddie as he prepares to step into the sand. 'I wouldn't worry about the club,' replies the caddie. 'Just make sure you take in plenty of food and water.'

✳ A woman is accompanying her husband on a round of golf. At the first stroke he hits the ball in the rough. She shakes her head in sympathy. On the second stroke he hits the ball into a bunker. She shakes her head and sighs. On the third stroke the man knocks the ball on the green and it rolls into the hole. 'Oh boy,' says his wife. 'Now you're in real trouble.'

✳ An avid golfer is so obsessed with the game he can't stand the idea of not playing when he's dead. To put his mind at rest he goes to a spiritualist to try and find out if there's golf in Heaven. The spiritualist communes with the spirits then says, 'I have good news and bad news.' 'What's the good news?' asks the man. 'Heaven does indeed have a golf course,' says the spiritualist. 'It's a beautiful course with 36 holes, 24-hour access, and the most magnificent clubhouse you can imagine.' 'Wow,' says the man. 'So what's the bad news?' The spiritualist replies, 'You're booked in for a game next Tuesday.'

✳ Every year Billy's father asked him what he wanted for his birthday and every year Billy said he wanted a pink golf ball. For years and years this was the only gift he ever requested. If it was his birthday he wanted a pink golf ball, if it was Christmas he only ever wanted a pink golf ball. Nothing else would tempt him. Eventually Billy's father got tired of buying his son pink golf balls, so for his 18th birthday he got him a surprise present – a car. Billy liked the car and took it into town for a spin. Passing a sporting goods store he saw they had some pink golf balls in the window so he parked on the kerb and crossed the road to take a closer look. Halfway across the road he was hit by a truck. Billy's father came to see him in hospital. He knew Billy wasn't going to make it and he wanted to ask his son one question before he died. 'Billy,' he said. 'You've never played golf, so why for all these years did you only ever want pink golf balls as gifts?' Billy looked up at his father, opened his mouth to speak, then died. And the moral of this story is, you should always look both ways before crossing the street.

✳ Golfer, to caddy, 'Say, do you think my game is improving?' Caddy, 'Certainly. You miss the ball much closer than you used to.'

✳ On their honeymoon a husband confesses a secret to his new wife: 'Darling, I'm a golf addict,' he says. 'You'll never see me at the weekends and all our holidays will be at golfing resorts.' 'I've got a confession too,' replies his new wife. 'I'm a hooker.' 'That's not a problem,' replies the husband. 'Just keep your head down and your arm straight.'

✳ Harry and Tom are on the golf course when Harry slices a shot deep into a wooded ravine. He takes his eight iron and clambers down the embankment in search of his lost ball. After fifteen minutes hacking at the underbrush, Harry spots something glistening among the leaves. He gets closer and discovers that it's an eight iron in the hands of a skeleton. Harry calls out to Tom, 'Hey! I've got trouble down here!' 'What's up?' shouts back Tom. 'Bring me my wedge!' replies Harry. 'You can't get out of here with an eight iron!'

✳ Harry and Tom are on the golf course. 'I wish my wife had never taken up golf,' says Harry. 'She spends so much time practising she's cut down our sex life to once a week.' 'Count yourself lucky,' replies Tom. 'She's cut some of us out altogether.'

✳ Harry is on the golf course lining up a perfect drive when a voice from the club-house calls out, 'Will the gentleman on the ladies' tee please move back to the men's tee!' Harry ignores the voice and continues his practice swings. The voice calls out again, 'Sir, will you please obey club rules and use the men's tee!' Harry prepares to take a swing when the voice calls out again, 'The player on the ladies' tee must move back to the men's tee immediately!' Harry's had enough, he turns and shouts back, 'Do you mind shutting up while I take my second shot!'

✳ How did the bad golfer hit two good balls? He stood on a rake.

✳ Jill takes up golf and has many lessons with her golf pro before embarking on her first game. Unfortunately she soon hits her ball into the rough and, while trying to find it, gets stung by a bee. She runs back to the clubhouse for help and sees her pro at the bar. 'Have you got any first aid? I got stung by a bee,' says Jill. 'Whereabouts?' asks the pro. 'Between the first and second hole,' she replies. 'Dammit, Jill,' says the pro. 'We really need to work on your stance.'

✳ One Sunday morning a vicar decides to bunk off to play golf. He leaves a note on the church door saying he's too ill to read the Sunday service, then sneaks off to the golf course. God and Saint Peter are watching this from above. 'I hope you're going to punish that man,' says Saint Peter. 'Watch this,' says God. The vicar tees off and his first ball ricochets off three trees, skips across a pond, bounces off a boulder, loops the loop, and drops neatly into the hole. 'I thought you were going to punish him?' says Saint Peter. 'I have,' says God. 'Who's he going to tell?'

gossip

A woman says to her friend, 'Peggy told me that you told her the secret I told you not to tell her.' 'Well,' replies her friend in a hurt tone, 'I told her not to tell you I told her.' 'Oh dear!' says the woman. 'Well, don't tell her I told you that she told me.'

GRAFFITI

✳ Graffiti in a toilet: 'I like grils.' Somebody had written underneath, 'You mean girls, stupid.' And underneath that someone else had written, 'What's the matter with us grils?'

✳ On a wall in a ladies' room: 'My husband follows me everywhere.' Written just below it: 'No. I don't.'

✳ Written in a women's toilet: 'Friends don't let their friends take home an ugly man.'

✳ Written over a mirror in a men's toilet: 'No wonder you always go home alone.'

✳ Written over a mirror in a women's toilet: 'You're too good for him.'

✳ Written over a urinal: 'Express lane – five beers or less.'

HAIR AND/OR THE LACK OF IT

✳ A bald man sees a sign outside a barber's shop saying, 'Baldies! Instant treatment! A head of hair just like mine for £5,000!' Underneath the sign is a picture of the barber with a fine mane of luxuriant hair. The bald man goes in and says, 'Can you guarantee my head will look like yours, instantly, for £5,000?' 'I sure can,' says the barber. 'It'll only take a few seconds for us to look exactly alike.' So the bald man hands over the £5,000, and the barber shaves his own hair off.

✳ A girl is at the hairdresser's chatting to her stylist. 'My boyfriend has terrible dandruff,' she says. 'Is there anything you can suggest?' The stylist replies, 'Why don't you give him Head & Shoulders?' The girl thinks for a moment then says, 'So how do you give shoulders?'

✳ How did they know the shark attack victim had dandruff? They found his head and shoulders on the beach.

✳ I do sometimes bleach my hair. It's the only way I can get it clean.

✳ It's such a shame to ruin such beautiful blonde hair by dying the roots black.

✳ She waxed the hair off her legs, she waxed the hair off her armpits, she waxed the hair off her bikini line. But when she tried to wax the hair out of her nostrils she asphyxiated herself.

✳ Tom sees Harry on the high street and shouts, 'What did you do to your hair? It looks like a wig!' Harry looks embarrassed and says, 'Well, it is a wig.' Tom replies, 'You know what, you'd never be able to tell.'

✳ What is the only true cure for dandruff? Baldness.

✳ What should you buy if your hair falls out? A good vacuum cleaner.

✳ Women will never be equal to men until they can walk down the street bald and still think they're gorgeous.

happiness

'Some cause happiness wherever they go; some whenever they go.' *Oscar Wilde*

'What's the use of happiness? It can't buy you money.'. *Henny Youngman*

Happiness: good health and a bad memory.

HARDWARE AND DIY

✹ 'If you nail a tool shed closed, how do you put the hammer away?' *George Carlin*

✹ I got a self-assembly wardrobe. It didn't work. I got it out of the box, it didn't do a thing.

✹ I used some of that quick drying wood stain the other day and, like they say, it did exactly what it said on the tin. It caused nausea and vomiting when ingested.

✹ I was doing some decorating, so I got out my step-ladder. I don't get on with my real ladder.

✹ My boyfriend's really into DIY. He's just built a set of shelves for our house and now he's writing some books to put on them.

HEALTH AND DOCTORS

✹ A half-drowned man washes up on a beach outside a hospital. A medical team rushes out, gives him the kiss of life, then pump out his stomach to get rid of any seawater. The pump brings up gallons of water, some seaweed, a number of small fish, and some crabs. The medical team keep pumping but after five minutes the brine, the fish, the seaweed, and the shellfish still keep coming in an endless stream. Finally a bystander taps one of the doctors on the shoulder and says, 'Excuse me, but should you be doing that while he's still sitting in the water?'

✹ A health specialist is giving a talk on well-being in a village hall. 'The best way to start the day is to do five minutes light exercise, and five minutes of deep breathing,' says the specialist. 'Then I take a short hot shower, and feel rosy all over.' A voice from the back of the hall shouts, 'Tell us more about Rosie!'

✹ A rat catcher walks into a doctor's office, 'I was putting down some poison when one of the little buggers bit off my finger.' 'Which one?' asks the doctor. 'How should I know?' says the rat catcher. 'They all look the same to me.'

✳ A man answers a knock at his front door. Outside is a six-foot ladybird which proceeds to head-butt him, kick him in the crotch, and stamp on his head. The man wakes up in hospital where he describes his ordeal to the doctor, 'You're the sixth case like this we've had in today,' says the doctor. 'There's a rather nasty bug going about.'

✳ A man goes to a psychiatrist. 'You've got to help me,' says the man. 'I can't stop deep-frying things in batter. I get up in the morning and deep-fry my boiled egg. I've deep-fried all my clothes and shoes. I've even deep-fried my bike and battered the cat! What's wrong with me?' 'It's obvious,' replies the psychiatrist. 'You're frittering your life away.'

✳ A man goes to the doctor and says, 'Doctor, I can't pronounce my Fs, Ts or Hs.' 'Well,' says the doctor. 'You can't say fairer than that.'

✳ How do you stop a head cold going to your chest? Tie a knot in your neck!

✳ I'm taking antenatal breathing classes. I'm not having a baby, I'm just having trouble breathing.

✳ A man is sitting in a doctor's waiting room. Every so often he says, 'Lord, I hope I'm sick!' After saying this about six or seven times the receptionist says, 'Excuse me, but why in the world would you want to be sick?' The man replies, 'I'd hate to be well and feel this crappy.'

✳ A man walks into a doctor's. The doctor says, 'I haven't seen you in a long time.' The man replies, 'I know, I've been ill.'

✳ An old man goes to a school reunion where he finds that his surviving class-mates are only interested in talking about their ailments: kidney stones, heart murmurs, liver pains, etc. When he gets home his daughter asks him how it went. 'It wasn't much of a reunion,' he replies. 'It was more like an organ recital.'

✳ Doctors can be frustrating. You wait a month and a half for an appointment and he says, 'I wish you'd come to me sooner.'

✳ Jack Benny receiving a showbusiness award: 'I don't deserve this. But I have arthritis and I don't deserve that either.'

✳ My doctor said he would have me on my feet in two weeks. He did, I had to sell my car to pay his bill.

✳ Tom spent many years trying to find a cure for his halitosis and acne only to find people didn't like him anyway.

✳ Tom, to Dick, 'Who gave you that black eye?' Dick, 'Nobody. I had to fight for it.'

✳ Never go to a doctor whose office plants have died.

✳ What good is mouthwash that kills germs? Who wants a mouth full of dead germs?

✳ Sam and John are at work in the timberyard when John accidentally chops his arm off with a saw. Sam wraps the arm in a plastic bag and takes John to a surgeon. Four hours later Sam is amazed to see John in the pub throwing darts. 'Wow!' thinks Sam. 'That surgeon is great.' A few weeks later John accidentally cuts his leg off. Sam puts the leg in a plastic bag and takes John back to the surgeon. That evening he's amazed to see John playing football. 'Wow!' thinks Sam. 'That surgeon is amazing.' A few weeks later John cuts his head off. Sam puts the head in a plastic bag and carries John to the surgeon. Next day the surgeon calls Sam and says, 'I'm sorry, but John is dead.' 'Don't blame yourself,' says Sam. 'I'm sure you did all you could.' 'I'm not blaming myself,' says the surgeon. 'I'm blaming you. If you'd put some holes in that plastic bag the poor bastard wouldn't have suffocated!'

health and doctors:
alternative therapy

'A friend of mine is into voodoo acupuncture. You don't have to go. You'll just be walking down the street, and... "Oh, that's much better".' *Steven Wright*

'I went to a massage parlour. It was self-service.' *Rodney Dangerfield*

⛄HEALTH AND DOCTORS: DOCTOR, DOCTOR...

✳ 'Doctor, doctor I have a ringing in my ears.' 'Don't answer!'

✳ 'Doctor, doctor I've hurt my arm in several places.' 'Well, don't go there any more.'

✳ 'Doctor, doctor I think I'm shrinking!' 'Now, settle down. You'll just have to be a little patient.'

✳ 'Doctor, doctor can I have second opinion?' 'Certainly. Come back tomorrow!'

✳ 'Doctor, doctor I feel like a pack of cards.' 'I'll deal with you later!'

✳ 'Doctor, doctor can you cure my sleepwalking?' 'Try these.' 'Are they sleeping pills?' 'No. They're tin tacks. Sprinkle them on the floor.'

✳ 'Doctor, doctor everyone I meet thinks I'm a liar!' 'I'm sorry but I can't believe that!'

✳ 'Doctor, doctor everyone keeps ignoring me.' 'Next please!'

✳ 'Doctor, doctor have you got something for a headache?' 'Yes. Take this hammer and hit yourself on the head.'

✳ 'Doctor, doctor I can't get to sleep.' 'Sit on the edge of the bed and you'll soon drop off.'

✳ 'Doctor, doctor I can't stop my hands shaking!' 'Do you drink a lot?' 'Of course not. I spill most of it!'

✳ 'Doctor, doctor I feel like a pair of curtains.' 'For goodness sake, pull yourself together.'

✳ 'Doctor, doctor I get a terrible pain in my eye when I drink a cup of coffee.' 'Try taking the spoon out.'

✳ 'Doctor, doctor I keep feeling like I'm a packet of savoury biscuits!' 'Oh no. You're crackers!'

✳ 'Doctor, doctor I keep thinking I'm a dog.' 'Sit on the couch and we'll talk about it.' 'I can't, I'm not allowed on the couch!'

✳ 'Doctor, doctor I keep thinking I'm invisible.' 'Who the hell said that?'

✳ 'Doctor, doctor I keep thinking there are two of me.' 'One at a time please.'

✳ 'Doctor, doctor I think I need glasses.' 'You certainly do. This is a garage.'

✳ 'Doctor, doctor I snore so loudly I keep myself awake.' 'Have you tried sleeping in another room?'

✳ 'Doctor, doctor I think I'm a bridge.' 'What's come over you?' 'Two cars, a truck, and a coach.'

✳ 'Doctor, doctor I think I'm a dog.' 'How long have you felt like this?' 'Ever since I was a puppy!'

✳ 'Doctor, doctor I've just swallowed a pen.' 'Well, sit down and write your name!'

✳ 'Doctor, doctor I think I'm a python.' 'You can't get round me just like that you know!'

✳ 'Doctor, doctor I think I'm suffering from déjà vu!' 'Hang on! Didn't I see you yesterday?'

✳ 'Doctor, doctor I think I'm turning into an apple.' 'We'll have to get to the core of this!'

✳ 'Doctor, doctor I'm a kleptomaniac!' 'Take these pills and if that doesn't work pick me up a DVD player.'

✳ 'Doctor, doctor I'm having trouble with my breathing.' 'Don't worry. I'll give you something that will put a stop to that!'

✳ 'Doctor, doctor I've got something wrong with my eyes. I keep seeing an insect spinning round my head.' 'Don't worry, that's just a bug going round.'

✳ 'Doctor, doctor I've got terrible wind. What can you give me for it?' 'Have you tried a kite?'

✳ 'Doctor, doctor I think I'm a moth.' 'Get out of the way, you're in my light!'

✳ 'Doctor, doctor I've had tummy ache since I ate three crabs yesterday.' 'Did they smell bad when you took them out of their shells?' 'What do you mean "took them out of their shells"?'

✳ 'Doctor, doctor I've lost my memory!' 'When did this happen?' 'When did what happen?'

✳ 'Doctor, doctor I've swallowed a bone!' 'Are you choking?' 'No, I really did!'

✳ 'Doctor, doctor my baby's swallowed a bullet.' 'Well, don't point him at anyone until I get there!'

✳ 'Doctor, doctor my sister thinks she's a lift!' 'Tell her to come in.' 'I can't, she doesn't stop at this floor!'

✳ 'Doctor, doctor my son has swallowed my pen. What should I do?' 'Use a pencil till I get there!'

✳ 'Doctor, doctor some days I feel like a tepee and other days I feel like a wigwam.' 'I think you're two tents.'

✳ 'Doctor, doctor there's a strawberry growing out the top of my head.' 'I'll give you some cream to put on that.'

✳ 'Doctor, doctor these pills you gave me for BO are rubbish!' 'What's wrong with them?' 'They keep slipping out of my armpits!'

✳ 'Doctor, doctor you've taken out my tonsils, my adenoids, my gall bladder, my varicose veins and my appendix, but I still don't feel well.' 'That's quite enough out of you!'

✳ 'Doctor, doctor I keep seeing images of Mickey Mouse and Donald Duck!' 'I see, and how long have you been having these Disney spells?'

✳ 'Doctor, doctor. I feel terrible!' 'What are the symptoms?' 'It's a cartoon show with yellow people.'

✳ 'Doctor, doctor I feel like a bee.' 'Buzz off. I'm busy!'

✳ 'Doctor, doctor I keep dreaming about necrophilia, sadism and bestiality!' 'Forget it, you're flogging a dead horse.'

✳ 'Doctor, doctor it hurts when I do this.' 'Then don't do that!'

✳ 'Doctor, doctor my wife keeps feeding me rubbish.' 'How do you feel?' 'Down in the dumps.'

✳ 'Doctor, doctor I can't control my aggression!' 'How long as this been going on?' 'Who the hell wants to know?'

✳ 'Doctor, doctor I keep thinking I'm a woodworm.' 'How boring for you!'

✳ 'Doctor, doctor I tend to flush a lot.' 'Don't worry, it's just a chain reaction!'

✳ 'Doctor, doctor I think I'm a bell.' 'Take these and if they don't help give me a ring!'

✳ 'Doctor, doctor I think I'm an adder.' 'Great, you can help me with my accounts!'

✳ 'Doctor, doctor I think I'm an electric eel.' 'That's shocking!'

✳ 'Doctor, doctor I've got a split personality.' 'Well, you'd better both sit down then!'

✳ 'Doctor, doctor I've just swallowed a pillow.' 'How do you feel?' 'A bit down in the mouth.'

✳ 'Doctor, doctor my little boy has just swallowed a roll of film.' 'Let's wait and see if anything develops!'

✹HEALTH AND DOCTORS: HYPOCHONDRIA

✳ 'There's no need for me to come out to the house,' says the doctor to a worried caller. 'I've checked my files and your uncle isn't ill at all, he just thinks he's sick.' A week later, the same caller phones back. 'And how's your uncle today?' asks the doctor. 'Worse,' replies the caller. 'Now he thinks he's dead.'

✳ A man goes to his doctor and tells him he's suffering from a long list of illnesses. 'The trouble with you,' says the doctor. 'Is that you're a hypochondriac.' 'Oh no,' says the man. 'Don't tell me I've got that as well.'

✳ Doctor, to patient, 'I have good news and bad news. The good news is that you're not a hypochondriac.'

✳ Hypochondria is the only disease I haven't got.

✳ Inscription on a hypochondriac's grave: 'I told you I was ill.'

✳ Mrs Smith is a hypochondriac and her doctor – fed up with her constant complaints about non-existent illnesses – starts palming her off with a mild sedative to keep her happy. One day Mrs Smith complains of chest pains and is prescribed her usual treatment. However, this time the pain is real and Mrs Smith dies of a heart attack. The doctor hears this and is so upset he dies of shock. Mrs Smith and the doctor are buried in adjoining plots. Next morning, the doctor hears a tapping on his coffin. A muffled voice calls out, 'Doctor, this is Mrs Smith! Do you have anything for worms?'

✹HELPFUL ADVICE

✳ Commuters. Keep the seat next to you on the train vacant by smiling and nodding at people as they walk up the aisle.

✳ A neighbour's car aerial, carefully folded, makes an ideal coat hanger in an emergency.

✳ Anorexics. When your knees become fatter than your legs, start eating cakes again.

✳ Clean the lavatory bowl at the same time as you urinate. Drink no other liquids apart from toilet cleaner.

✳ Clumsy? Avoid cutting yourself while slicing vegetables by getting someone else to hold them.

✳ Cooks. Thicken up runny low-fat yoghurt by stirring in a spoonful of lard.

✳ Don't waste money buying expensive binoculars, simply stand closer to what you want to look at.

✳ Employees. Only empty your bowels at work. Not only will you save money on toilet paper, you'll also be getting paid for it.

✳ Hijackers. Avoid a long stressful siege and the risk of arrest, simply make sure you book a flight to your intended destination in the first place.

✳ Husbands. Avoid arguments with your wife about lifting the toilet seat. Just piss in the sink.

✳ Men. Create instant designer stubble by sucking a magnet and dipping your chin in a bowl of iron fillings.

✳ Motorists. Enjoy the freedom of cycling by removing your windscreen, sticking half a melon skin on you head, then jumping red lights and driving the wrong way up one-way streets.

✳ Nissan Micra drivers. Attach a lighted sparkler to the roof of your car before starting a long journey. You drive it like a dodgem car anyway, so it might as well look like one.

✳ Oversleeping? A mousetrap placed on top of your alarm clock will prevent you from going back to sleep.

✳ Tell me what you need, and I'll tell you how to get along without it.

🐛 HORSE RACING

✳ 'Betting on horses is a funny old game,' says a man to his friend. 'You win one day and lose the next.' The friend replies, 'So why not bet every other day?'

✳ I bet on a great horse yesterday! It took seven horses to beat him.

✳ Man, to friend, 'I don't fancy the chances of that horse you bet on.' Friend, 'Why's that?' Man, 'I just saw the jockey buy a book to read on the journey.'

✳ Riding the favourite at Cheltenham, a jockey is well ahead of the field. Suddenly he's hit on the head by a salmon sandwich and a pork pie. He manages to keep control of his mount and pulls back into the lead, only to be struck by a tin of caviar and a dozen Scotch eggs. With great skill he manages to steer the horse to the front of the field once more when, on the final furlong, he's struck on the head by a bottle of Chardonnay and a Bakewell tart. Thus distracted, he only manages second place. Furious he immediately goes to the stewards to complain that he's been seriously hampered.

✳ The horse I bet on was so slow, the jockey kept a diary of the trip.

housework

'I'm an excellent housekeeper. Every time I get a divorce, I keep the house.' Zsa Zsa Gabor

A woman is complaining to her friend about the amount of housework she has to do, 'I spend all day at the office then come home and wash the clothes and dishes. And every weekend I have to wash the kitchen floor and all windows.' 'But what about your husband?' asks her friend. 'I make him wash himself,' says the woman.

My idea of housework is to sweep the room with a glance.

You know the greatest labour-saving device around the house – tomorrow.

✤ HUNTING

✳ A couple of rednecks are hunting in the woods when one suddenly collapses. His friend dials the emergency services on his mobile and shouts to the operator, 'Help me. My friend is dead! What can I do?' The operator tries to calm him down. 'Take it easy,' she says. 'The first thing to do is make sure he really is dead.' Next thing the operator hears the man putting the phone down, then a rifle shot. The man picks up the phone again, 'Okay. So what next…?'

✳ A hunter goes into a butcher's shop and asks for a duck. 'I'm sorry,' says the butcher. 'We're out of duck. How about a chicken?' 'Oh, yes.' replies the hunter. 'And how do I tell my wife I shot a chicken?'

✳ A man takes his wife hunting for the first time. He impresses upon her the need to claim a kill quickly before anyone has the chance to step in and bag your deer. The wife is suitably impressed by this and they both stalk off into the woods. A little while later the wife shoots and makes a kill. The brush is too thick for the husband to see what's going on but he can hear his wife arguing with another man. 'This is my kill,' shouts his wife. 'There is no other hunter in the vicinity and I can categorically prove that my bullet killed this deer.' 'I'm not arguing with you,' says the man. 'But can I take *my* saddle off *your* deer, before you take it home?'

✳ A young man from the city goes to visit his farmer uncle. For the first few days, the uncle shows him the usual things; chickens, cows, crops, etc. However, it's obvious the nephew is getting bored so the uncle suggest he goes on a hunt. 'Why don't you grab a gun, take the dogs, and go shooting?' This cheers up the nephew and off he goes with the dogs in trail. After a few hours, the nephew returns. 'Did you enjoy it?' asks his uncle. 'It was great!' exclaims the nephew. 'Got any more dogs?'

✳ The Alaskan hunters usually dined on deer in the evenings – it was far too cold to hunt bear.

✳ What has 100 balls and screws rabbits? A shotgun cartridge.

✳ Obituary: Mr Thomas Gunner died in a hunting accident last Thursday. He is survived by a wife, two sons, and a rabbit.

❋ Two blondes decide to go duck hunting. Neither one of them has ever been hunting before and after several hours they still haven't bagged any. One blonde looks at the other and says, 'I just don't understand it. Why aren't we getting any ducks?' Her friend replies, 'I keep telling you, I just don't think we're throwing the dog high enough.'

❋ A rich lawyer is grouse shooting when one of his birds falls in an adjacent field. The lawyer sees an old yokel standing in the field and asks him to pick up the grouse. 'Not doing that,' says the old man. 'This be my field, so that be my bird.' This infuriates the lawyer. 'Listen,' he says. 'I know the law and that bird belongs to me. If you don't hand it over I'll sue you.' The old man replies, 'Round here we settle things with the Three Wack Rule. I gives you three whacks with my stick, then you give me three whacks. Whoever gives the biggest whacks wins.' The lawyer is sure he can whack harder than the old yokel so he agrees. The old man takes his walking stick and gives the lawyer a terrific whack across the legs, then another across his nose, and another across the back of his head. The lawyer has been knocked to his knees but manages to stagger to his feet, 'Right. My turn,' he says. 'Naahh,' says the old yokel. 'You win. Keep the rotten bird.'

❋ A hunter is stalking through the jungle when he finds a ravishing young woman lying naked on a blanket. After staring at her breathlessly for a second he asks, 'Are you game?' 'I sure am,' replies the girl. So he shoots her.

❋ Tom and Dick go hunting in the woods and get lost. Tom remembers that the international SOS signal in this situation is to fire three shots in the air. Dick fires three shots and they wait, but no one comes. Tom fires three shots, again they wait, but still no one comes. It starts to snow heavily and the sun is fast dropping below the horizon. 'Well, this is it,' says Dick. 'If this doesn't work we're done for. We only have three arrows left.'

❋ Two hunters are dragging a dead deer back to their truck, when a man approaches them and says, 'Y'know it's much easier if you drag it the other way – then the antlers won't dig into the ground and slow you up.' The hunters try this method and make good progress. The first hunter says to the other, 'That guy really knew what he was talking about, didn't he?' 'Yes,' replies the second hunter. 'But on the other hand we are getting further away from the truck.'

☺ IDEAS AND INVENTIONS

✳ 'I had a great idea this morning but I didn't like it.' *Samuel Goldwyn*

✳ Harry has invented a new gadget for speeding up work on production lines – he calls it a whip.

✳ Man to friend, 'Did you hear about the man who invented a rubber suit to protect construction workers if they fell off tall buildings?' Friend, 'Did it work?' Man, 'Yes, but when he tried it out he bounced around for so long he starved to death.'

✳ Tom made a fortune in the dog food business. He invented a canned meat that tastes just like a postman's leg.

✳ When he was younger Harry invented a two-rung ladder – it was for women who wanted to elope from bungalows.

✳ A man approaches one of the speakers at an inventors' conference and says, 'Correct me if I'm wrong, but didn't you invent Tipp-Ex?'

☺ INSULTS

✳ 'I have had a perfectly wonderful evening – but this wasn't it.' *Groucho Marx*

✳ 'There's no beginning to your talents.' *Clive Anderson to Jeffrey Archer*

✳ 'You know, I could rent you out as a decoy for duck hunters.' *Groucho Marx*

✳ Any friend of yours – is a friend of yours.

✳ Any similarity between you and a human being is purely coincidental.

✳ Are you depriving a village somewhere of an idiot.

✳ At least you're not obnoxious like so many other people – you're obnoxious in different and worse ways!

✳ Before you came along we were hungry. Now we are fed up.

✳ Did the aliens forget to remove your anal probe?

✳ Do you want me to accept you as you are, or do you want me to like you?

✳ God could still use you for miracle practice.

✳ Don't you realise that there are enough people to hate in the world already, without your working so hard to give us another?

✳ He could be described as charming, intelligent and witty. And who knows, perhaps one day he will be.

✳ Don't get me wrong. I'm not trying to make a monkey out of you. I can't take the credit.

✳ Here's 20 cents. Call all your friends and bring back the change!

✳ He's a difficult man to forget. But well worth the effort.

✳ He's a lesson to us all. He's a man who started out with nothing and to this day he still has most of it.

✳ He's a man of hidden talents. As soon as we find one we'll let you know.

✳ His own father looks on him as the son he never had.

✳ I believe in respect for the dead – in fact I could only respect you if you were dead!

✳ I bet I know what you use for contraception? Your personality.

✳ I can tell you always manage to keep your head above water – just by the colour of it.

✳ I knew the day would come when you would leave me for my best friend. So here's his leash, water bowl and chew toys.

✳ I know you're a self-made man – it's nice of you to take the blame!

✳ I like your approach, now let's see your departure.

✳ I must admit, you brought religion into my life. I never believed in Hell till I met you.

✳ I see you in my dreams – if I eat too much.

✳ I thought I saw your name on a loaf of bread this morning. But when I looked again what it actually said was, 'Thick cut'.

✳ I thought of you all day today. I was at the zoo.

✳ I used to think you were a pain in the neck. Now I have a much lower opinion of you.

✳ I want nothing out of you but breathing, and very little of that!

✳ I won't mind you talking as long as you won't mind me not listening.

✳ I'd like to give you a going-away present – but you have to do your part.

✳ I'd like to leave you with one thought – but I'm not sure you have a place to put it!

✳ I'd like to see things from your point of view but I can't seem to get my head that far up my arse.

✳ If God tried to help you, we'd have an eight-day week.

✳ If I said anything to you that I should be sorry for, I'm glad.

✳ If I throw a stick, will you leave?

✳ If I want your stupid opinion, I'll beat it out of you.

✳ If truth is stranger than fiction, you must be truth!

✳ If we killed everybody who hates you, it wouldn't be murder; it would be genocide!

✳ If you ever had a bright idea, it would be beginner's luck!

✳ If you think people are the same as you, you have a very low opinion of them.

✳ I'm busy now – can I ignore you some other time?

✳ I'm not rude. You're just insignificant.

✳ I'm so miserable without you, it's almost like you're here.

✳ I'm trying to imagine you with a personality.

✳ Instead of being born again, why don't you just grow up?

✳ It's mind over matter – I don't mind, because you don't matter.

✳ I've only got one nerve left – and you're getting on it.

✳ I've seen people like you before – but I had to pay admission!

✳ Just because you have one doesn't mean you have to act like one!

✳ Keep talking – I always yawn when I'm interested.

✳ Learn from your parents' mistakes – use birth control!

✳ Nice suit. Were you there for the fitting?

✳ Of all the people I've met, you're certainly one of them.

✳ One day you stopped to think then forgot to start again.

✳ Ordinarily people live and learn – you just live.

✳ Pardon me, but you've obviously mistaken me for someone who gives a damn.

✳ People can't say that you have absolutely nothing – you have inferiority!

✳ Please breathe the other way – you're bleaching my hair.

✳ She's a treasure. I wonder who dug her up?

✳ Some people are one in a million. He was won in a raffle.

✳ Some people say you're superficial – but that's just on the surface.

✳ Someone said you're not fit to sleep with pigs. I stuck up for the pigs.

✳ Sorry if I looked interested. I'm not.

✳ The more I think of you, the less I think of you.

✳ The only thing you brought to your job was your car.

✳ The smaller the pip, the louder the squeak.

✳ The ultimate proof of the overwhelming nature of the sex drive is the fact that someone was willing to father you.

✳ There's nothing wrong with you that reincarnation won't cure.

✳ There's one too many in this room and I think it's you.

✳ They say opposites attract. I hope you find someone good-looking and intelligent who doesn't stink.

✳ We all sprang from the apes – but you didn't spring far enough.

✳ We have been friends for a very long time, what say we call it quits?

✳ We know you'd go to the end of the world for us – but would you stay there?

✳ We think of you when we are lonely. Then we are content to be alone.

✳ You used to be arrogant and obnoxious, now you're the opposite – obnoxious and arrogant.

✳ When they made him they kept the mould and threw him away.

✳ When you ran away from home your folks sent you a note saying, 'Don't come home and all will be forgiven.'

✳ When you were a child your mother tried to hire someone to take care of you – but the Mafia wanted too much.

✳ Whoever told you to just be yourself couldn't have given you worse advice.

✳ Why don't you bore a hole in yourself and let the sap run out?

✳ You are a prime candidate for natural deselection.

✳ You couldn't hit sand if you fell off a camel.

✳ You couldn't organise a piss-up in a brewery.

✳ You did some soul searching, but didn't find one.

✳ You don't know the meaning of the word fear, but then again you don't know the meaning of most words.

✳ You fear success, but really have nothing to worry about.

✳ You got into the gene pool while the lifeguard wasn't watching.

✳ You have a great deal of pride, but very little to be proud of.

✳ You have a lot of well-wishers – they'd all like to throw you down one.

✳ You have a mechanical mind. Too bad you forgot to wind it up this morning.

✳ You have a nice personality, but not for a human being.

✳ You have a room-temperature IQ

✳ You have an inferiority complex – and it's fully justified.

☻INSULTS: STUPIDITY

☀ 'To call you stupid would be an insult to stupid people.' *John Cleese*

☀ A guy with your IQ should have a low voice too!

☀ Are you always so stupid, or is today a special occasion?

☀ Calling you stupid would be an insult to the stupid.

☀ Don't go to a mind reader – go to a palmist. I know you've got a palm.

☀ Don't let your mind wander too far. It's too little to be out alone.

☀ Go ahead, tell them everything you know. It'll only take ten seconds.

☀ Have you considered suing your brains for non-support?

☀ He has to be careful. He's not allowed anything sharp – like a mind.

☀ I bet your brain feels as good as new, seeing that you've never used it.

☀ I don't think you're a fool. But then what's my opinion against thousands of others?

☀ I must say you're very open-minded. So much so your brains have fallen out.

☀ I refuse to enter a battle of wits with you – I can't attack an unarmed person.

☀ I would like to insult you, but with your intelligence you wouldn't get offended.

☀ If brains were dynamite you'd have nothing to worry about.

☀ If I gave you a penny for his thoughts, I'd get change back.

☀ If idiots could fly, this would be an airport.

☀ If intelligence was rain, you'd be holding an umbrella.

✳ If what you don't know can't hurt you, you're practically invulnerable.

✳ If you stand close enough to your head, you can hear the ocean.

✳ If you were any more stupid, you'd have to be watered twice a week.

✳ I'm glad to see you're not letting your education get in the way of your ignorance.

✳ Looking on the bright side, you're immune from serious head injury.

✳ Please sit down and give your mind a rest.

✳ Stupidity does not qualify as a handicap, park elsewhere!

✳ There sits a man with an open mind – you can feel the draught from here.

✳ What you lack in intelligence, you more than make up for in stupidity.

✳ What's on your mind, if you'll forgive the overstatement?

✳ What's the latest dope – besides yourself?

✳ When I look into your eyes – I see the back of your head.

✳ Why don't you go to the library and brush up on your ignorance?

✳ Would you cover one of your ears, please? You're causing a draught.

✳ You have an IQ one lower than it takes to grunt.

✳ Your brain waves fall a little short of the beach.

✳ Your mouth's in gear but your brain's in neutral.

✳ Your reaction time is longer than your attention span.

✳ Your verbosity is exceeded only by your stupidity.

kangaroos

A kangaroo keeps getting out of his enclosure at the zoo. Knowing how high he can jump, the zoo keepers put up a ten-foot fence. However, next morning the kangaroo is out again. Next time they try putting up a twenty-foot fence but, again, the kangaroo is out the next morning. Frustrated the zoo keepers build a forty-foot-high fence. A camel in the next enclosure says to the kangaroo, 'How much higher do you think they'll go?' The kangaroo replies, 'About a thousand feet, unless somebody remembers to lock the gate!'

What do you call a kangaroo at the North Pole? Lost.

KIDNAPPING

※ 'I remember the time I was kidnapped and they sent a piece of my finger to my father. He said he wanted more proof.' *Rodney Dangerfield*

※ 'When I was a kid I got no respect. The time I was kidnapped and the kidnappers sent my parents a note they said, "We want five thousand dollars or you'll see your kid again."' *Rodney Dangerfield*

※ I was a lovely baby. My parents used to fake my kidnapping just to see my picture in the papers.

LAW AND ORDER

※ A bank had been robbed three times by the same bandit. An FBI agent interviews one of the bank tellers looking for clues. 'Have you noticed anything distinctive about the man?' he asks. 'Not really,' replies the teller. 'But each time he turns up he's better dressed.'

※ A sleuth is a detective who discovers who slue who.

✳ A government inspector visits a prison. After being shown round he has tea with the Governor. 'You seem to have a lot of social events here,' says the inspector. 'Do we?' queries the Governor. 'Well, yes,' says the inspector. 'One of the prisoners sold me a ticket for the Warden's Ball. Didn't you know about it?' 'Well, yes I did,' says the Governor. 'But that's not a dance, that's a raffle.'

✳ A man walks into a police station and drops a dead cat in front of the duty sergeant. 'Someone threw this in my front garden,' says the man. 'I'll take your name, sir,' says the sergeant. 'And if no one claims it in three months you can keep it.'

✳ A judge finds two young men guilty of drug abuse. However, since it's their first offence, he decides to be lenient; instead of jail he tells them to go out and convince their friends about the evils of drugs. They do so, and a week later they report back and tell the judge how they've got on. The first young man says, 'I convinced twelve young people to give up drugs. I showed them this piece of paper with two circles on it; a big one and a little one. I told them the big circle represented their brain size before drug use and the little circle showed their brain size after drug use.' 'That's very impressive,' says the judge. He turns to the second young man and says, 'So how many young people did you manage to convert?' The young man replies, 'Two hundred and fourteen.' 'Holy cow!' exclaims the judge. 'How did you manage so many?' The young man replies, 'Well, I used two circles too. I pointed to the small circle and said, "This is your asshole before prison…"'

✳ A bank was held up by a criminal with a sawn-off shotgun. Luckily no one was injured – he'd sawn off the wrong end.

✳ A man is about to be put into the electric chair and the prison chaplain asks him if there's anything he can do for him in his dying moments. 'Yes,' says the man. 'Will you hold my hand?'

✳ A masked man runs into a bank and points a banana at the cashier. 'This is a cock-up!' he shouts. 'Don't you mean a hold-up?' asks the cashier. 'No,' says the man. 'It's a cock-up. I left the gun on the bus.'

✳ How do you recognise an idiot rape suspect? He steps out of the police line-up and says, 'That's the girl!'

✳ My grandfather was the unluckiest criminal in the country. He made a deathbed confession of all his crimes – then got better.

✳ It was half an hour before curfew in a Mexican town and a tourist sees a soldier gun down a man in the street. 'Why did you do that?' asks the tourist. 'Breaking the curfew,' replies the soldier. 'But it's half an hour till the curfew,' says the tourist. 'I know,' says the soldier. 'But I know where he lives and he was never going to get home in thirty minutes.'

✳ My grandmother gave me £1 and said, 'Not a word about this to your parents.' I said, 'It's going to cost you a lot more than that.'

✳ The police have reported the theft of a shipment of filing cabinets, document folders and labelling machines – it's believed to have been the work of organised crime.

✳ To find out which is the best law enforcement agency in the USA, the President sets a test for the CIA, the FBI and the LAPD. He releases a rabbit in a forest and challenges them to find it. The CIA goes in first and, after months of interviewing forest dwellers and conducting forensic tests, they deduce that the rabbit never existed. The FBI go in next and burn down half the forest claiming the rabbit provoked them. The LAPD go in last and after half an hour drag out a badly beaten bear yelling, 'Okay, okay. I'm a rabbit, I'm a rabbit...'

✳ We have 35 million laws to enforce the Ten Commandments.

✳ What did the idiot burglar do when he saw his 'Wanted' poster outside the police station? He went in and applied for the job.

✳ Why did the doctor fail when he turned kidnapper? No one could read his ransom notes.

✳ Why did the escaped convict saw the legs off his bed? He wanted to lie low.

✳ Why in movies are detectives only able to solve cases once they've been suspended from duty?

✳ You can always spot a real crook – even his cash bounces.

✳ A corruption trial is in progress and the prosecuting lawyer is attacking a witness. 'Isn't it true,' he bellows, 'that you accepted five thousand pounds to compromise this case?' The witness stares out of the window. The attorney again shouts, 'Isn't it true that you accepted five thousand pounds to compromise this case?' The witness still does not respond. The lawyer asks yet again, but there's still no response. Finally, the judge leans over and says, 'Sir, please answer the question.' 'Oh, sorry,' says the startled witness. 'I thought he was talking to you.'

✳ Crime might not pay, but at least you're your own boss.

✳ Harry is waiting at a bus stop when he notices someone knock on the door of a nearby house. A woman answers, announces the time in a loud voice and closes the door again. A second visitor calls and gets the same response, then a third, and then a fourth. Bob turns to another waiting passenger, 'Excuse me, but why do people keep asking that woman the time?' The passenger replies, 'She's the local neighbourhood watch.'

✳ Policeman, to driver, 'You passed the breathalyser test but I'm still going to ask you accompany me to the station.' Driver, 'Why?' Policeman, 'There's a dark alley on the way back and I'm afraid to go down it by myself.'

🍊LAW AND ORDER: COURT

✳ A magistrate is speaking to three men brought before him for a misdemeanour. He ask the first man why he's there. The man replies, 'For throwing peanuts in the lake.' The judge asks the second man why he's there. The man replies, 'For throwing peanuts in the lake.' The judge asks the third man why he's there. He says, 'I'm Peanuts.'

✳ After his motion to suppress evidence was denied by the court the attorney addressed the judge, 'Your Honour. What would you do if I called you a stupid, degenerate old fool?' The judge replies, 'I would hold you in contempt and seek to have you suspended from practising before this court again!' 'What if I only thought it?' asks the attorney. 'In that case,' says the judge, 'there is nothing I could do. You have the right to think whatever you like.' 'I see,' says the attorney. 'Then, if it pleases the court, I "think" you're a stupid, degenerate old fool.'

✳ A man has to appear in court for a minor traffic summons. He grows increasingly restless as he waits hour after hour for his case to be heard. When his name is called it's late in the day and he stands before the judge only to hear that the court is going be adjourned until the next day. 'What for?' he snaps at the judge. The judge shouts back, 'Twenty pounds – contempt of court. That's why!' Then, noticing the man checking his wallet, the judge relents, 'That's all right. You don't have to pay now.' The man replies, 'I'm not paying. I'm just seeing if I have enough for two more words.'

✳ A man is on trial for murder. There's strong evidence of guilt; but no corpse. In the defence's closing statement the man's lawyer says, 'Ladies and gentlemen of the jury, I have a surprise for you. Within one minute, the person presumed dead in this case will walk into this courtroom.' The jury watch the door but after a minute has passed the lawyer says, 'Ladies and gentlemen, I made up the previous statement. But you all watched the door in anticipation. I therefore put it to you that there is reasonable doubt as to whether anyone was killed and insist that you return a verdict of not guilty.' The jury retires to deliberate. A few minutes later, they return and the foreman declares a verdict of guilty. 'What?' says the lawyer. 'You must have had some doubt; You were all staring at the door.' The foreman replies, 'Yes, we were all looking, but your client wasn't.'

✳ Accused, to judge, 'As the Lord is my judge, I am not guilty.' Judge, 'He's not, I am, you are, six months.'

✳ Barrister, to witness, 'And did you actually see the accused bite off Mr Smith's nose?' Witness, 'No, but I saw him spit it out.'

✳ Clerk, 'Prisoner at the bar, how do you plead, guilty or not guilty?' Prisoner, 'How can I tell till I've heard the evidence?'

✳ Judge, to accused, 'You admit murdering that old lady for a paltry fifty pence?' Accused, 'Fifty here, fifty there. It soon adds up.'

✳ Judge, to disruptive witness, 'Are you showing contempt for this court?' Witness, 'No, I'm doing my best to hide it.'

✳ Judge, to man, 'Are you the defence lawyer?' Man, 'No, I'm the bloke who stole the chickens.'

☺ LAW AND ORDER: MURDER

✳ A defence lawyer meets with his client. 'The blood tests have come back and we have good news and bad news.' 'So what's the bad news?' asks the client. 'Your DNA matches the blood found on the victim, the murder weapon, and the getaway car.' 'Okay,' says the defendant. 'So what the good news?' The lawyer replies, 'Your cholesterol is down to 120.'

✳ I'd like to smother my mother-in-law in diamonds. Then again, there has to be a cheaper way to do it.

✳ Mick is in court for a double murder. The judge says, 'You are charged with beating your wife to death with a spanner.' A man at the back of the courtroom yells out, 'You bastard!' The judge continues, 'You are also charged with beating your wife's lover to death with a spanner.' The man yells out, 'You absolute bastard!' The judge looks at the man and says, 'Sir, I can understand your anger at this crime, but I will have no more outbursts. If you have anything to say, say it now.' The man gets up and says, 'For fifteen years I lived next door to that bastard. And every time I asked to borrow a bloody spanner, he said he didn't have one!'

✳ Mr Smith, to judge, 'Your Honour, my wife is being ridiculous. Most women would love to have a chivalrous husband. Who could object to having a car door opened for them?' 'Mr Smith,' replies the judge. 'It might be chivalrous to open a car door for your wife, but not when you're driving at 65 miles per hour.'

✳ Why did Mrs Jones shoot her husband with a bow and arrow? She didn't want to wake the children.

☺ LAW AND ORDER: POLICE

✳ A hole has appeared in the ladies' changing rooms at the sports club. The police are looking into it.

✳ A salesman, tired of his job, gives it up to become a policeman. Several months later a friend asks him how he likes it. 'Well,' he replies. 'The pay is good and the hours aren't bad, but what I like best is that the customer is always wrong.'

✳ A woman finds her house has been robbed, so she calls the police and demands they send a patrol car immediately. The dispatcher tells her that the only patrol car near her home is a canine car. She yells, 'I don't care, just send him over!' The car stops by, but when the woman sees the officer get out of the car with his Alsation, she wails, 'Just my luck! My house gets robbed and they send me a blind policeman!'

✳ A police officer stops a woman and asks for her licence. He reads it and says, 'Lady, it says here that you should be wearing glasses.' The woman answers, 'I have contacts.' 'I don't care who you know!' says the officer. 'You're getting a ticket!'

✳ A policeman is at scene of a terrible accident. Body parts are everywhere and the officer is making notes of what is where. He comes across a head and writes in his notebook, 'Head on boolevard'. This doesn't look right so he crosses it out and writes, 'Head on bullevard'. That doesn't look right either so he writes 'Head on boullavard' which still doesn't seem right. The officer looks around to make sure no one is watching, and kicks the head. Then he writes, 'Head in garden'.

✳ Two guys are driving through Texas when they get pulled over by the highway patrol for speeding. The driver rolls down the window and the patrolman hits him across the face with his flashlight. 'Ow! What was that for?' asks the driver rubbing his face. The patrolman replies, 'In Texas, drivers have their licence and registration ready when I come to the window.' The patrolman writes the driver a ticket and gives it to him. The driver is about to roll up his window when the patrolman hits him again. 'Ow!' yells the man. 'What the hell was that for?' 'In Texas, when we give you a ticket. You say, thank you,' replies the patrolman. The driver quickly says thank you and rolls up his window. The patrolman then walks around to the passenger side and taps on the window. The passenger rolls down his window and the officer hits him over the head. The passenger yells, 'Ouch! Why did you do that?' The patrolman says, 'I was making your wish come true.' 'What wish?' asks the passenger. The patrolman replies, 'Five yards down that road you would have turned to your buddy and said "I wish that son of a bitch had tried that shit with me."'

✳ It's a tough job being a policeman these days. So many things have changed. Violence, drunkenness, attacks on the defenceless, obscene language – and that's just the Chief Inspector.

☻LAWYERS

✳ A doctor and a lawyer are involved in a car crash. The lawyer, seeing that the doctor is a little shaken up, offers him a drink from his hip flask. The doctor accepts, has a drink and hands back the flask. The lawyer puts it in his pocket. 'Aren't you having one yourself?' asks the doctor. 'Sure,' says the lawyer. 'But I'll wait till after the police leave.'

✳ A widow goes to her doctor and asks him to explain the human reproductive process. 'But you've been married three times,' says the doctor. 'Surely you've had sex?' 'Never,' replies the woman. 'My first husband was a gynaecologist, and all he did was look at it. My second husband was a psychiatrist, and all he did was talk about it. And my third husband was a explorer who was never around to do it.' 'So why do you want to know now?' asks the doctor. 'I'm getting married to a lawyer,' replies the woman. 'So I'm bound to get screwed somehow.'

✳ A doctor and a lawyer are talking at a party but their conversation is constantly interrupted by people asking the doctor for free medical advice. After an hour of this the doctor says to the lawyer, 'What do you do to stop people from asking you for legal advice when you're out of the office?' 'I give it to them,' replies the lawyer. 'Then I charge them for it.' The doctor is shocked. 'Does that really work?' 'Certainly does,' replies the lawyer. 'And that'll be £400 thank you.'

✳ A lawyer buys a farm as a weekend retreat. While walking round his new property he looks down and sees that his feet are in the middle of a huge cowpat. The lawyer starts yelling, 'Oh my God! Help me, help me!' His wife runs up and asks what's the matter. The lawyer points to his feet and screams, 'I'm melting! I'm melting…!'

✳ A lawyer dies in a car accident on his 40th birthday and finds himself greeted at the Pearly Gates by a brass band. Saint Peter runs over, shakes his hand and says, 'Congratulations!' 'Congratulations for what?' asks the lawyer. 'We're celebrating the fact that you lived to be 160 years old.' 'But that's not true,' says the lawyer. 'I only lived to be forty.' 'That's impossible,' replies Saint Peter. 'We've added up your time sheets.'

✳ A lawyer is paid £950 in new bills but, on counting the money, he discovers that two notes have stuck together and he's been overpaid by £50. This leaves him with an ethical dilemma – should he tell his partner?

✳ A lawyer opens the door of his BMW. Another car speeds by and hits the door, ripping it off completely. When the police arrive, the lawyer is complaining bitterly. 'Officer, look what they've done to my car!' he whines. 'You lawyers are so materialistic, you make me sick,' replies the officer. 'You're so worried about your stupid car, you haven't even noticed your left arm was ripped off!' 'Oh my God!' replies the lawyer. 'Where's my Rolex?'

✳ A woman drives home with the front of her car covered in branches, sticks, leaves, mud, and lots of blood. 'I'm really sorry about the car,' says the woman to her husband. 'But I hit a lawyer on the way home.' 'Well, that explains the blood,' says the husband. 'But what about the other stuff?' 'I had to chase him through the park,' says the woman.

✳ A lawyer with insomnia consults his doctor. 'Which side is it best to lie on?' he asks. 'The side that pays your fee,' replies the doctor.

✳ A man is stuck in a traffic jam. Looking out of his car window he sees a kid on a skateboard weaving his way towards him. 'Hey, what's the hold up?' he asks. 'It's some crazy lawyer,' replies the boy. 'He's lying in the middle of the road. He's doused himself with petrol and is threatening to set fire to himself. We're taking up a collection for him.' 'How much have you got so far?' asks the man. The boy replies, 'About thirty boxes of matches and twenty-three lighters.'

✳ A man walks into a bar with a alligator. He says to the bartender, 'Do you serve lawyers here?' 'Sure do,' replies the bartender. 'Good,' says the man. 'Give me a beer, and a lawyer for my 'gator.'

✳ An incompetent attorney can delay a trial for months or years. A competent attorney can delay one even longer.

✳ After having a big operation a lawyer slowly comes out of anaesthesia. He looks round his room and says, 'Doctor, why are all the blinds drawn in my room?' 'There's a big fire across the street,' replies the doctor. 'We didn't want you to think the operation had been a failure.'

✳ A man wanders into an antique shop in San Francisco's Chinatown. He picks through the curios on display and comes across a bronze sculpture of a rat. The craftsmanship is very good, and the price is low, so he buys it. Taking the rat statue outside the man walks towards the waterfront but is alarmed when he realises he's being followed by a pair of real rats. Soon the two rats are joined by others, then more arrive, until a horde of rats is following the man. Terrified, the man starts to run and the rats run after him, more joining all the time. Finally the man reaches a pier where he's cornered by a host of rats. Figuring this behaviour has something to do with the bronze rat sculpture, the man throws it into the sea. Immediately all the rats fling themselves into the water and drown. The man rushes back to the antique shop and accosts the old Chinese man who owns it. 'About that statue…' gasps the man. 'Yes, I probably should have warned you,' says the owner. 'The statue is cursed…' 'Never mind that,' says the man. 'Have you got any statues of lawyers?'

✳ A woman is told she needs two kilos of brain for a transplant. She's informed that two kilos of doctor brain will cost £500, and the two kilos of architect brain will cost £600. She replies that, since her father was a famous lawyer, she'd prefer a lawyer's brain. 'Okay,' says the doctor. 'That'll cost you £10,000.' 'What?' she says. 'How can two kilos of lawyer's brain cost £10,000?' The doctor replies, 'Do you have any idea how many lawyers we have to pop open to get that much?'

✳ An airliner is having engine trouble. The pilot instructs the cabin crew to prepare for an emergency landing. A few minutes later the pilot asks the flight attendants if everyone is buckled in and ready. 'All set back here, Captain,' comes the reply. 'Except one lawyer. He's still going around passing out business cards.'

✳ An elderly patient needs a heart transplant and discusses his options with his doctor. The doctor says, 'We have three possible donors. One is a young, healthy athlete. The second is a middle-aged businessman who never drank or smoked, and the third is an attorney who just died after practising law for 30 years.' 'I'll take the lawyer's heart,' says the patient. 'Why?' asks the doctor. The patient replies, 'It's never been used.'

✳ Did you hear about the lawyer who was hurt in an accident? The ambulance he was chasing stopped too suddenly.

✳ He was a very keen lawyer, he even named his daughter 'Sue'.

✳ How can you tell when a lawyer is lying? His lips are moving.

✳ How do you get a lawyer out of a tree? Cut the rope.

✳ If a lawyer and a tax official were both drowning and you could only save one of them, what would you do; go to lunch or read the paper?

✳ How do you stop a lawyer from drowning? Shoot him before he hits the water.

✳ How do you stop a lawyer from drowning? Take your foot off his head.

✳ How many lawyers does it take to stop a moving bus? Never enough.

✳ If an apple a day keeps the doctor away, how many orchards does it take for a lawyer?

✳ If it wasn't for lawyers, we wouldn't need them.

✳ Jerry is charged with stealing a Mercedes Benz, and after a long trial, the jury acquits him. Later that day Jerry comes back to speak to the judge that tried his case. 'Your Honour,' he says. 'I want to get out a warrant for that dirty lawyer of mine.' 'Why?' asks the judge. 'He won your acquittal. Why do you want to have him arrested?' Jerry replies, 'I didn't have the money to pay his fee, so the bastard went and took the car I stole.'

✳ Lawyer, 'Let me give you my honest opinion.' Client, 'No, no. I'm paying for professional advice.'

✳ Lawyer's creed – a man is innocent until proven broke.

✳ Man, to lawyer, 'If I give you £500, will you answer two questions?' Lawyer, 'Absolutely. What's the other question?'

✳ Old lawyers never die, they just lose their appeal.

✳ Terrorists have hijacked a planeload of lawyers bound for a legal convention. They've threatened to start releasing the lawyers one by one until their demands are met.

✳ Mister Smith is on his deathbed and comes up with a plan to take some of his wealth with him. He calls for the three men he trusts most – his lawyer, his doctor and his clergyman. 'I'm going to give you each £30,000 in cash before I die,' says Mister Smith. 'At my funeral, I want you to place the money in my coffin so that I can try to take it with me.' At the funeral, each approaches the coffin and places an envelope inside. Later, while riding in the limousine to the cemetery, the clergyman says, 'I have to confess I only put £20,000 in the coffin. The church needs a new baptistery very badly, so I took £10,000 out of the envelope.' The doctor says, 'Well, I didn't put the full £30,000 in the coffin either. I used £20,000 of the money to buy a dialysis machine for the hospital.' The lawyer then says, 'I'm ashamed of both of you. When I put my envelope in that coffin it held my personal cheque for the full £30,000.'

✳ Santa Claus, the tooth fairy, an honest lawyer and a drunk are in a bar when they spot a hundred pounds on the floor. Who gets it? The drunk – the other three are mythological creatures.

✳ Ninety-nine percent of lawyers give the rest a bad name.

✳ Three men are travelling in the countryside when their car breaks down. They go to a farmhouse to seek shelter. The farmer only has two spare beds but says that one of the men can sleep in the barn. The first man, a rabbi, volunteers to sleep outside, but a few minutes after he leaves, there's a knock at the door. It's the rabbi. It turns out there's a pig in the barn and the rabbi doesn't feel comfortable sleeping there. To get round the problem the second man, a Hindu, volunteers to take the rabbi's place. He leaves for the barn, but a few minutes later, there's a knock at the door. It's the Hindu. It turns out there's also a cow in the barn and the Hindu doesn't feel comfortable sleeping near it. The third man, a lawyer, says he doesn't have any religious hang-ups and walks out to sleep in the barn. A few minutes later the rabbi and the Hindu hear a knock. The rabbi opens the door. Standing outside are a pig and a cow.

✳ What do you call ten lawyers buried up to their necks in the sand? Football practice.

✳ Two lawyers are walking down the road when they see a beautiful woman walking towards them. 'What a babe,' one says. 'I'd sure like to screw her!' 'Really?' replies the other. 'Out of what?'

✷ Two lawyers make a suicide pact and plan to jump from the top of their office block. The building is 20 storeys high, each lawyer has the same body type, and both weigh the same. One is wearing a brown suit, the other is wearing a blue suit. Question: which of them hits the street first? Answer: who cares?

✷ Two tigers are prowling through the jungle in single file and the one behind keeps licking the arse of the tiger in front. 'Will you stop that,' says the first tiger. 'It's getting really annoying.' 'I'm sorry,' says the second tiger. 'But I just ate a lawyer and I'm trying to get the taste out of my mouth.'

✷ What can a goose do, a duck can't, and a lawyer should? Stick his bill up his rear.

✷ What do you call 5,000 dead lawyers at the bottom of the ocean? A good start.

✷ What do you call a lawyer with an IQ of 50? Your Honour.

✷ What happens when a lawyer takes Viagra? He gets taller.

✷ What's the difference between two lawyers in a Porsche and a porcupine? The porcupine has pricks on the outside.

✷ What's a foot long, transparent and lies in the gutter. A lawyer once the crap's been kicked out of him.

✷ What's black and tan and looks great on a lawyer? A Dobermann pinscher.

✷ What's the difference between a dead lawyer in the road and a dead skunk in the road? There are skid marks in front of the skunk.

✷ What's the difference between a female lawyer and a pit bull? Lipstick.

✷ When a person assists a criminal in breaking the law before a crime, we call him an accomplice. When a person assists a criminal in breaking the law after a crime, we call him a defence lawyer.

✷ What's the difference between a shame and a pity? If a busload of lawyers goes over a cliff and there are no survivors – that's a pity. If there were any empty seats – that's a shame.

✳ Why do they bury lawyers in 20ft holes? Because deep down they're all really nice guys.

✳ Why does the bar association prohibit lawyers and clients from having sex? To prevent clients from being billed twice for the same service.

✳ Why don't lawyers enjoy fishing? Because it's too much like work, what with all the lying involved.

✳ Why don't you see lawyers on the beach? Cats keep covering them with sand.

✳ A lawyer dies but his firm keeps receiving calls asking to speak with him. The receptionist keeps saying, 'I'm sorry, he's dead.' But the calls keep coming. Eventually the receptionist realises that most of the calls are coming from the same woman. 'Why do you keep phoning?' says the receptionist. 'You know he's dead.' 'Yes, I know he's dead. He was my husband,' says the female caller. 'I just like to hear you say it.'

✳ A lawyer is sitting in his office when the Devil appears before him. The Devil says, 'I have a proposition for you. You can win every case you try. Your colleagues will stand in awe of you, and you will make embarrassing sums of money. All I want in exchange is your soul, and the souls of all your relatives.' The lawyer thinks about it for a second, then says, 'Okay. So, what's the catch?'

✳ Do you know how to save a drowning lawyer? No? Good!

✳ A lawyer once grew so huge that when he died they couldn't find a coffin big enough to bury him in. In they end they had to give him an enema and bury what was left in a shoe-box.

✳ A man is giving his local priest a lift in his car when he sees a lawyer crossing the road, without thinking he turns the car to run the lawyer over. Suddenly he remembers he's got holy company, hauls on the wheel and just misses the startled lawyer. The man turns to the priest and says, 'I'm sorry about that, Father. I don't know what came over me.' The priest replies, 'Don't worry, my son. I got him with my door.'

✳ Why won't sharks attack lawyers? Professional courtesy.

life

Life may not be worth living, but what else can you do with it?

The first half of life if ruined by your parents, the second by your kids.

There's one good thing about life. It's only temporary.

🍊 LIGHT BULB

✳ How many boring people does it take to change a light bulb? One.

✳ Do you know how many musicians it takes to change a light bulb? No, but you hum it and I'll play it.

✳ How many actors does it take to change a light bulb? Only one. They don't like to share the spotlight.

✳ How many chiropractors does it take to change a light bulb? Only one, but it takes 15 visits.

✳ How many Christian Scientists does it take to change a light bulb? Just one, to heal the old light bulb.

✳ How many civil servants does it take to change a light bulb? 45. One to change the bulb, and 44 to do the paperwork.

✳ How many existentialists does it take to change a light bulb? Two. One to screw it in, the other to observe how the light bulb symbolises a single, incandescent beacon of subjective reality in a netherworld of endless absurdity.

✳ How many consultants does it take to change a light bulb? I'll have an estimate for you a week on Monday.

✳ How many cops does it take to screw in a light bulb? None. It turned itself in.

✳ How many divorced men does it take to screw in a light bulb? Who knows, they never get the house.

✳ How many divorced women does it take to screw in a light bulb? Four. One to screw in the bulb, and three to form a support group.

✳ How many economists does it take to screw in a light bulb? None. If the light bulb really needed changing, market forces would have already caused it to happen.

✳ How many folk singers does it take to screw in a light bulb? Two: one to change the bulb, and one to write a song about how good the old one was.

✳ How many football managers does it take to change a light bulb? Who knows, they're never around long enough for anyone to find out.

✳ How many Hollywood directors does it take to change a light bulb? One, but he'll want to do it 19 times.

✳ How many Irish people does it take to change a light bulb? 257. One to hold it and 256 to turn the room.

✳ How many Jewish mothers does it take to change a light bulb? None, 'Never mind me, I'll just sit here in the dark…'

✳ How many Jewish-American princesses does it take to screw in a light bulb? Two. One to get a Tab, and one to call Daddy.

✳ How many jugglers does it take to change a light bulb? One, but it takes at least three light bulbs.

✳ How many managers does it take to change a light bulb? Three. One to get the bulb and two to get the phone number to dial one of their subordinates to actually change it.

✳ How many LA cops does it take to change a light bulb? Five. One to screw in a new bulb, and four to beat the crap out of the old one.

✳ How many witches does it take to change a light bulb? Into what?

✳ How many male chauvinists does it take to change a light bulb? None – she can do it when she's finished the dishes.

✳ How many Marxists does it take to screw in a light bulb? None, the seeds of revolution and change are within the light bulb itself.

✳ How many medical students does it take to change a light bulb? Five. One to change the bulb and four to pull the ladder out from under him.

✳ How many men does it take to screw in a light bulb? One. He holds it and waits for the world to revolve around him.

✳ How many men does it take to screw in a light bulb? One. Men will screw anything.

✳ How many Microsoft programmers does it take to change a light bulb? None. Microsoft declare that darkness comes as standard with Windows 2000.

✳ How many necrophiliacs does it take to screw in a light bulb? None. Necrophiliacs prefer dead bulbs.

✳ How many New Yorkers does it take to screw in a light bulb? None of your damn business!

✳ How many Valley Girls does it take to change a light bulb? Oooh, like, manual labour? Gag me with a spoon! For sure.

✳ How many pessimists does it take to change a light bulb? None, the old one is probably screwed in too tight.

✳ How many philosophers does it take to replace a light bulb? Three. One to change it, and two to argue over whether or not the light bulb really exists.

✳ How many poets does it take to change a light bulb? Three. One to curse the darkness, one to light a candle, and one to change the bulb.

✳ How many politicians does it take to change a light bulb? It depends on how many it took under the previous government.

✳ How many nihilists does it take to change a light bulb? There is nothing to change.

✳ How many professors does it take to change a light bulb? Only one, but they get three tech reports out of it.

✳ How many programmers does it take to change a light bulb? None. That's a hardware problem.

✳ How many psychiatrists does it take to change a light bulb? Only one. But the light bulb has really got to want to change.

✳ How many punk rockers does it take to change a light bulb? Two. One to change the bulb, and one to eat the old one.

✳ How many Real Women does it take to change a light bulb? None. A Real Woman would have plenty of Real Men around to do it.

✳ How many Roman Catholics does it take to change a light bulb? Two. One to do the screwing, and one to hear the confession.

✳ How many stand-up comedians does it take to change a light bulb? Two, one to screw it in, and another to say, "Sock it to me".'

✳ How many straight San Franciscans does it take to change a light bulb? Both of them.

✳ How many surrealists does it take to change a light bulb? Two. One to hold the giraffe, and the other to fill the bathtub with brightly coloured machine tools.

✳ How many telemarketers does it take to change a light bulb? One. But he has to do it while you're having dinner.

✳ How many televangelists does it take to screw in a light bulb? None. Televangelists screw in motels.

✳ How many US Marines does it take to change a light bulb? 50. One to screw in the bulb and 49 to guard him.

✳ How many Ukrainians does it take to screw in a light bulb? None. People who glow in the dark don't need light bulbs.

✳ How many accountants does it take to screw in a light bulb? What kind of answer did you have in mind?

✳ How many bikers does it take to change a light bulb? Two. One to change the bulb, and the other to kick the switch.

✳ How many mystery writers does it take to screw in a light bulb? Two: one to screw it almost all the way in and the other to give it a surprising twist at the end.

✳ How many mathematicians does it take to screw in a light bulb? One. He gives it to six Californians, thereby reducing the problem to an earlier joke.

logic

I think sex is better than logic, but I can't prove it.

Someone who thinks logically provides a nice contrast to the real world.

✪LOST AND FOUND

✳ 'Once when I was lost I saw a policeman, and asked him to help me find my parents. I said to him, "Do you think we'll ever find them?" He said, "I don't know, kid. There are so many places they can hide."' *Rodney Dangerfield*

✳ A man loses his donkey and gets down on his knees to thank God. A passer-by asks, 'Why are you thanking God when you've lost your donkey?' The man replies, 'Well, thank goodness I wasn't on it at the time or I'd be lost too.'

✳ Two little boys come home with a football. 'Where did you get that from?' asks their mother. 'We found it,' they say. 'Are you absolutely sure it was lost?' says Mum. 'Yes,' say the kids. 'We saw the people looking for it.'

☙ MARRIAGE

✳ 'Before we were married, you told me you were well off.' 'Yes. Unfortunately I didn't realise just how well off.'

✳ 'Husbands are like fires. They go out when unattended.' *Zsa Zsa Gabor*

✳ 'I was married by a judge. I should have asked for a jury.' *Groucho Marx*

✳ A couple come across a wishing well. The husband leans over, makes a wish and throws in a penny. The wife makes a wish too, but she leans over too far, falls into the well and drowns. The husband says, 'Wow! It really works!'

✳ 'My marriage is on the rocks again. Yeah, my wife just broke up with her boyfriend.' *Rodney Dangerfield*

✳ 'Why do you and your wife fight all the time?' 'I don't know. She never tells me.'

✳ A husband and wife are driving along when they see an injured skunk lying by the roadside. They decide to take it to a vet but don't have anything to carry it in. 'Why not wrap it in your skirt?' suggests the husband. 'What about the stink?' protests his wife. Her husband replies, 'It'll just have to get used to it.'

✳ A husband and wife visit a marriage guidance counsellor. The wife complains that her husband doesn't pay her enough attention, so the counsellor decides on some shock treatment. He leans over the desk and gives the woman a long passionate kiss. He then turns to the husband and says, 'Your wife needs that kind of attention at least twice a week.' 'Okay,' replies the husband. 'But I can only get her here Tuesdays and Thursdays.'

✳ A man approaches a beautiful woman in a supermarket. 'I've lost my wife somewhere,' he says. 'Do you mind if I talk to you for a moment?' 'Okay,' replies the woman. 'But how's that going to help you find your wife?' 'Easy,' replies the man. 'She always turns up when I start chatting to strange women.'

✳ A husband is living proof that a wife can take a joke.

✳ A little girl runs into her parents' room and demands that her mother tells her a story. 'It's three in the morning, dear,' says her mother. 'Can't you just go back to bed?' The girl replies, 'I tried, Mummy, but I can't sleep. Please tell me a story.' Mother sighs and says, 'Tell you what, you jump in bed with me, and when your daddy finally gets home, we'll both get to hear a story!'

✳ A husband says to his wife, 'I was a fool when I married you.' 'I know,' she replies. 'But I was in love and didn't notice.'

✳ A little boy says, 'Dad, I've heard that in some parts of Africa a man doesn't know his wife until he marries her.' 'Son,' says the dad. 'That happens everywhere.'

✳ A man comes home and finds his wife packing her bags. 'Where are you going?' he asks. 'To Las Vegas!' she replies. 'Why should I have sex with you for free when there are men out there who'll pay £400 for a good time!' The man picks up a suitcase and starts packing too. 'What d'you think you're doing?' asks the wife. 'I'm going to Las Vegas with you,' replies the man. 'I want to see how you'll live on £800 a year!'

✳ A man boards a plane. Sitting next to him is an elegant woman wearing the largest, most stunning diamond ring he's ever seen. He asks her about it. 'This is the Klopman diamond,' she says. 'It's beautiful, but there is a terrible curse that goes with it.' 'What's the curse?' asks the man. The woman replies, 'Mister Klopman.'

✳ A man comes home from an exhausting day at work, collapses on the couch in front of the TV, and says to his wife, 'Get me a beer before it starts.' His wife gets him a beer. Fifteen minutes later he says, 'Get me another beer before it starts.' She looks cross, but fetches another beer. A few minutes later he says, 'Quick, get me another beer, it's going to start any minute.' His wife is furious. She yells, 'Is that all you're going to do tonight? Drink beer and sit in front of that TV? You're nothing but a lazy, drunken, fat slob, and furthermore …' The man sighs and says, 'It's started…'

✳ A man rushes into his house and yells to his wife, 'Martha, pack up your things! I just won the Lottery!' Martha shouts back, 'Shall I pack for warm weather or cold?' The man replies, 'I don't care, just as long as you're out of the house by noon!'

✳ A man has a check-up and the doctor finds something seriously wrong. He decides the news is too bad to tell the man directly so he breaks it to his wife. 'Your husband is seriously ill,' says the doctor. 'The only way you can save his life is to offer him a completely stress-free existence. You must not contradict him in any way. He must give up his job so he can concentrate on restful hobbies. He must have three home-cooked meals every day, and live in an environment that is as tranquil, tidy and germ free as possible.' In the car home the husband says, 'So what's going to happen to me?' The wife answers, 'You're going to die.'

✳ A man is on his deathbed. 'Grant me one last wish, my dear,' he gasps pitifully to his wife. 'Six months after I die I want you to marry Joe.' 'But I thought you hated Joe,' says his wife. 'I do,' says the man.

✳ A woman marries a man expecting he will change, but he doesn't. A man marries a woman expecting that she won't change, and she does.

✳ A woman puts an ad in the paper saying, 'Husband wanted'. Next day she gets a hundred letters all saying the same thing: 'You can have mine.'

✳ A man is walking down the street when he hears a voice shouting, 'Stop! Take one more step and you'll be killed!' The man stops and a brick crashes on to the path in front of him. The man looks around but can't see who shouted the warning. A few moments later the man is crossing a road when the same voice yells, 'Stop! Don't step off the kerb!' A car jumps a red light and zooms past just missing the man. Again he looks round but can't see who shouted. An hour later the man is getting on a ferry when the voice yells, 'Don't do it! You'll drown!' The man steps off the ferry then watches it sink midstream a few minutes later. The man looks round but still can't see who shouted. He calls out, 'Who's there?' 'It's me. Your guardian angel,' replies the voice, 'I watch over everything you do.' 'You rotten bastard!' shouts the man. 'What d'you mean?' replies the voice. 'I just saved your life three times.' 'Yes,' replies the man, 'but where were you on my wedding day?'

✳ A policeman on a motorcycle pulls over a car. 'What's up?' says the driver. 'Your wife fell out the passenger door three miles back,' says the policeman. 'Thank goodness for that,' says the driver. 'I thought I'd gone deaf.'

✳ A third-grade teacher is getting to know her pupils on the first day of school. She turns to one little girl and says, 'And what does your daddy do?' The girl replies, 'Whatever Mummy tells him to.'

✳ A woman worries about the future until she gets a husband. A man never worries about the future until he gets a wife.

✳ A tramp approaches a man in the street and asks for money. 'Will you spend the money on drink?' asks the man. The tramp shakes his head. 'Will you waste it on card games?' asks the man. The tramp shakes his head. 'Then come home with me,' says the man. 'Why?' asks the tramp. The man replies, 'I want my wife to meet the kind of man who doesn't drink or gamble.'

✳ A widower goes to a psychic to see if he can contact his late wife. The séance starts and he finds himself talking to her. 'Honey,' he says. 'Are you happy?' 'Yes, my husband,' replies his wife. 'Happier than you were with me?' asks the husband. 'Much, much happier,' replies his wife. 'Heaven must be an amazing place,' says the husband. 'I'm not in Heaven,' replies his wife.

✳ A woman finds her husband sobbing in the kitchen. 'What's the matter?' she asks. 'You remember when your father found out you were pregnant and threatened me with 20 years in jail if I didn't marry you,' says the husband. 'Yes,' says the woman. 'Well, today was my release date.'

✳ A woman is sick of her husband's drinking and decides to teach him a lesson. She dresses up like Satan, and when her husband returns after another bender, she jumps out on him from behind the door. 'You don't scare me,' slurs the man. 'I married your sister.'

✳ A woman turns to her husband on their silver wedding anniversary and says, 'Darling, will you still love me when my hair turns grey?' Her husband replies, 'Why not? I stuck with you through the other six shades.'

✳ A woman's house has been ransacked but she doesn't report the crime till next day. When a police officer calls round he asks her why she delayed reporting the robbery. 'I didn't know I had been robbed,' replies the woman. 'When I came in I thought my husband had been looking for a clean shirt.'

✳ According to the latest survey, married men's favourite fantasy when making love is that their wives aren't fantasising.

✳ Going to a party with your wife is like going fishing with a game warden.

✳ Attending a wedding for the first time, a little girl whispers to her mother, 'Why is the bride dressed in white?' Mother decides to keep things simple and replies, 'Because white is a happy colour and today is the happiest day of her life.' The girl thinks for a second, then says, 'So why is the groom wearing black?'

✳ Courtship is like looking at the pictures in a seed catalogue. Marriage is what comes up in your garden.

✳ For sale: Twenty-volume encyclopaedia. Good condition. No longer needed. Wife knows everything.

✳ For twenty years my wife and I were very happy. Then we met.

✳ Getting married is very much like going to a restaurant with friends. You order what you want, then when you see what the other person's got, you wish you'd ordered that.

✳ Harry invites his friend Dick for dinner. At the dinner table Harry talks to his wife using endearing terms such as Honey, My Love, Darling, Sweetheart, Pumpkin, etc. When Harry's wife is out of the room Dick says, 'That's really nice. After all these years of marriage, you still call your wife pet names.' Harry whispers back, 'It sounds good but to tell the truth, I forgot her real name three years ago.'

✳ Harry went into town and got a bottle of wine for his wife – it was one of the best deals he'd ever made.

✳ He asked for her hand in marriage after an evening in the pub. It was very romantic. He actually climbed up on one knee to propose.

✳ He joined the Foreign Legion to forget his wife, unfortunately the sergeant major looked just like her.

✳ He never got married. He said he didn't want to make the same mistake once.

✳ He was in a position to marry anyone he pleased. Unfortunately he didn't please anyone.

✳ I got married to Miss Right. I just didn't realise her first name was 'Always'.

✳ Husband, to wife, 'I hear you've been telling everyone that I'm an idiot.' Wife, 'Sorry, I didn't know it was a secret.'

✳ Husband, to wife, 'Put your coat on, I'm going to the pub.' Wife, 'Oh that's nice, are you taking me for a drink?' Husband, 'No, I'm turning the heating off.'

✳ Husband, to wife, 'You have a flat chest and hairy legs. Tell me, have you ever been mistaken for a man?' 'No,' replies his wife. 'Have you?'

✳ I came downstairs this morning and my wife asked me what I wanted for breakfast. So I said, 'Eggs, bacon, fried bread and mushrooms.' At least that's what I meant to say. What I actually said was, 'You've ruined my life, you fat ugly witch.'

✳ I joined Bachelors Anonymous. Every time I feel like getting married they send round a woman in curlers to nag me for a while.

✳ I live like a medieval knight. Every night I go to sleep with a battleaxe at my side.

✳ I never married because there was no need – I have three pets which serve the same purpose as a husband. I have a dog that growls every morning, a parrot that swears all afternoon, and a cat that comes home late every night.

✳ I take my wife everywhere, but she keeps finding her way back.

✳ I took two marriage vows. Silence and poverty.

✳ I wouldn't say she's been married a lot but the church is trying to get her to pay for a new aisle carpet.

✳ If it weren't for marriage, men would go through life thinking they had no faults at all.

✳ It's not true that married men live longer than single men. It only seems longer.

✳ If you want your wife to pay attention to every word you say, try talking in your sleep.

✳ I've been happily married for ten whole years. And ten out of thirty isn't bad.

✳ I've been very depressed lately. My wife's threatened to leave me. But even that hasn't cheered me up.

✳ I've often wanted to drown my troubles, but I can't get my wife to go swimming.

✳ Ladies, don't forget the jumble sale. It is a good chance to get rid of those things not worth keeping around the house. Bring your husbands.

✳ Lady Astor to Winston Churchill, 'If you were my husband I'd poison your brandy.' Churchill, 'If you were my wife I'd drink it.'

✳ Losing a wife can be hard. In most cases, it's damned near impossible.

✳ Make love, not war. Or if you want to do both – get married!

✳ Man is incomplete until he's married. Then he's finished.

✳ Man, to friend, 'When did you first realise your wife had stopped loving you?' Friend, 'When she pushed me through the window, and wrote for an ambulance.'

✳ Marriage is a bed of roses – without the flowers.

✳ Marriage is love. Love is blind. Marriage is an institution. Therefore: marriage is an institution for the blind.

✳ Marriage is not a lottery – you get a chance in a lottery.

✳ My wife and I have agreed never to go to bed angry with one another. So far we've been up for three weeks.

'One night I came home. I figured, let my wife come on. I'll play it cool. Let her make the first move. She went to Florida.'
Rodney Dangerfield

✳ Marrying a man for his good looks is like buying a house for its paint.

✳ Marriages are made in Heaven – but then again, so are thunder and lightning.

✳ My wife and I have the secret to making a marriage last. Two times a week, we go to a nice restaurant and have a little wine and good food. She goes Tuesdays, I go Fridays.

✳ My wife and I lead a quiet life. The last time we went out together was when the gas boiler exploded.

✳ My wife constantly complains that I never listen to her... Or something like that.

✳ My wife has a contract to give lectures – it's called a marriage licence.

✳ On the way home from a party, a wife says to her husband, 'Have I ever told you how handsome, sexy and irresistible to women you are?' The husband is very flattered, 'Why no, I don't think you have.' His wife replies, 'Then what in hell's name gave you that idea at the party?'

✳ Remember your wife is a romantic who still loves flowers and chocolates. Show her you remember as well by referring to them occasionally.

✳ She has her husband eating out of the palm of her hand – it saves on the washing-up.

✳ The best way to get your husband to do something is to suggest he's too old to do it.

✳ The husband who wants a happy marriage should learn to keep his mouth shut and his chequebook open.

✳ The trouble with some women is that they get all excited about nothing – and then they marry him.

✳ A woman applies for a job in a lemon grove. 'Have you got any experience picking lemons?' asks the foreman. 'I certainly have,' says the woman. 'I've been married four times.'

✳ The CIA advertises for an assassin and three applicants, Tom, Dick and Harry, are chosen for a final test. Tom is given a gun and shown a door. 'Inside this room, you will find your wife sitting in a chair. Kill her!' says the CIA agent. Tom replies, 'You can't be serious. I could never shoot my wife.' 'Then you're not the right man for this job,' says the agent. Dick is given the same instructions. He takes the gun and goes into the room. After a few minutes he emerges in tears and says, 'I tried, but I can't kill my wife.' The agent says, 'You don't have what it takes. Take your wife and go home.' Finally, it's Harry's turn. He's given the same instructions, takes the gun and goes into the room. Several shots are heard, then lots of screaming, crashing and banging. Eventually Harry emerges wiping sweat from his brow. 'That damn gun you gave me was loaded with blanks. I had to beat her to death with the chair.'

✳ Since I got married I haven't looked at another woman. My wife put me off them.

✳ Two aerials met on a roof, fell in love, and got married. The ceremony was rubbish but the reception was brilliant.

✳ There's a lot to be said about marriage, but we try not to say it in front of the children.

✳ They are a fastidious couple. She's fast and he's hideous.

✳ Two married men are talking over the telephone. One says, 'Ever since we got married, my wife has tried to change me. She got me to stop drinking, smoking and running around until all hours of the night. She taught me how to dress well, enjoy the fine arts, gourmet cooking, classical music, even how to invest in the stock market.' 'Sounds like you may be bitter because she changed you so drastically,' remarks his friend. 'I'm not bitter,' replies the first. 'It's just now that I'm so improved, I've realised she isn't good enough for me.'

✳ Two women meet on the street. One asks the other about her husband. 'Well, liquor doesn't agree with him and he doesn't know how to play poker,' says the first. 'That's wonderful,' says her friend. 'It would be,' says the first woman. 'If he didn't drink and play poker.'

✳ What is the difference between a girlfriend and a wife? About 40 lb.

✳ Two strangers, a man and a woman, find themselves in the same sleeping carriage of a train. They both go to sleep, the man on the top bunk, the woman on the bottom. In the middle of the night the man leans over and says, 'I'm sorry to bother you, but I'm awfully cold and I was wondering if you could possibly get me another blanket?' 'I have a better idea,' replies the woman with a glint in her eye. 'Just for tonight, let's pretend that we're married.' 'Sounds good to me,' says the man. 'Great,' replies the woman. 'Now go and get your own damn blanket!'

✳ Why is marriage a three-ring circus? First the engagement ring, then the wedding ring, then the suffering.

✳ Wife, to husband, 'I need a new dress.' Husband, 'What's wrong with the dress you've got?' Wife, 'It's too long and the veil keeps getting in my eyes.'

✳ Wife, to husband, 'Let's go out and have some fun tonight!' Husband, 'Okay, but if you get home before I do, leave the hall light on.'

✳ Wife, to husband, 'My mother says I should never have married you. She says you're effeminate.' Husband, 'Compared to her everyone is.'

✳ Wife, to husband, 'When I married you you said you had an ocean-going yacht!' Husband, 'Shut up and row.'

✳ A factory sets up in a small town and advertises for workers, however, the advertisements say that they will only be hiring married men. A local woman is outraged at this and calls on the factory manager. 'Why are you only hiring married men?' asks the woman. 'Don't you think women can do the job?' 'Not at all, madam,' replies the manager. 'It's because we like employees who are used to obeying orders, are accustomed to being pushed around, know how to keep their mouths shut, and don't pout when I yell at them.'

✳ A trainee marriage guidance counsellor sits in on a senior colleague while he interviews a couple. The counsellor interviews the husband and wife separately. First he listens to the man's story, then agrees it's all his wife's fault. 'You're so right,' he says. Then he listens to the wife's story and agrees it's all the husband's fault. 'You're so right,' he says. The assistant collars the counsellor outside and says, 'What sort of counselling is that? They can't both be right.' The counsellor nods and says, 'You're so right.'

MARRIAGE: ADULTERY

✳ 'Eighty per cent of married men cheat in America. The rest cheat in Europe.' *Jackie Mason*

✳ 'Men would like monogamy better if it sounded less like monotony.' *Rita Rudner*

✳ A couple are celebrating their golden wedding anniversary when the husband asks his wife if she's ever been unfaithful. 'Three times,' answers the wife. 'Remember when you needed money to start up your business and no one would give you any? Well I slept with the bank manager to secure you a loan.' 'You made that sacrifice for me?' asks the astonished husband. 'That was wonderful of you. What was the second time?' 'Remember that operation you needed that no one would perform because it was too dangerous? Well, I slept with the surgeon so he'd do it.' 'Oh my God,' says the husband. 'You saved my life. And what was the third time?' 'Well,' says his wife. 'Remember when you wanted to be president of the golf club and you were fifty-two votes short...?'

✳ A couple are sitting in a restaurant when the man suddenly slips under the table. His female companion doesn't seem to notice so the waiter says, 'Madam. Is your husband all right? He's slipped on the floor.' The woman replies, 'He's not my husband. My husband just walked through the door.'

✳ A husband suspects his wife is having an affair. He needs to go on a business trip for several days, so he sets a trap for her. He puts a bowl of milk under the bed. From the bed springs he suspends a spoon. He has it calibrated so that her weight on the bed will not drop the spoon into the milk. But, if there is any more weight than that, the spoon will drop into the milk and he will detect it upon his return. He comes home several days later. The first thing he does is reach under the bed and retrieve the bowl – which is now full of butter.

✳ A farmer comes home from the fields early and sees a light on in his bedroom. Suspecting foul play, he grabs his shotgun and creeps up the stairs. He bursts into the bedroom and finds one of his farmhands naked, in bed with his wife. The farmhand stands up and shouts, 'Don't shoot! For God's sakes give me a chance!' The farmer aims his gun and says, 'Okay, I'll give you a chance – now swing 'em!'

✳ A farmer's son accompanies his father on a trip to buy a cow. The farmer prods the cow all over, strokes its sides, looks in every nook and cranny, and even lifts its tail so he can peer up its rear end. 'Y'see,' explains the farmer. 'You have to give it a real going over before you know if it's worth paying money for.' Next day the boy runs up to his father and says, 'Dad! I just saw Mummy and the postman behind the barn. I think he's planning on buying her!'

✳ A husband and wife are trying to save for their holidays. The husband suggests that he puts a £20 note in a jar every time they have sex. Three months later the man counts the money and finds over £700. 'How did that happen?' asks the husband. 'We only had sex six times.' His wife replies, 'Yes, but not everyone's as stingy as you are.'

✳ A husband comes home early and finds his wife, Mary, lying naked on the bed dying of a heart attack. He picks up the phone to ring the doctor when his young son shouts out, 'Dad! There's a nude man in the wardrobe!' The husband opens the wardrobe door and finds his best friend naked inside. 'I don't believe it!' shouts the man. 'Mary's dying on the bed and you're playing games with the kids?'

✳ A knight goes off on the crusades, but defends his wife's honour by equipping her with a chastity belt embedded with razor blades. A year later he returns and orders all his retainers to drop their trousers. They do so and the knight sees that all but one man have shredded privates. He stands before the unshredded man and says, 'For your loyalty I shall give you my best horse and one hundred acres of land.' The man replies, 'Oh, hank u ery uch.'

✳ A little boy goes to his mother and says, 'Mummy, every night I hear you and Daddy making noises and when I look in your room you're bouncing up and down on him.' His mother thinks quickly and says, 'Oh, well, I'm bouncing on Daddy's tummy because he's fat and that makes him thin again.' The boy says, 'Well, that won't work.' 'Why not?' asks his mother. The boy replies, 'Because the lady next door comes by every afternoon and blows him back up again!'

✳ A man gets arrested for making love to a dolphin. His wife is furious and embarrassed. 'How could you?' she says. 'Caught making love to a dolphin. That's it! I'm leaving you.' 'Doesn't bother me,' he says. 'There's plenty more fish in the sea.'

✳ A little girl goes up to her father and says, 'Daddy when my cat died, why did it lie on its back with its legs in the air?' Daddy replies, 'Well, its legs were up like that to make it easier for Jesus to grab hold of him and pull him up to Heaven.' 'Oh my gosh,' says the girl. 'That means Mummy almost died this morning!' 'What d'you mean?' asks Dad. 'Well,' replies the girl. 'When I looked into Mummy's room she was lying on the bed with her legs in the air shouting, "Jesus! Jesus! I'm coming!" and if it hadn't have been for the postman holding her down, he would have got her!'

✳ A Mafia don is on his death bed and calls his eldest son to him. 'My boy,' he says. 'I want you to have this family heirloom.' So saying he pulls out a gun and hands it to his boy. 'Gee, Pop,' replies the son. 'Y'know I don't like guns. If you want to leave me something, why not give me your watch?' 'I see,' says the indignant don. 'You don't want my gun, huh. So tell me, when you get home and find your wife in bed with the mailman, wadya going to do? Shoot him? Or point at your watch and say, "Hey, buddy, time's up?"'

✳ A man comes home and finds his best friend in bed with his wife. 'You bastard,' he says. 'I've known you since school. You were my best man and my son's godfather. I lent you money...Stop doing that when I'm talking to you!'

✳ A man comes home and finds his wife in bed with the milkman. 'What are you doing?' shouts the man. The woman turns to the milkman and says, 'There. I told you he doesn't know the first thing about sex.'

✳ A man finds a young woman crying on a park bench and asks her what's the matter. 'My husband's been caught having sex with one of his patients. He's cheated on me and now it looks like he'll be struck off.' 'That's terrible,' says the man. 'But look on the bright side – news like that can't get any worse.' 'Yes it can,' sobs the woman. 'He's a vet.'

✳ A man wants to find out if both his wife and his mistress are faithful to him, so he sends them on the same cruise. When they're back he casually asks his wife about the behaviour of the passenger he knew to be his mistress. 'She was terrible,' replies his wife. 'She slept with every man on the ship.' The disappointed man then asks his mistress about the passenger he knew was really his wife. 'She was a real lady,' says the mistress. 'She came on board with her husband and never once left his side.'

'Last night my wife met me at the front door. She was wearing a sexy negligee. The only trouble was, she was coming home.'
Rodney Dangerfield

✳ A man goes into a magic shop and sees a pair of 'nudie' glasses for sale. 'What do they do?' asks the man. 'They let you see everyone in the nude,' says the storekeeper. 'Why not try them on?' So the man tries on the glasses and straight away everyone he looks at is in the nude. The storekeeper is nude, his assistant is nude, even a passer-by looking in the window is nude. The man buys the glasses and goes out into the street to look at everyone in the nude. After an hour of fun he decides to sneak home and surprise his wife with his new toy. He gets back, creeps in the living room, and finds his wife and his neighbour nude on the couch. 'Surprise!' he shouts, coming into the room. 'What do you think of my new glasses?' He takes them off and is surprised to see that his wife and neighbour are still naked. 'Damn!' he says. 'I've only had them an hour and they're broken already!'

✳ A man is in the back of his car having sex with a woman he picked up in a bar. The woman is insatiable and keeps demanding more. Finally the man has to have a break and steps out to smoke a cigarette. Once out of the car he notices a man nearby struggling to change the tyre on his pick-up truck. The first man goes over and says, 'Look, I've got a really hot date in that car and I can't keep up with her. If I change your tyre will you go in there are have sex with her? I really need a rest. It's pitch black in there so she won't know the difference.' The second man agrees and jumps in the back of the car which soon starts to rock rhythmically. A passing policeman spots this and shines a torch in the back of the car. 'What's going on in there?' he says. The man replies, 'I'm having sex with my wife.' 'Why can't you do that at home?' asks the policeman. The man replies, 'Because I didn't realise it was my wife till you shone that torch in her face.'

✳ A marine is stationed on a remote Pacific island. He writes to his wife asking for something to while away the hours and keep his mind off all the beautiful native women. His wife sends him a harmonica and suggests he learn to play it. A year later the marine comes home to his wife and says, 'Baby, I'm so love-starved! Let's go to bed right now!' 'Sure,' she says. 'But first, play me something on the harmonica.'

✳ A man walks into a bar and orders a beer. 'Certainly, sir,' replies the barman. 'That'll be one penny.' 'One penny for a beer!' exclaims the man. 'That's incredible! How much is the food in this place?' 'I'd recommend the steak dinner,' says the barman. 'You get a 16-ounce steak, potatoes, salad and a dessert for three pennies.' 'That's amazing,' says the man. 'How do manage to make a profit with such low prices?' 'You'd have to ask the owner,' replies the barman. 'But he's not here right now, he's upstairs with my wife.' 'What's he doing up there?' asks the man. 'The same as I'm doing to his business,' replies the barman.

✳ A pair of newly-weds are arguing on their honeymoon. The couple promised to be open and honest with each other but the husband still won't tell his wife how many sex partners he's had. 'Look,' he says. 'If I tell you, you'll just get angry.' 'No, I won't,' she replies. 'Cross my heart and hope to die.' 'Okay, then,' says the man. 'Let me think. There was one, two, three, four, five, you, seven, eight...'

✳ A police officer gets off work four hours early and gets home at two in the morning. Not wanting to wake his wife he undresses in the dark, creeps into the bedroom and starts to climb into bed. As he does so his wife says, 'Dear, would you go down to the all-night drugstore and get me some aspirin? I've got a splitting headache.' 'Certainly, honey,' says the policeman and, feeling his way across the dark room, he gets dressed and walks over to the drugstore. When he arrives the pharmacist looks at him in surprise, 'Don't I know you?' he says. 'I thought you were a policeman?' 'I am a policeman. What about it?' says the officer. 'Just curious,' replies the pharmacist. 'I just wondered what the heck you're doing dressed like a fire chief?'

✳ A private detective is reporting to his female client. 'Yesterday I followed your husband to two bars on Elm Street, three on Maple, and finally to the Humpmore Motel,' he says. 'I see,' says the woman. 'And d'you think that's enough grounds for divorce?' 'I'm not sure,' says the detective. 'After all he was following you at the time.'

✳ Guns don't kill people – husbands who come home early kill people.

✳ A woman is in bed with her husband's best friend. The phone rings, and the friend hears her say, 'Uh-huh, sure, wonderful. Okay. Uh-huh. Yep. That's fine. Okay, bye.' She turns to her lover and says, 'That was John. Don't worry, he won't be home for hours – he's out playing cards with you.'

✳ A wife is in bed with her lover when they hear hubby coming up the stairs. There's no time to get dressed. The man runs to hide in the en-suite bathroom while the wife pushes his clothes under the bed. The husband bursts through the bedroom door. 'What are you doing lying naked on the bed?' he asks. 'Darling, I heard you coming and got ready to receive you,' she replies. 'Great,' says her husband. 'I'll just nip into the bathroom to clean up.' The husband goes into the bathroom and finds a man clapping his hands together in mid-air. 'Who the devil are you?' he asks. 'I'm from the exterminator company,' replies the man. 'Your wife called me in to get rid of these pesky moths.' The husband yells, 'But you've got no clothes on!' The man looks down at his body, jumps backwards in surprise and shouts, 'The little bastards!'

✳ A woman goes to hospital to have a baby and is shown a new machine that can transfer all the pain of childbirth to the father. The woman's husband agrees to give it a go and the machine is hooked up. The labour is long and difficult but the husband feels no pain at all. The doctors are mystified as to why no one is suffering but everything seems okay so they send the couple and their baby home. Next day the husband rings the hospital and says, 'I think I know why I wasn't feeling anything. When we got home we found the milkman dead on our doorstep.'

✳ A woman is in bed with her lover when she hears her husband come in the front door. There's no time for the lover to escape so the wife makes him stand in the corner and covers him with talcum powder. 'Just stay still and pretend you're a statue,' she tells him. The husband comes in and his wife says, 'Hello dear. I was just admiring our new statue. You remember the Smiths bought one for their bedroom? Well, I thought we could have one for ours.' The husband admires the statue then the couple go downstairs for dinner. An hour later the husband returns with a glass of milk and a sandwich. He puts them on a table and says, 'There you go. When I was playing statues at the Smiths I stood there for three days without so much as a drink of water.'

✳ After twenty years of marriage they are still in love. She loves the gardener, and he loves the lady next door.

✳ Harry goes to confession and tells the priest he's been having affairs with four different women from the neighbouring villages. 'How could you do such a thing?' asks the priest. 'It's easy,' says Harry. 'I've got a moped.'

❋ An artist and his model are kissing on the sofa when they hear the front door open. 'Oh my God! It's the wife,' shouts the artist. 'Quick! Get your clothes off!'

❋ Bob calls home one afternoon to see what his wife is making for dinner. 'Hello?' says a little girl's voice. 'Hi, honey, it's Daddy,' says Bob. 'Is Mummy near the phone?' 'No, Daddy,' says the girl. 'She's upstairs in the bedroom with Uncle Frank.' Bob says, 'But you don't have an Uncle Frank.' 'Yes, I do,' says the girl. 'He's upstairs in the bedroom with Mummy!' 'Okay, then,' says Bob. 'Here's what I want you to do. Put down the phone, knock on the bedroom door and shout to Mummy and Uncle Frank that Daddy's car has just pulled up outside the house.' A few minutes later, the little girl comes back to the phone. 'I did what you said, Daddy. When they heard me Mummy jumped out of bed and ran around screaming. Then she tripped over the rug and fell out of the window and now she's all dead.' 'Oh my God!' says Bob. 'And what about Uncle Frank?' 'He jumped out the back window into the swimming pool,' says the girl. 'But he must have forgotten that you took out all the water last week, so now he's dead as well.' There's a long pause, then Bob says, 'Swimming pool? Is this 555 7039?'

❋ Contrary to popular belief, Harry's mother and father were married. Not to each other. But they were married.

❋ Dick and Harry die and go to Heaven. Saint Peter meets them at the Pearly Gates and tells them that they will each get a car depending on how faithful they were in life. Harry's record is very good, he was married for 24 years and was completely faithful so he gets a Rolls-Royce. Dick, on the other hand, had five affairs during his marriage and only gets a third-hand Ford Fiesta. A week later Dick is driving through Heaven when he passes Harry crying by the roadside. 'What's the matter?' asks Dick. 'I thought you'd be really enjoying that Rolls-Royce.' 'I was,' sobs Harry. 'But then I saw my wife on a skateboard.'

❋ I got home and found a man in bed with my wife. I said, 'Who said you could sleep with my wife?' He said, 'Everybody.'

❋ I have the most wonderful wife in the whole world, I just hope her husband never finds out.

❋ In all my years of marriage I've never stopped being romantic, but if my wife finds out she'll kill me.

✴ Two men are sitting at a bar. One says to the other, 'I heard about this great place. You get all your drinks paid for and at the end of the evening you get laid for free.' 'That sounds fantastic,' says his friend. 'Have you ever been?' 'No,' says the first. 'But my wife goes there all the time.'

✴ A couple have four sons. The oldest three are tall with red hair, while the youngest, Jason, is short and dark. After a long illness, the father is facing death. He turns to his wife and says, 'Dearest, before I die, be honest – is Jason my son?' His wife replies, 'Yes, he is, my darling. I swear it.' Hearing this the husband passes away peacefully. His wife lets out a sigh of relief, 'Thank God he didn't ask about the other three.'

✴ A husband comes into the living room and complains to his wife. 'I'm getting our phone number changed. That's the third time this week someone's rung thinking we're the coastguard.' 'The coastguard?' says the wife. 'Yes,' says the husband. 'Some idiot keeps ringing to ask if the coast is clear.'

✴ A husband suspects his wife of having an affair and bursts into their high-rise apartment to catch her in the act. His wife is alone, but looking out of the window he sees a man hurrying down the stairs. The husband waits till the man is in the open then drops a fridge on him. However, the strain of lifting the fridge is too much, and he has a heart attack. Later the husband is standing at the Pearly Gates with two other men and they start discussing how they died. The first man says, 'I was out collecting rents one afternoon when someone dropped a fridge on me.' 'Really?' says the embarrassed husband. 'I had a heart attack.' 'That's nothing,' says the second man. 'I was hiding in this fridge...'

✴ Harry has been summoned to his attorney's office. 'Do you want the bad news first or the terrible news?' says his lawyer. 'Give me the bad news first,' says Harry. 'Your wife found a picture worth a half-million dollars,' says the lawyer. 'That's the bad news?' asks Harry. 'I can't wait to hear the terrible news.' The lawyer replies, 'The picture's of you and your mistress.'

✴ Harry was a smooth talker. He even made his wife feel sorry for the poor hitch-hiker who lost her bra in his car.

✴ Married people who often hold hands in restaurants are not often married to each other.

MARRIAGE: DIVORCE

✳ 'As soon as I get through with you, you'll have a clear case for divorce – and so will my wife.' *Groucho Marx*

✳ 'Instead of getting married again, I'm going to find a woman I don't like and give her a house.' *Lewis Grizzard*

✳ A doctor tells a woman she can no longer touch anything alcoholic – so she gets a divorce.

✳ A man goes to court to get a divorce. 'Why do you want a divorce?' asks the judge. The man replies, 'Because I live in a two-storey house.' 'That's not much of a reason to leave your wife,' responds the judge. 'Sure it is,' replies the man. 'Whenever I want some action in bed she just has two stories; either she has a headache, or it's her time of the month.'

✳ A quarter of all married men kiss their wife goodbye when they leave the house. Of these same men, 90 per cent will kiss their house goodbye when their wife leaves.

✳ After forty years of marriage Harry asks his wife June for a divorce. 'A divorce? After all these years?' says June. 'After we've been through so much together? What about the time you had your heart attack, who nursed you back to health? When your business went bust, who convinced the bank manager to give you a loan? After the house burned down, who helped you rebuild? After your sister died, who helped you get over it? What would you have done without me?' 'Probably a lot better,' says Harry. 'After all these years I've finally figured out you're bad luck.'

✳ An elderly man and his wife tell a friend they're getting divorced. 'But you're 95 and your wife is 93. You've been married for 72 years!' says the friend. 'Why do you want to separate now?' The wife replies, 'To be honest we haven't been able to stand the sight of each other for a long time. But we thought we should wait till all the children died before we split up.'

✳ Dick had been trying to lose annoying weight for some time, unfortunately he couldn't afford to get divorced.

✳ Did you hear about the new 'divorced' Barbie doll? It comes with all of Ken's stuff.

✳ Hell hath no fury like the lawyer of a woman scorned.

✳ Judge, to woman, 'On what grounds do you wish to divorce your husband?' 'Adultery,' says the woman. 'On what evidence?' queries the judge. The woman replies, 'I'm certain he's not the father of my fourth child.'

✳ Keep your marriage licence in a very safe place. It's one of the most important documents you'll ever have. You can't get a divorce without it.

✳ My friend is engaged in a major custody battle. His wife doesn't want him and his mother won't take him back.

✳ What do a hurricane, a tornado, a fire and a divorce have in common? They are four ways you can lose your house!

✳ Why would you ever want to remarry an ex-husband? It's like finding some sour milk, putting it in the trash for a couple of days, and then saying to yourself, 'Gee, I wonder if it'll taste any better now?'

✳ Harry always felt the shine went out of his life when his wife left him – she took the family silver with her.

✳ Love is grand. Divorce is a hundred grand.

✳ Woman, to lawyer, 'I want to divorce my husband. He has a lousy memory!' Lawyer, 'Why would you want to divorce him for that?' Woman, 'Every time he sees a young woman, he keeps forgetting he's married!'

✇MARRIAGE: NEWLY-WEDS

✳ A man returns from his honeymoon and his friend asks him how it went. 'Terrible,' replies the man. 'On the first night I got up to go to the bathroom and without thinking I put a £50 note on her pillow.' 'Well, that's not so bad,' replies the friend. 'If she's upset tell her it was a joke.' 'She wasn't upset,' replies the man. 'I got upset when she gave me £30 change.'

✻ For a brief period we were lovers. It was for the two weeks after we got married.

✻ Two newly-weds are on their honeymoon. As they undress for bed the husband tosses his trousers to his bride, saying, 'Here, put these on.' She puts them on but the waist is twice the size of her body. 'I can't wear your trousers,' she says. 'That's right,' says her husband. 'And don't you ever forget it. I wear the pants in this family.' With that the bride throws him her panties. 'Try these on,' she says. The husband tries them on but finds he can only get them as far as his knees. 'Hell,' he says, 'I can't get into your panties!' His bride replies, 'That's right, and that's the way it's going to stay until you change your attitude.'

marriage – proposals

'Marry me and I'll never look at another horse!' *Groucho Marx*

A young lady comes back from a date looking sad. She says to her mother, 'Jeff proposed to me.' 'Then why are you so sad?' asks her mother. 'Because he also told me he was an atheist,' says the girl. 'He doesn't even believe there's a hell.' Her mother replies, 'Marry him anyway. Between the two of us, we'll show him how wrong he is.'

MARRIAGE: WEDDINGS

✻ 'Now what is a wedding? Well, Webster's dictionary describes a wedding as the process of removing weeds from one's garden.' *Homer Simpson*

✻ A couple apply for a wedding licence. 'Can I have your name?' asks the clerk. 'David Smith,' replies the man. 'Jenny Smith,' replies the woman. 'Any connection?' asks the clerk. 'Only the once,' replies the woman. 'That's when he knocked me up.'

✻ I got a note from the bride thanking me for the wedding present I sent. She said it was just what she wanted and she'd use them every time she entertained guests. I'm a bit worried. I gave her bedsheets.

✳ A man goes up to a vicar and says, 'Excuse me, Reverend, but do you think a man ought to profit by the mistakes of others?' 'No, I don't think he should,' replies the vicar. 'In that case can I have my £40 back?' says the man. '£40? What d'you mean?' replies the vicar. The man says, 'That's what you charged for my wedding ceremony.'

✳ I like to watch my wedding video running backwards so I can watch myself walk out of the church a free man.

✳ What did the idiot bridegroom do to make sure he had a successful wedding? He took out a maritime insurance policy.

✳ A police officer stops a motorist speeding down Main Street. 'But officer,' the man says, 'I can explain—' 'Be quiet,' snaps the officer. 'I'm going to let you cool your heels in jail until the chief gets back.' 'But, officer, I just wanted to say—' says the driver. 'And I say keep quiet! You're going to jail!' replies the officer. A few hours later the officer looks in on his prisoner and says, 'Lucky for you the chief is at his daughter's wedding. He'll be in a good mood when he gets back.' 'Don't count on it,' answers the motorist. 'I'm the groom.'

✳ During a wedding rehearsal the groom takes the vicar to one side and says, 'Listen, when you get to the part about me "loving and honouring" her, and "forsaking all others" I want you to leave all that out. Okay?' So saying he hands the vicar £100. During the service the vicar comes to the vows and says, '…and do you promise to love and honour her, and forsaking all others promise never to even look at another woman, never question her credit card bills, and do all the housework for ever and ever, amen…' The groom is appalled, 'But, vicar,' he cries. 'We had a deal!' 'We did, my son, 'replies the vicar. 'But the bride made me a better offer.'

martial arts

'Karate is a form of martial arts in which people who have had years and years of training can, using only their hands and feet, make some of the worst movies in the history of the world.' *Dave Barry*

My brother-in-law died. He was a karate expert who joined the army. The first time he saluted, he killed himself.

MENTAL HEALTH

✳ 'Hello. Allow me to introduce myselves.'

✳ 'My brother thinks he's a chicken, we don't talk him out of it because we need the eggs.' *Groucho Marx*

✳ A doctor is making the rounds of a mental home when he comes across a room with two new patients in it. One patient is sawing an imaginary plank in half while the other is hanging from a roof beam. 'What's your friend doing up there?' asks the doctor. 'He thinks he's a light bulb,' replies the patient. 'Shouldn't you get him down?' says the doctor. 'He might hurt himself.' 'What?' replies the patient. 'And work in the dark?'

✳ A Freudian slip is when you say one thing but mean your mother.

✳ A guy walks into a psychiatrist's office wearing shorts and Y-fronts made entirely out of cling film. The psychiatrist says, 'Well, I can clearly see you're nuts.'

✳ A man walks into a psychiatrist's dressed in a tutu, a diving mask and flippers. 'Doctor!' he says. 'I'm worried about my brother.'

✳ A man walks into a psychiatrist's and says, 'You've got to help me! I keep thinking I'm a goat!' 'How long have you had these delusions?' asks the psychiatrist. The man replies, 'Ever since I was a kid.'

✳ A woman is chatting with her friend. 'My husband bought me a mood ring the other day,' she says. 'It lets him monitor my emotional state.' 'Oh yes?' says the friend. 'How does it work?' The woman replies, 'When I'm in a good mood it turns green, and when I'm in a bad mood it leaves a big red mark on his forehead.'

✳ A woman worked for a psychiatrist but in the end she had to give the job up. If she was late, he said she was hostile. If she was early, he said she had an anxiety complex. And if she was on time, he called her a compulsive.

✳ Did you hear about the advertising executive who made a fortune out of insanity? He sold poster space on psychiatrists' ceilings.

✳ Do you hear about the paranoid man with low esteem? He thought no one important was out to get him.

✳ Everyone is someone else's weirdo.

✳ Fred has been away for a week on an anger management course. Actually the course only lasted two days, the rest of the time he spent arguing with them about the fee.

✳ Harry goes to a psychiatrist. 'Doctor, every time I get into bed, I think there's somebody under it,' says Harry. 'Then, if I get under the bed, I think there's somebody on top of it. Top, under, top, under. You gotta help me!' 'I can cure you,' says the psychiatrist. 'But it will take weekly visits over six months at £100 an hour.' 'I'll think about it,' says Harry and leaves the office. A month later the psychiatrist meets Harry on the street. 'Why didn't you come to see me again?' he asks. 'For a hundred pounds a visit?' says Harry. 'A bartender cured me for ten quid.' 'How did he manage that?' asks the psychiatrist. Harry replies, 'He told me to cut the legs off the bed!'

✳ I don't suffer from insanity; I enjoy every minute of it.

✳ I feel like a reggae group without a bass player.

✳ I feel like I'm diagonally parked in a parallel universe.

✳ I tried to get in touch with my inner child – but he's not allowed to talk to strangers.

✳ I used to be schizophrenic, but we're all right now.

✳ If the left side of the brain controls the right hand, then only left-handed people are in their right mind.

✳ If you want to know more about paranoids, follow them around.

✳ Madness takes its toll. Please have exact change ready.

✳ My inferiority complex isn't as good as yours.

✳ Man, to psychiatrist, 'Last week my wife bought 20lb of wire wool. I think she should be put in a mental home.' Psychiatrist, 'Well, that's certainly unusual, but it doesn't mean she needs treatment.' Man, 'Yes, but then she started knitting a gas stove.'

✳ Roses are red, violets are blue, I'm schizophrenic, and so am I.

✳ Therapy is expensive. Popping bubble-wrap is cheap. You choose.

✳ Two cows are standing in a field. One says to the other, 'Are you scared about all of this mad cow business?' The other says, 'Nope.' The first cow asks, 'How come you're not scared?' The second cow says, 'Because I'm a chicken.'

✳ Two mental patients, Harry and Tom, are waiting for an interview with their doctor. If they can each answer two simple questions they've been told they will be free to leave the asylum. The first patient, Harry, goes in for his interview. 'Harry,' says the doctor. 'If I were to poke out one of your eyes what would happen?' 'I would be half blind,' replies Harry. 'And what would happen if I poked out the other eye?' asks the doctor. 'I would be completely blind,' replies Harry. The doctor sends Harry out of the room and prepares the paperwork for his release. Meanwhile Harry whispers the answers to Tom. Tom is then brought in for his interview. 'Tom, what would happen if I cut off your ear?' asks the doctor. 'I would be blind in one eye,' replies Tom. 'I see,' replies the puzzled doctor. 'And what would happen if I cut off your other ear?' 'I would be completely blind,' answers Tom. 'Why do you think you'd be blind if you had no ears?' asks the doctor. Tom thinks for a second, then replies, 'Because my hat would fall over my eyes.'

✳ What do you call Maoris on Prozac? Once were worriers.

✳ Why did Cleopatra think she didn't need a psychiatrist? Because she was the Queen of Denial.

✳ A man goes to a psychiatrist and tells him that, every night, he's troubled by visions of a huge, ugly, fire-breathing monster with two heads. 'Well, I can cure you,' says the psychiatrist. 'But the treatment will cost £10,000.' 'Are you crazy?' says the man. 'For that kind of money I'd rather go home and make friends with it.'

✳ A man is being interviewed prior to his release from a mental hospital. 'And how will you try to ensure that you don't have another breakdown?' asks the doctor. 'I'll stay away from stressful occupations,' says the patient. 'In my former life I worked in a high-pressure city job, but I'm planning to start a new life in the country.' 'I see,' says the doctor. 'And what will happen if that doesn't work out?' 'Well,' replies the patient. 'I suppose I can always go back to being a teapot.'

✳ A man rings a psychiatrist. 'Doctor, my wife thinks she's a horse.' 'A horse? That sounds serious,' says the psychiatrist. 'It could mean a long and expensive course of therapy.' 'Money's no object,' replies the man. 'She's just won the National!'

✳ A strange thing happened to me the other day. I was in the checkout line at the supermarket when I noticed a woman staring at me. She asked me if my name was Ernest. I said, 'No, it isn't.' She said I looked just like her long-lost son, whose name was Ernest. I said that I was very sorry to hear he was lost. She showed me a picture of him and there was some resemblance between us. She then said, 'Do you mind if I call you Ernest?' I replied, 'Well, yes, I do.' Then I paid for my groceries. As I left the store, I noticed her waiting for me. I stepped out into the car park and she mumbled something to me but I just kept going. Then she started yelling, 'Wait, Ernest! Wait!' I quickly put my groceries in the car but as I was getting into the driver's seat, she began pulling and pulling on my leg, just like I'm pulling yours…

✳ A woman goes to a psychiatrist with a duck under her arm. The psychiatrist asks her what her problem is. 'I haven't got a problem,' says the woman, holding up the duck. 'It's my husband with the problem.'

✳ Out of my mind. Back in five minutes.

✳ Three mental patients are being assessed prior to their release. The doctor asks the first patient what two plus two is. 'Eleven,' replies the patient. The doctor asks the second patient what two plus two is. 'Blue,' replies the patient. The doctor turns to the third patient and again asks, 'What is two plus two?' The patient replies, 'Four.' 'Excellent,' says the doctor. 'You're the only one to get it right.' 'It's simple,' explains the patient. 'Two times two is eleven, divide by blue makes four.'

models

Harry gets stranded on a desert island with Cindy Crawford. One day he goes up to her and asks her to put on some of his old clothes. She does so. Then he asks if he can call her Pete. Cindy is surprised but says it's okay by her. Harry then takes a piece of charcoal from the campfire and draws a moustache on Cindy's upper lip. 'What on earth are you doing?' says Cindy. 'Never mind that, Pete,' says Harry. 'Listen, you'll never believe who I've been sleeping with for the last six months...'

MOTHERS-iN-LAW

❋ A big-game hunter goes on safari with his wife and his mother-in-law. One evening the wife wakes up to find her mother gone. She rushes to find her husband, he picks up his rifle, and they go out to look for her. In a clearing not far from the camp, they come upon a chilling sight – the mother-in-law is backed up against a rock with a fierce lion facing her. 'Oh no,' cries the wife. 'What are we going to do?' 'Nothing,' says her husband. 'That lion got himself into this mess. He can get himself out of it.'

❋ A man is playing golf with his mother-in-law when she slices the ball into a field with a cow in it. They climb the fence and start looking for the ball. They search everywhere but can't find it. Eventually the man realises that the one place they haven't looked is by the cow. He goes over, pokes around, then sees something sticking in the cow's backside. He lifts up the cow's tail, sees a ball lodged in the hole, and shouts over to his mother-in-law, 'Hey! Does this look like yours?'

❋ A man receives a telegram informing him about the death of his mother-in-law. It also asks him whether she should be buried or cremated. The man telegraphs back, 'Take no chances. Burn the body and bury the ashes.'

❋ Did you know you can calculate the age of your mother-in-law by counting the rings in her bath tub.

❉ Fred, to Steve. 'You're looking down in the mouth today, what's the matter?' Steve, 'I had a quarrel with my mother-in-law. She swore she wouldn't talk to me for a month.' Fred, 'That's not so bad.' Steve, 'Yes it is, that was four weeks ago!'

❉ I saw six men kicking and punching my mother-in-law. My wife said, 'Aren't you going to help?' I said, 'No. Six should be enough.'

❉ Of course Adam was the only married man not to have a mother-in-law. And he lived in paradise.

❉ What's the best way to talk to your mother-in-law? Through a medium.

❧NUDISM, NUDITY AND NUDENESS

❉ A streaker runs through a golf club with a towel over his face and passes three female members. 'Well, that's not my husband,' says the first woman. 'No, it isn't,' says the second woman. 'He's not even a member of the club,' says the third woman.

❉ At a nudist colony for intellectuals, two old men are sitting on the porch. One turns to the other and says, 'I say, old boy, have you read Marx?' The other says, 'Yes, it's these wicker chairs.'

❉ Two small children are spying on the inhabitants of a nudist colony through a hole in the fence. 'Are they men or ladies?' asks one. 'I can't tell,' replies the other. 'They haven't got any clothes on.'

❧OPTIMISM AND PESSIMISM

❉ 'There is no sadder sight than a young pessimist, except an old optimist.' *Mark Twain*

❉ Remember, whenever one door closes, another slams in your face.

✳ Today may be the first day of the rest of your life, but on the other hand it's also the last day of your life so far.

✳ Y'know there's always someone worse off than yourself – hello.

✳ You should always borrow money from pessimists. They don't expect it back.

orphans

'When they asked Jack Benny to do something for the actors' orphanage, he shot both his parents and moved in.' *Bob Hope*

PERSONAL HYGIENE

✳ A couple have just got married but they each have a terrible secret. He has smelly feet and she has bad breath. As they get ready for bed on their wedding night he throws his socks in the bath and she sprays in some breath freshener. Once in bed he decides to make a confession. 'Darling! I think there's something you should know. I have very smelly feet.' 'I have a confession for you as well,' says his wife. 'I think I know what it's going to be,' said her husband. 'You've eaten my socks, haven't you?'

✳ How do you get a hippie out of the bath? Turn on the water.

✳ How do you starve a hippie? Hide his giro under the soap.

✳ I tried some of that revitalising shampoo. My hair was awake all night.

✳ If your slippers smell fill them with cat litter then leave them overnight. By morning all the odour will have been absorbed – as long as you don't have a cat.

✳ They show you how detergents take out bloodstains, but if you've got a T-shirt with bloodstains all over it, maybe your laundry isn't your biggest problem.

phones

'If I called a wrong number why did you answer it?'

'My phone number is seventeen. I got one of the early ones.'
George Carlin

🐛PLANES AND FLYING

✳ 'If God had intended us to fly, He'd have sent us tickets.' *Mel Brooks*

✳ A man pays to go for a spin in a two-seater plane at an air show. The pilot does a corkscrew, loops the loop, then free-falls towards the crowds below. 'Half the people down there think we're going to have an accident!' jokes the pilot. The man replies, 'Half the people up here *have* had an accident.'

✳ A photographer wants to take some aerial shots of his neighbourhood and arranges a flight at his local aerodrome. The photographer is directed to the runway and told that his plane is waiting for him. The photographer sees a light aircraft with its engine running and gets in. 'Let's go,' he tells the pilot and the plane taxis down the runway and takes off. 'Okay,' says the photographer. 'If you do a low pass over the bridge I'll take some pictures.' 'Why do you want to do that?' asks the pilot. 'It's what I do,' says the photographer. 'I'm a photographer, I take pictures.' The pilot replies, 'Y'mean – you're not the flight instructor?'

✳ A plane carrying an Englishman, a Frenchman, a Mexican and a Texan is about to crash. The pilot shouts back at them, 'We have to lose weight! If three of you jump, the fourth might be saved!' The Englishman stands up, shouts, 'God Save the Queen!' and jumps. The Frenchman stands up, shouts, 'Vive la France!' and jumps. The Texan stands up and shouts, 'Remember the Alamo!' – and throws out the Mexican.

✳ I used to be an airline pilot but they sacked me when I left the handbrake off a 747. Before I knew it the whole thing had slipped straight back up in the air.

✳ I wouldn't say he was reckless pilot but he never checked the railway time-tables before he flew through the tunnels.

✳ A plane carrying Mike Tyson, Bill Gates, the Dalai Lama and a hippie is about to crash into the sea and there are only three parachutes. Tyson stands up and says, 'I am the world's greatest boxer and I deserve a parachute!' With these words he grabs a parachute and jumps out of the plane. Bill Gates then stands up and says, 'Gentlemen, I am the world's smartest man and I should have a parachute also.' So saying he grabs one and jumps. The Dalai Lama and the hippie look at one another. The Dalai Lama says, 'My son. I have lived a satisfying life and have known the bliss of true enlightenment. You have your whole life ahead of you. You take the parachute and I will go down with the plane.' The hippie smiles and says, 'Don't sweat it, dude. The world's smartest man just jumped out wearing my backpack.'

✳ A plane is about to crash into the sea. A little old lady grabs a stewardess and asks, 'Are there any sharks in the ocean below?' 'Yes, I'm afraid there are some,' replies the stewardess. 'But not to worry, we have a gel designed especially for emergencies like this. Just rub the gel on to your arms and legs.' 'And if I do that the sharks won't eat me?' asks the old lady. 'Oh, they'll still eat you,' replies the stewardess. 'They just won't enjoy it as much.'

✳ A rich businessman is forced to charter a light aircraft to get to an appointment but is horrified at the cost of the flight. He gets on board with his wife and moans non-stop to the pilot about the price of the charter. Eventually the pilot says, 'Tell you what. If you can make it through the rest of the trip without opening your mouth I'll give you the flight for free, but if you can't, you have to pay double.' The businessman agrees but the pilot decides to have some fun and starts looping the loop, going into spins, and indulging in all sorts of aerobatics. Despite this activity the businessman keeps his mouth shut until the plane lands. The pilot congratulates him. 'You beat me,' he says. 'I never thought you'd stay quiet through all of that.' 'Well, it wasn't easy,' says the businessman. 'Especially when my wife fell out.'

✳ An aircraft landing is simply a controlled mid-air collision with a planet.

✳ Definition of the jet age: breakfast in Rome, lunch in Paris, dinner in London, bags in Singapore.

✳ How do you know if there's a pilot at your party? He'll tell you.

✳ I got strip-searched at the airport. Why those customs officers had to take their clothes off I've no idea.

✳ If flying is so safe, why do they call the airport the terminal?

✳ One of the airlines recently introduced a special half-fare rate for wives accompanying their husbands on business trips. Anticipating some valuable testimonials, the airline sent out letters to all the wives of businessmen who used the special rates, asking how they enjoyed their trip. Responses are still pouring in, asking, 'What trip…?'

✳ Passenger, to stewardess, 'How often do these types of plane crash?' Stewardess, 'Once.'

✳ RAF pilot, to navigator, 'Have you figured out where we are yet?' Navigator, 'Yes, and I think we ought to stand to attention and take off our hats.' Pilot, 'How come?' Navigator, 'According to this map we're in Westminster Abbey.'

✳ Strange isn't it? You stand in the middle of a library and go 'Aaaaaagghhhh!!' and everyone stares at you. Do it on an aeroplane and everyone joins in.

✳ What's the purpose of an aircraft propeller? To keep the pilot cool (if you don't think so, just watch him sweat when it stops).

✳ The pilot of a jumbo jet is getting ready to take off. He announces all the usual stuff over the intercom but forgets to turn it off. The co-pilot asks him how he's feeling. 'I could really use some hot sex and a cup of coffee,' replies the pilot. A stewardess hears this and runs to the cockpit to tell them the intercom is on. As she passes one of the passengers shouts, 'Don't forget the coffee!'

✳ The plane is about to crash. 'Does anyone onboard believe in the power of prayer?' the captain asks the passengers. A vicar puts his hand up. 'That's great,' says the captain. 'We're one parachute short.'

✳ You know you're flying in a crappy aeroplane when you have a bird strike – from behind.

🐱PLUMBERS

✳ A Texan is admiring the Niagara Falls when a local approaches him and says, 'Bet you've got nothing like that where you come from.' 'No,' admits the Texan. 'But we've got plumbers who could fix it.'

✳ A pipe burst in a doctor's house so he calls a plumber. The plumber arrives, unpacks his tools, fixes the leak then hands the doctor a bill for £400. The doctor exclaims, 'This is ridiculous! I don't even make that much as a doctor!' The plumber replies, 'Neither did I when I was a doctor.'

✳ A plumber calls at a house to do some emergency work. The door is answered by a women wrapped in a towel who's obviously had her bathtime interrupted. 'I'm afraid you've caught me in a terrible dilemma,' says the lady. 'That's all right,' says the plumber. 'The last lady I caught was in a dirty kimono.'

✳ A plumber is called to a house to repair a leaking pipe. When he arrives he is pleased to discover that the lady of the house is both beautiful and very friendly. One thing leads to another and the two end up in the bedroom. Suddenly the phone rings and the woman answers it. 'That was my husband,' she says when she puts down the receiver. 'He's on his way home, but he's taking a flight out of town at eight. If you come back then we can take up where we left off.' The plumber looks at the woman in disbelief. 'What?' he says. 'On my own time?'

🐱POLITICS

✳ A Liberal is a man who makes enemies left and right.

✳ A politician is in bed asleep with his wife when there's a massive storm and a bolt of lightning lights up the entire bedroom. The politician leaps up and shouts, 'I'll buy the negatives! I'll buy the negatives!'

✳ Apologies for the mess. We've got the Conservatives in.

✳ Capitalism is the exploitation of one man by another. Communism is the opposite.

✳ For every action, there is an equal and opposite Government programme.

✳ He's the finest politician money can buy.

✳ If voting really could change anything it would be illegal.

✳ A US politician goes to an Indian reservation to try and drum up support. He stands on a barrel and delivers a rousing speech. First he promises less taxes and his audience reply by shouting, 'Hoya! Hoya!' 'Hey, they like me,' thinks the politician. He then promises the Indians better public facilities. 'Hoya! Hoya!' shouts his audience. The politician is delighted and then promises to increase the reservation lands by fifty per cent. The crowd yells back, 'Hoya! Hoya!' 'This is fantastic!' thinks the politician. 'They're eating out of my hand.' He gets off his barrel and asks one of the chiefs if he can give another speech next week. 'We'll talk about it while I walk you back to your car,' says the chief. The chief escorts the politician to his limo parked by a cattle pen. 'I did pretty good back there,' says the politician. 'You think so?' answers the chief. 'Hey, watch your shoes! You almost stepped in that big pile of hoya.'

✳ An Englishman, a Swede and a Russian are looking at a painting of Adam and Eve in the Garden of Eden. 'Look at that beautiful garden,' muses the Englishman. 'Only an Englishman could grow a garden as beautiful as that.' 'Nonsense,' says the Swede. 'They're naked and unashamed. They must be Scandinavian.' 'Rubbish,' says the Russian. 'No clothes, no house, one apple between them, and they're told it's paradise – definitely Russian.'

✳ In the days of the Cold War three men are sitting in a Bulgarian café. One man looks at a newspaper, shakes his head and sighs. The second man looks at his newspaper shakes his head and sighs. The third man reaches for his hat and coat and says, 'If you two are going to discuss politics, I'm off.'

✳ No matter who you vote for the Government always seems to get in.

✳ Politicians and babies' nappies have one thing in common. They should both be changed regularly, and for the same reason.

✳ The Prime Minister has left the country on a tour of friendly countries. He's expected home tomorrow.

✳ There are three kinds of lie: a small lie, a big lie and politics.

✳ To succeed in politics, it is often necessary to rise above your principles.

✳ Tony Blair is skating on a frozen pond when the ice cracks and he falls in. Luckily three little boys are on hand to pull him out. 'You've saved my life,' says Tony. 'How can I repay you?' 'I'd like a toy car,' says one boy. 'I'd like a toy plane,' says another boy. 'I'd like a motorised wheelchair,' says the third boy. 'Why do you want a wheelchair?' asks Tony. 'You look very healthy to me.' 'I am,' says the little boy. 'But I'm going to need one when my dad discovers I saved Tony Blair.'

✳ What do Japanese men do when they have elections? Vote.

✳ Why did the Israelis stay out of the Gulf War? Because the last time they spoke with a Bush they spent forty years wandering in the desert.

✳ Why do we use the word 'politics' to describe the process of Government? 'Poli' in Latin meaning 'many' and 'tics' meaning 'bloodsucking creatures'.

✳ An older couple have a son still living at home. The son is unable to decide on his future career so his parents decide to do a small test. They take a ten-dollar bill, a Bible, and a bottle of whisky, and put them on the front hall table. Then they hide in a closet. Father says to Mother, 'If our son takes the money, he'll be a businessman, if he takes the Bible, he'll be a priest, but if he takes the bottle of whisky, I'm afraid our son will be a drunkard.' The son arrives home, picks up the ten-dollar bill, looks at it against the light, and slips it in his pocket. He then takes the Bible, flicks through it, and puts it under his arm. Then he grabs the bottle, opens it to take a sniff, then tucks it under his other arm and goes to his room. 'Dang it!' says Father. 'He's going to be a senator!'

✳ Diplomacy is the art of saying 'good doggie' – until you find a rock.

✳ If we quit voting, will they all go away?

praise

'He has not a single redeeming defect.' *Benjamin Disraeli*

'It's more than magnificent – it's mediocre.' *Samuel Goldwyn*

🎃PUNS

✳ A boat carrying red paint and a boat carrying blue paint crashed into each other. Apparently the crew were marooned.

✳ A brown paper bag goes to his doctor feeling unwell. The doctor takes all sorts of samples and asks the bag to come back next week. Next week the bag returns and the doctor says, 'I'm afraid I have bad news. We discovered from your blood tests that you have haemophilia.' 'Haemophilia?' says the bag. 'How can that be? I'm a brown paper bag.' 'Yes,' replies the doctor, 'but it seems your mother was a carrier.'

✳ A frog walks into a bank, goes up to the teller, Ms Patty Black, and says, 'I'd like a loan.' Patty Black replies, 'Do you have any collateral?' The frog says, 'Yes, I have a pink ceramic elephant.' Patty Black goes to the manager's office and says, 'Sir, there's a frog out there who wants a loan. He has a pink ceramic elephant for collateral. What should I do?' The manager says, 'It's a knick-knack, Patty Black, but give the frog a loan.'

✳ A good pun is its own reword.

✳ A man always buys his wife anemones on her birthday, but one day he goes to the florist and finds they've run out. There's no time to go anywhere else so the man buys the only plant they've got left, a large fern. As luck would have it his wife is delighted by the novel gift. 'With fronds like these,' she says. 'Who needs anemones?'

✳ A tourist couple are visiting Moscow with their Russian guide, Rudolph. One day the couple decide they want to visit Gorky Park, but Rudolph looks at the sky and tells them they can't as it will rain soon. Sure enough a couple of hours later it starts to rain. Next day the couple want to go to Red Square, but again Rudolph looks at the sky and predicts rain. Sure enough a few hours later it starts to pour down. The next day the couple decide they want to go to the Moscow woods but Rudolph looks at the sky and tells them it will rain. 'It can't rain,' complains the husband. 'Look at the sky. There's not a cloud to be seen.' His wife pipes up, 'I think we'd better give the woods a miss today. By now we know that Rudolph the Red knows rain, dear.'

✳ A vicar offers Harry £500 to paint his church. Harry buys some paint and starts working but discovers he's using more paint than he expected. Harry adds some thinner to the paint to make it last but finds he's still using too much, so he add yet more thinner. The paint is now too thin to use properly, but Harry carries on regardless. Suddenly there's a crack of thunder and a voice booms out from the clouds, 'Harry! Repaint and thin no more!'

✳ A Viking called Leif comes home after a long voyage to find that his name has been removed from the town register. He complains to the council. 'I'm sorry,' says the official. 'I must have taken Leif off my census.'

✳ A vulture boards an aeroplane, carrying two dead racoons. The stewardess looks at him and says, 'I'm sorry, sir. Only one carrion allowed per passenger.'

✳ A woman has twins and gives them up for adoption. One of them goes to a family in Egypt and is named Ahmal. The other goes to a family in Spain and they name him Juan. Years later, Juan sends a picture of himself to his natural mother. When she gets the picture, she tells her husband she wishes she had a picture of Ahmal too. Her husband says, 'They're twins! If you've seen Juan, you've seen Ahmal.'

✳ Did you hear about the Buddhist who refused Novocaine during the root canal treatment? He wanted to transcend dental medication.

✳ Did you hear about the painter who was fired for dropping things on people? He couldn't hold his lacquer.

✳ Fork, to spoon, 'Who was that ladle I saw you with last night?' Spoon, 'That was no ladle. That was my knife.'

✳ Four men are in a boat. They decide to have a smoke, but discover no one has any matches. One of the men comes up with a solution and throws a cigarette into the sea – thus making the boat a cigarette lighter.

✳ Harry is tried for bigamy after marrying Kate and Edith. In court the prosecuting barrister declares that Harry wanted to have his Kate, and Edith too.

✳ He worked for MI5 as an undercover shepherd. He was a shepherd spy.

✳ How do you catch a bra? Set a boobie trap.

✳ How do you catch a one-of-a-kind rabbit? Unique up on him.

✳ How do you make a hormone? Don't pay her.

✳ How many ears did Davy Crockett have? Three – his left ear, his right ear and his wild front ear.

✳ Julius Caesar is addressing the crowd in the Coliseum. 'Friends, Romans and countrymen. I have returned from my campaign in France where I killed 50,000 Gauls!' The crowd rises to its feet cheering, 'Hail mighty Caesar!' At this point Brutus jumps up and yells, 'Caesar lies. I've discovered he only killed 25,000!' Caesar replies, 'Yes, but remember that away Gauls count double in Europe.'

✳ Mahatma Gandhi walked barefoot everywhere and developed callouses over his feet. He also ate very little which made him rather frail, while his odd diet gave him bad breath – he was indeed a super-calloused fragile mystic plagued with halitosis.

✳ Nelson Mandela is sitting at home when he hears a knock at the door. When he opens it, he's confronted by a little Chinese man clutching a clipboard yelling, 'You sign! You sign!' while pointing at a truckful of car exhausts. Nelson says, 'Look, you've obviously got the wrong address.' And shuts the door. Next day Nelson hears another knock at the door. When he opens it the little Chinese man is back with a truckload of brake pads. He thrusts the clipboard under Nelson's nose, yelling, 'You sign! You sign!' Nelson pushes the little Chinese man away, 'Clear off! You've got the wrong man!' And slams the door. The following day the little Chinese man is back. He thrusts the clipboard under Nelson's nose, shouting, 'You sign! You sign!' Behind him are two trucks full of windscreens. This time Nelson loses his temper. 'Look, I don't want these! You must have the wrong name! Who do you want to give these to?' The little Chinese man looks at him puzzled, consults his clipboard, and says 'So, you not Nissan Main Dealer?'

✳ Three roosters get caught in the rain. Two run for the barn, the third makes a duck under the porch.

✳ Tom comes across a man in the street wearing a parka. The hood on the parka keeps leaping about and people are throwing money into it. Tom says to the man, 'D'you earn a lot doing that?' 'Yes,' says the man. 'It's my livelihood.'

✳ Some friars were behind in their belfry payments, so they opened up a small florist shop to raise funds. Since everyone liked to buy flowers from the men of God, a rival florist across town thought the competition was unfair. He asked the monks to close down, but they refused. He went back and begged them to close. They ignored him. So the rival florist hired Hugh MacTaggart, the roughest, most vicious thug in town to persuade them to close. Hugh beat up the monks and trashed their store, saying he'd be back if they didn't close up shop. Terrified, they did so. Thereby proving that Hugh, and only Hugh, can prevent florist friars.

✳ The ashes of a famous general are due to be flown home for burial but it's discovered that all the airlines are fully booked. Eventually a helicopter is found to take the urn home. Next day the newspaper headline reads, 'The Whirly Bird Gets the Urn'.

✳ Three animals, a hawk, a lion and a skunk, are arguing about which is the most fearsome. The hawk says it's the most fearsome as it's the fastest. The lion says it's the most fearsome because it's the strongest. The skunk says it's the most fearsome as it's the worst smelling. Just then a bear came along and swallowed them all: hawk, lion and stinker.

✳ Three legionnaires are walking through the desert under a baking sun. The trio have plenty of water but little food and soon start to see tempting mirages. Suddenly one of them stops and points at the horizon. 'Regardez, mes amis,' says one of the legionnaires. 'Is not zat a bacon tree?' The others stare into the distance and, sure enough, a tree is standing there festooned with rashers of bacon. The legionnaire runs towards it and is within a stone's throw when a shot rings out. The legionnaire collapses into the sand. His two friends hurry to bring him aid. 'Alas, mes amis,' says the dying legionnaire. 'Zat was no bacon tree, zat was an 'am bush.'

✳ Three men are stranded in a small boat. After bobbing about for a week they see a huge hand slowly rise out of the water. As they watch, the hand slowly dips to the right, then slowly to the left. It then submerges beneath the waves. 'Streuth!' says one of the men. 'Did you see the size of that wave?'

✳ Two men are lost in the desert, slowly dying of thirst. They crawl over a sand dune and see a Bedouin market laid out before them. Overjoyed, they stumble towards the first stall and ask for water. The stallkeeper says, 'Sorry, I have no water. All I can offer you is some sponge cake, some custard, or maybe some jelly.' The two men go to the next stall where, again, they beg for water. 'Alas no,' replies the stallholder, 'I can give you jelly, custard or sponge cake, but no water.' Desperate, the men approach the last stall and again beg the owner for water. Again the reply is, 'We have plenty of custard, sponge cake and jelly, but no water.' Despondent the two men crawl back into the desert. One says to the other, 'That market was very odd.' 'Yes,' replies his friend. 'It was a trifle bazaar.'

✳ What are the people who come round to your house to demonstrate vacuum cleaners called? Je-hoover's witnesses.

✳ What did the zookeeper say when he was charged by a baby aardvark? 'A little aardvark never hurt anybody.'

✳ While he was hiding in Iraq, Saddam Hussein had a concealed bunker in a ziggurat. Unfortunately he burnt his lunch one day and the smoke alerted the Americans. Saddam ran for it – he knew that smoking ziggurats were bad for his stealth.

✳ Why did the Mexican shoot his wife? Tequila.

✳ Why was the Irish folksinger unable to perform? She'd left her harp in Sam Frank's disco.

✳ A man goes into a shop and complains about the cost of gherkins. 'It's not the gherkins that cost so much,' explains the shopkeeper. 'It's the stuff they're pickled in. Dill waters run steep.'

✳ A man learns carpentry in prison and starts doing odd jobs for the prison staff. All goes well until the Governor asks the prisoner to fit a new kitchen counter – the prisoner refuses. 'Why won't you fit a new counter?' asks the Governor. The prisoner replies, 'It was counter fitting that got me in here in the first place.'

✳ After work a doctor is in the habit off stopping off at his local bar for a hazel-nut daiquiri. One day the barman realises he's run out of hazelnuts and knocks up a daiquiri with hickory nuts instead. The doctor notices the substitution and asks what sort of drink he's been given. The barman replies, 'It's a hickory daiquiri, Doc.'

recycling

Marrying a man who's been married before is ecologically responsible. There are more women than men in the world so it's good sense to recycle.

One woman says to another, 'Do you recycle?' 'Of course,' says her friend. 'After we divorced, I slept with my ex.'

REFUSE COLLECTION

✳ A dustman is collecting the bins when an old woman comes out of her house in her nightdress and curlers. 'Am I too late for the rubbish?' she asks. 'Course not, dear,' says the dustman. 'Hop in.'

✳ Junk is something you've kept for years – then throw away a week before you need it.

RELIGION

✳ A boy is wandering through a hotel when he hears amorous sounds coming from a room. Curious he opens the door to an unlit room. 'Wow,' he says. 'It's dark in here!' A man shouts out, 'Clear off and leave us alone!' Startled, the boy shuts the door and runs away. Later that evening the boy passes the hotel laundry room and, again, hears amorous sounds coming from inside. He opens the door and says, 'Wow. It's dark in here!' Again, a man shouts, 'Go away and leave us alone!' And the boy shuts the door and runs away. Next day the boy's mother takes him to his first confession. The boy enters the confessional box and says, 'Wow. It's dark in here.' The priest says, 'Are you following me around, you little bastard?'

✳ A man has some churchmen to his house for dinner. He offers a glass of whisky to an Anglican bishop, who gratefully accepts, then does the same to a teetotal Scottish minister of the Free Church. 'Sir,' says the minister. 'I would rather commit adultery with your wife, than let a drop of that whisky pass my lips.' 'Blimey,' says the bishop. 'I didn't know we had a choice.'

✳ A mother is preparing pancakes for her sons, Kevin, five, and Ryan, three. The boys begin to argue over who gets the first pancake and their mother sees the opportunity for a moral lesson. 'If Jesus were sitting here,' she says. 'He would say, "Let my brother have the first pancake. I can wait."' Kevin turns to his brother and says, 'Okay, Ryan. You be Jesus.'

✳ A Sunday school teacher reads a Bible passage to her class. 'And the Lord appointed a great fish to swallow up Jonah; and Jonah was in the belly of the fish three days and three nights. Then Jonah prayed to the Lord his God from the belly of the fish, saying, "I called to the Lord of my distress and He answered me." … and the Lord spoke to the fish, and it vomited out Jonah upon the dry land.' When she's finished reading, the teacher says, 'Now, children. What does this story teach us?' Little Johnny raises his hand and says, 'You can't keep a good man down?'

✳ At a church gathering the priest stacks a pile of apples at one end of a table with a sign saying, 'Take only one apple please – God is watching'. On the other end of the table is a pile of cookies, Little Johnny places a sign by it saying, 'Take all the cookies you want – God's watching the fruit'.

✳ Little Johnny comes home from school and says, 'Dad. Today we found out what God's name is. He's called Harold.' 'Harold?' replies his father. 'What gave you that idea?' 'It said so in the poem,' replies Johnny. 'Our Lord who art in heaven. Harold be they name.'

✳ My husband and I divorced over religious differences. He thought he was God. I didn't.

✳ Remember there are seven deadly sins. One a day. So, have a good week.

✳ Teacher, 'Johnny, please list the Ten Commandments in any order.' Johnny, 'Okay: 3, 6, 1, 8, 4, 5, 9, 2, 10, 7.'

✳ What did the Virgin Mary say when she saw the wise men? 'Typical, you wait ages then three come at once.'

RELIGION: ATHEISTS AND AGNOSTICS

✳ An atheist is taking a hike through the woods when a huge bear starts chasing after him. The bear corners the atheist in a cave and he falls on his knees, shouting, 'Lord, save me!' God calls down, saying, 'You hypocrite. All these years you've denied me and now you want my help.' The atheist replies, 'You're right. It is hypocritical to proclaim myself a Christian after all these years, but could you meet me halfway and make the bear a Christian.' 'I suppose so,' says God and gives the bear religion. The atheist breathes a huge breath and walks past the startled bear. The bear turns and bites the atheist in the neck, killing him. The bear then puts its paws together and says, 'Lord, for this bounty...'

✳ I swear to God I'm an athiest!

✳ Did you hear about the 'Dial-A-Prayer' telephone service for agnostics? You dial the number and no one answers.

✳ What's an atheist's favourite Christmas movie? *Coincidence on 34th Street.*

RELIGION: GOD

✳ 'God don't make mistakes. That's how He got to be God.' *All in the Family*

✳ 'I played the part of God, in *Gideon*. It was method acting, so two weeks beforehand, I started to live the part offstage, y'know. I really came on God, there, I was really fabulous, I put on a blue suit, I took taxi cabs all over New York. I tipped big, 'cause he would have. I got into a fight with a guy, and I forgave him. It's true. Some guy hit my fender and I said unto him, "Be fruitful and multiply", but not in those words.' *Woody Allen*

✳ 'If triangles had a God, he'd have three sides.' *Yiddish proverb*

✳ 'Not only is there no God, but try getting a plumber on weekends.' *Woody Allen*

❋ God did not create the world in seven days; he messed around for six days then pulled an all-nighter.

❋ God is not dead but alive and working on a much less ambitious project.

❋ God is planning a holiday but can't decide where to go. 'What about visiting Mercury?' suggests an angel. 'No, too hot,' says God. 'Then how about Mars?' says the angel. 'Nah,' says God. 'Too dry and dusty.' 'What about Earth?' says the angel. 'You've got to be kidding,' says God. 'I went there 2,000 years ago, knocked up some bird, and they're *still* going on about it.'

❋ God is sitting in Heaven when a scientist flies up in a rocket and says, 'God, we don't need you any more. Science has figured out a way to create life out of nothing. We can now do what you did in the beginning.' 'Really?' replies God. 'What exactly do you mean?' 'Well,' replies the scientist. 'We can take dirt and form it into your likeness and make it live.' 'That's something I'd like to see,' says God. 'Why don't you show me?' So the scientist bends down and starts to mould the dirt into the shape of a man. God grabs his arm and pulls him back. 'Hey. Not so fast,' he says. 'Go and get your own dirt.'

❋ I know God won't give me more than I can handle. I just wish He didn't trust me so much.

❋ If there is no God, who pops up the next Kleenex in the box?

❋ Yes, I believe God will provide. But if only He would till He does.

🎃 RELIGION: NUNS

❋ A man is enjoying a drink outside a bar when a nun comes along and starts lecturing him on the evils of booze. The man argues back and it turns out that the nun has never had a drink in her life. 'Tell you what,' says the man. 'I'll buy you some alcohol, you drink it, and tell me what you think.' 'Out of the question,' replies the nun. 'I could never be seen to be drinking in public. But I suppose if you put the liquid in a coffee cup I might have a sip.' The man agrees, goes inside and orders a double brandy in a coffee cup. 'Oh no,' replies the barman. 'It's not that bloody nun again is it?'

❋ A man rushes into a pub and orders a brandy. While the barman is pouring, the man says, 'How tall does a penguin grow?' 'About two foot,' replies the barman. 'Dammit!' says the man, knocking back his drink. 'I've just run over a nun.'

❋ Two nuns are driving through Transylvania when Count Dracula suddenly jumps on their car. 'Quick, show him your cross!' says one of the nuns. The other nun shouts, 'Hey, Dracula! Get off the God damn car!'

religion: the pope

The Pope is visiting a town and all the residents are lining the street hoping for a blessing. The Mayor is sure the Pope will stop and talk to him, but is surprised when the Pope ignores him completely and whispers a few words to a filthy old tramp standing on the other side of the road. 'Of course!' thinks the Mayor. 'The Pope cares more for the poor and homeless, not the rich like me!' With this he dashes over to the tramp, buys his clothes, gets into them, then runs to the end of the street and lines up again. Sure enough the Pope sees the Mayor and walks over to talk to him. 'Hey, stinky,' whispers the Pope. 'I thought I told you to get lost.'

RESTAURANTS

❋ 'At the all-you-can-eat barbecue near my house, you have to pay the regular dinner price if you eat less than you can.' *Steven Wright*

❋ 'Waiter! This water is very cloudy.' 'No, sir, you just have a very dirty glass.'

❋ A customer is ordering food in an Indian restaurant. 'Waiter, what's this chicken tarka?' The waiter replies, 'It's the same as chicken tikka, but it's a little 'otter.'

❋ A man goes into a restaurant and the waitress comes to take his order. 'I want a quickie,' says the man and the waitress slaps his face. Another waitress passes and the man says, 'Please, can I have a quickie?' Again the waitress slaps his face. A third waitress passes. The man says, 'All I want is a quickie.'

Again the man gets his face slapped. A diner on the next table leans over and says, 'It's pronounced "Keesh".'

✳ Harry took his date to a posh restaurant and ordered the entire meal in French. Even the waiters were impressed – especially as it was a Chinese restaurant.

✳ It's a very authentic Spanish restaurant. They bring you a glass of water then warn you not to drink it.

✳ Mister Smith and his wife enter an expensive restaurant. 'I'm sorry,' apologises the maître d', 'but there are no tables available.' Mister Smith replies, 'I bet if the President came in and asked for a table, there'd be one available. 'Yes,' admits the maître d', 'I suppose there would.' 'Then I'll take that one,' says Mister Smith. 'The President isn't coming.'

✳ There are two things you should avoid approaching from the rear – horses and restaurants.

✳ Two ladies go for their regular restaurant appointment and order a meal. 'And make sure I have a clean glass,' says one of the ladies. 'The one I had last week was filthy.' A few minutes later the waiter returns, sets out the food, and says, 'And which one of you ordered the clean glass?'

✳ We were eating in an open air café when it started raining really heavily. It took us an hour and a half to finish our soup.

RESTAURANTS: WAITER

✳ 'Waiter! Do you have frogs' legs?' 'Oui, monsieur.' 'Then hop over the counter and get me some cigarettes.'

✳ 'Waiter! There's a fly in my soup!' 'That's not a fly, that's a vitamin Bee.'

✳ 'Waiter! This food isn't fit for a pig.' 'In that case I shall take it away and bring you some that is.'

✳ 'Waiter! This plate is wet.' 'No, that's your soup.'

※ 'Waiter! This soup tastes funny.' 'Then why aren't you laughing?'

※ 'Waiter! What's this fly doing in my soup?' 'It looks like the backstroke.'

※ 'Waiter! Why is there a dead cockroach in my soup?' 'Surely don't expect a live one at these prices?'

※ 'Waiter! There's a fly in my soup!' 'In that case I'll get you a fork.'

※ 'Waiter! There's a dead grasshopper in my soup.' 'I'm sorry, sir, they're not very good swimmers.'

※ 'Waiter! What's the meaning of this fly in my soup?' 'How should I know? I'm a waiter not a fortune teller.'

※ 'Waiter! What's this in my bowl?' 'It's bean soup, sir.' 'I don't care what it's been, what is it now?'

royalty

It was announced that the Queen had gone on a short informal walkabout today shortly after hitting her thumb with a hammer.

Prince Charles arrives in Iran on an official visit. He says to the President, 'Where's the Shah?' 'What do you mean?' says the President. 'There is no Shah. We got rid of the Shah years ago.' 'Okay,' says Prince Charles. 'In that case I'll have a bath.'

SCIENCE

※ 'If I melt dry ice, can I swim without getting wet?' *Steven Wright*

※ A neutron walks into a bar. 'I'd like a beer,' he says. The bartender promptly serves up a beer. 'How much will that be?' asks the neutron. 'For you?' replies the bartender. 'No charge.'

✳ 'If you were in a vehicle and you were travelling at the speed of light, and then you turned your lights on, would they do anything?' *Steven Wright*

✳ 'It's a good thing we have gravity, or else when birds died they'd just stay right up there.' *Steven Wright*

✳ How many balls of string would it take to reach the moon? Just one – if it's long enough!

✳ A day without radiation is a day without sunshine.

✳ A man is playing Trivial Pursuit. He rolls the dice and lands on Science & Nature. The question is, 'If you are in a vacuum and someone calls your name, can you hear it?' The man thinks for a moment before asking, 'Is the vacuum on or off?'

✳ A mathematician, a physicist and an engineer were all given a red rubber ball and told to find the volume. The mathematician carefully measured the diameter and evaluated a triple integral. The physicist filled a beaker with water, put the ball in the water, and measured the total displacement. The engineer looked up the model and serial numbers in his red-rubber-ball table.

✳ A physics professor is giving a lecture on lighting. 'The moon is more useful than the sun because the moon shines at night when you want the light, whereas the sun shines during the day when you don't need it.'

✳ A research scientist drops a piece of buttered toast on the floor and is astonished to find that it lands butter-side up. He takes the toast to a colleague and asks him how on earth the toast landed butter-side up when, according to experience, it always lands butter-side down. The colleague thinks for a moment then comes up with the answer. 'It's easy,' he says. 'You must have buttered the wrong side.'

✳ A Russian, an American and a blonde get talking. The Russian says, 'We were the first in space!' The American says, 'We were the first on the moon!' The blonde says, 'So what? We're going to be the first on the sun!' 'You can't land on the sun, you idiot!' says the Russian. 'You'll burn up!' The blonde replies, 'Duhhhh. We're going at night!'

✳ I went live on the Internet myself the other day – I was plugging in my modem and got my finger stuck in the socket.

✳ Statistics are like a lamp-post to a drunken man – more for leaning on than for illumination.

✳ An astronomer, a physicist and a mathematician are holidaying in Scotland. Glancing from a train window, they observe a black sheep in the middle of a field. 'How interesting,' observes the astronomer. 'All Scottish sheep are black.' The physicist responds, 'No, no! Only some Scottish sheep are black!' The mathematician tells them, 'In Scotland there exists at least one field, containing at least one sheep, at least one side of which is black.'

✳ A seminar on Time Travel will be held two weeks ago.

✳ Astronomers, go outside during the night of the next spring equinox and face south. Bend over to an angle of 45 degrees, slightly relax your knees, and lower your head so you can look back between your legs. Now hold a small mirror in your left hand and adjust the angle so it's parallel with your face. With luck you should now see Uranus.

✳ Did you know that Hannibal was the first man to experiment with genetics? He crossed a mountain with an elephant.

✳ Does the name Pavlov ring a bell?

✳ The thing I really like about the *Oxford Dictionary of Differential Calculus* is that it doesn't try to glamorise the subject in any way.

✳ Two hydrogen atoms are talking. One says, 'I think I've lost an electron.' The other asks, 'Are you sure?' The first replies, 'Yes, I'm positive.'

✳ How do you get a baby astronaut to sleep? You rocket.

'I put tape on the mirrors in my house so I don't accidentally walk through into another dimension.' *Steven Wright*

🍎 SEX

✳ 'I'd like to meet the man who invented sex and see what he's working on now.' *George Carlin*

✳ 'She's the original good time that was had by all.' *Bette Davis*

✳ 'When my old man wanted sex, my mother would show him a picture of me.' *Rodney Dangerfield*

✳ Did you hear about the transvestite who wanted a night on the town? He wanted to eat, drink and be Mary.

✳ A circus owner advertises for a lion tamer. Two people show up, one is a young man and the other is a gorgeous girl. The circus owner says, 'I'm not going to lie to you. This is a ferocious lion. He ate my last tamer so you guys better be good. Here's your equipment; a chair, whip and a gun. Who wants to try out first?' The girl volunteers. She walks past the whip and the gun, steps into the lion's cage and sits in the chair. The lion charges but the girl throws open her coat revealing that she's naked underneath. The lion stops dead in his tracks, licks her legs, then rests its head in her lap. The circus owner is astonished, 'I've never seen anything like that in my life.' He turns to the young man and says, 'Can you top that?' The young man replies, 'Sure I can – as soon as you get that damn lion out of the way.'

✳ A little boy is always biting his nails. In the end his mum gets cross and says, 'If you carry on biting your nails. You'll get bigger and bigger and bigger until you blow up like a balloon!' A few days later the little boy is on the bus when a very pregnant woman sits opposite him. After a few minutes she realises the boy is staring at her. 'Do you know me?' she asks. 'No,' says the boy. 'But I know what you've been doing.'

✳ A man picks up a gorgeous woman at a bar and they go back to her place. The man is surprised to see how many teddy bears and stuffed toys the woman has at her apartment – every surface is piled high with them. After a night of passion the man rolls over and says, 'So. How was I?' The woman replies. 'Take any prize from the bottom shelf.'

✳ 'Women need a reason to have sex. Men just need a place.' *Billy Crystal*

✳ A man takes early retirement and leaves the big city for a crofter's cottage in the Scottish Highlands. After a month of isolation he hears a knock on his door. He answers it and sees an enormous Scottish farmer standing outside. 'I hear you're new around here,' says the farmer, 'Yes, I am,' replies the man. 'I thought I'd introduce myself and ask you to a party I'm having,' says the farmer. 'That's very nice. I'd love to come,' says the man. 'I'd better warn you there'll be lots o'drinking,' says the farmer. 'I don't mind, I like a drink,' replies the man. 'And nee doubt they'll be a few fights breaking out,' says the farmer. 'That's okay, I can take care of myself,' replies the man. 'And things get a bit frisky in the wee hours,' says the farmer. 'There'll be lots of sex.' 'That's fine by me,' says the man. 'I haven't had any female company for a long time.' 'Och, there'll be no lassies,' says the farmer. 'It's just the two of us.'

✳ A new monk arrives at the monastery and starts to help copying old texts by hand. However, the monk notices that there are errors in the text and that the monks are copying copies, not the original books. The new monk goes to the abbot of the monastery and points out that if there was an error in the first copy, that error would be continued. The abbot agrees and decides to go and check the original books in the cellar. Hours later abbot still hasn't returned, so one of the monks goes to look for him. The monk hears sobbing coming from the back of the cellar and finds the abbot leaning over one of the books crying. 'What's wrong?' asks the monk. The abbot looks at him and says, 'The word is "celebrate".'

✳ A newly-wed couple didn't know the difference between putty and Vaseline. A week after the marriage all their windows fell out. Which was the least of their worries.

✳ At the retreat, Jill and John are each told to write a sentence using the words 'sex' and 'love'. Jill writes, 'When two mature people are both passionately and deeply in love with one another to a high degree and they respect each other very much, just like John and I, it is spiritually and morally acceptable for them to engage in the act of physical sex with one another.' John writes, 'I love sex.'

✳ Harry is very quick with the ladies, before they can tell him they're not that sort of girl, it's usually too late.

'I wouldn't mind being the last man on Earth – just to see if all of those girls were telling me the truth.' *Ronnie Shakes*

✳ How do girls get minks? The same way minks get minks.

✳ I think you'll find that any of my lady companions will tell you I'm a 'five times a night man'. I really shouldn't drink so much tea before I go to bed.

✳ I wish my girlfriend had warned me about the ceiling mirror in her bedroom. I lay down ready for her, then ran out screaming – I'd looked up and thought I was being attacked by a naked skydiver.

✳ Man cannot live on bread alone – he needs a bit of crumpet too.

✳ Man, to woman, 'Am I the first man you ever made love to?' Woman, 'You might be. Now you come to mention it, your face does look familiar.'

✳ Man, to woman, 'Do you want sex?' Woman, 'Your place or mine?' Man, 'Well, if you're going to argue. Forget it.'

✳ Patrick and Michael go to a pub for a drink and see a sign saying, 'Buy a double whisky and get a chance of free sex.' They both buy a double then ask the barman how to get the sex. 'It's simple,' he says. 'I think of a number between one and ten, and if you can guess what it is, you get laid.' 'Okay,' says Patrick. 'I'll guess, three.' 'Sorry,' says the barman. 'You're out of luck.' Next day the pair return and, again, Patrick tries his luck at the free sex quiz, he guesses four. 'Sorry,' says the barman. 'Better luck next time.' Next day the pair come back and Patrick guesses, two. 'Sorry,' says the barman. 'Wrong again.' Patrick turns to Michael and says, 'Y'know I'm beginning to think this contest is rigged.' 'Oh no,' says Michael. 'My wife tried it last week and she won three times.'

✳ The vicar never entertained lewd thoughts – they always entertained him.

✳ Two men are having a drink together. One says, 'I had sex with my wife before we were married. What about you?' 'I don't know,' says the other. 'What was her maiden name?'

✳ There is nothing wrong with sex on TV – as long as you don't fall off.

✳ Two teenage boys go to confession. In the booth the first boy admits having sex with a girl but refuses to name her. The priest asks, 'It wasn't Mary Jones, was it?' The boy says, 'No, Father, it wasn't.' The priest asks, 'Was it Angela Brown?' The boy replies, 'No, Father, it wasn't.' The priest asks, 'It wasn't Jane Carter, by any chance?' The boy says, 'No, Father it wasn't.' The priest gives up and says, 'Well, for your penance say fifty Hail Marys and leave half your pocket money in the poor box.' When the boy leaves his friend asks him how it went. The boy replies, 'Not bad, a £5 fine and three great leads.'

✳ What's a man's definition of safe sex? Meeting his mistress at least 30 miles from his house.

✳ When I was young my sister used to play with dolls and I played with soldiers, now we do it the other way round.

✳ Why is it called sex? Because it's easier to spell than Uhhhhh.. oooohh… Ahhhhhh…AIIEEEEEEE!

sheep

Two sheep are talking in a field. 'Baaaaaa,' says the first. 'Damn,' says the second. 'I was going to say that.'

Where do you get virgin wool from? Ugly sheep.

☻SHOPS AND SHOPPING

✳ 'I bought some used paint the other day. It was in the shape of a house.'
Steven Wright

✳ A man goes into a bookshop. He approaches a woman behind the counter and says, 'Do you keep stationery here?' 'No,' replies the woman. 'Sometimes I wriggle about a bit.'

✹ A man goes into a grocery store to buy a bar of soap when he realises he's been followed around by a little old lady. The old lady shadows him as he goes up and down the aisles and then follows him to the till. The old lady comes up to him and says, 'I'm sorry if I made you uncomfortable with my staring, but you look just like my dead son. Listen, I hate to ask, but it would make me so happy if you could say goodbye to me. My son was taken suddenly and never had the chance.' The man is touched by this request and waves her goodbye as she leaves the shop pulling her bag of groceries with her. 'Goodbye, Mother,' he cries. 'Goodbye!' He then turns to the assistant at the till and pays for his soap. 'That's £112.90,' says the assistant. 'What?' replies the man. 'I only bought soap.' 'Yes,' replies the assistant. 'But you mother said you'd be paying for her shopping too.'

✹ A man is a person who will pay two pounds for a one-pound item that he wants. A woman will pay one pound for a two-pound item that she doesn't want.

✹ A man walks into an alarm clock and Jack-in-the-box store. He says to the owner, 'What are you? Some kind of wind-up merchant?'

✹ A woman picks up a jumper in a clothes store. 'This is a little overpriced, isn't it?' she says to the shop assistant. 'Not really, madam,' the assistant replies. 'The wool comes from a rare breed of albino sheep only found in the highest mountains of Tibet. It's a beautiful yarn.' 'Yes,' replies the woman. 'And you tell it so well.'

✹ A woman goes to buy a fancy teasmade with all the latest gadgets. The salesman explains how everything works; how to plug it in, fill it up, and set the timer so that she'll awake to a fresh cup of tea. A few weeks later she's back in the store. The salesman asks her how she likes the teasmade. 'It's wonderful!' she says. 'But there's one thing I don't understand. Why do I have to go to bed every time I want a cup of tea?'

✹ An attractive girl walks into a fabric shop. 'I want to buy this material for a dress,' she says. 'How much does it cost?' 'Only one kiss per metre,' replies the male clerk. 'Fine,' replies the girl. 'In that case I'll take ten metres.' The clerk gives her the fabric and the girl points to a little old man standing next to her, 'Thanks,' she says. 'Grandpa's paying the bill.'

✹ Ever wondered about those people who pay a fortune for those little bottles of Evian water? Try spelling Evian backwards…

✳ An elderly gentleman goes into a West End furriers with his young lady and buys her a mink coat costing £15,000. 'Will a cheque be okay?' asks the man. 'Certainly, sir,' says the sales assistant. 'But we'll have to wait a few days for it to clear. Can you come back on Monday to take delivery?' 'Certainly,' replies the old man and he and his girlfriend walk out arm in arm. Next Monday the man returns. The sales assistant is furious, 'You've got a nerve coming back here. It turns out there's hardly a penny in your bank account, your cheque was worthless.' 'Yes, sorry about that,' replies the man. 'I just came in to apologise – and thank you for the greatest weekend of my life.'

✳ Customer, to shopkeeper, 'When I bought this rug you said it was used but in perfect condition. I get it home and find it's got a hole in the middle!' Shopkeeper, 'That's correct, sir. But if you'll recall, I did say it was in mint condition.'

✳ A woman is shopping in an exclusive shoe shop when she sees a beautiful pair of stilettos. The store owner comes over and says, 'They're very expensive, but if you go to bed with me I'll let you have them for nothing.' 'Well, okay,' says the woman. 'But don't expect me to enjoy it.' The owner gives her the shoes and takes her home. In the bedroom they get down to business. The owner drops his trousers, takes off the woman's underwear, pushes her back over the bed, and hoists her legs over his shoulders. As he thrusts away the woman says, 'Oh God, yes! Yes. Fantastic! Absolutely fantastic…' 'Oh really?' says the owner. 'And I thought you said you wouldn't enjoy sex with me?' 'I don't,' replies the woman. 'I'm admiring my new shoes.'

✳ For a few months I worked in one of those sweat shops – but after a while people just seemed to stop buying sweat.

✳ How do you identify people who can't count to ten? Simple. They're the ones in front of you in the supermarket express lane.

✳ I had a good talk to my wife about cutting down on her extravagant shopping bills. As a result there's definitely going to be some changes – I'm giving up smoking.

✳ I went to a bookstore and said to the saleswoman, 'Where's the self-help section?' She said, 'If I told you it would defeat the purpose.'

✳ My wife and I always hold hands. If I let go, she goes shopping.

✳ I went to the 24-hour grocery. When I got there, the guy was locking the front door. I said, 'Hey, the sign says you're open 24 hours.' He said, 'Yes. But not all at once.'

✳ I went to the shops yesterday and treated myself to a toilet brush. It's no good though. I'm going to have to go back to paper.

✳ The Church of England is opening its own string of supermarkets. They're going to be called Jesus Christ Superstores.

✳ The service at our local shop is so slow you can queue up to get Christmas cards and end up buying Easter eggs.

✳ Two lions are walking down the aisle of a supermarket, one turns to the other and says, 'Quiet in here today, isn't it?'

✳ They have quite a good offer on at the local shop. If you buy something then see the same product in another shop for a lower price, tell them – then they'll go round and smash the other shop's windows.

🍎 SHORTNESS

✳ Harry invited us round to his house to see the 'little woman'. We thought he wanted us to meet his wife, but it turned out his lodger is a midget.

✳ He was so small he had turn-ups in his underpants.

✳ He's so short he thinks it's unlucky to walk under a black cat.

✳ He's so short he was offered a job standing around in a bar. They reckoned he made the drinks look bigger.

✳ He's very short. In fact he's the one who poses for trophies.

✳ What did the midget order in the café? A glass of condensed milk and some shortbread.

✳ What's ET short for? Because he has little legs.

signs

At the electric company: We'd be delighted if you send in your bill. However, if you don't, you will be.

In a funeral home: Drive carefully – we can wait.

In a music library: Bach in a minuet.

In a vet's waiting room: Back in five minutes. Sit! Stay!

On a maternity room door: Push, Push, Push.

SKIING

* Two men are arguing about the best way to ski down a particular hill. They ask a man pulling a sledge for his opinion. 'Sorry,' says the man. 'There's no use asking me. I'm a tobogganist.' 'Oh,' says one of the men. 'In that case, could I have a pack of Marlboro Lights?'

* Two men, Jack and John, go on a skiing trip and get caught in a blizzard. They pull into a farm and ask the lady of the house, a good-looking widow, if they can sleep on her couch. She agrees and they turn in for the night. Next morning they go on their way and enjoy a weekend of skiing. A few months later, Jack gets a letter from the widow's lawyer. He says to John, 'You remember that good-looking widow we met on our skiing holiday?' 'Yes,' says John. 'In the middle of the night, did you go up to her room and have sex with her?' asks Jack. 'Yes,' admits John, a little embarrassed. 'I see,' says Jack. 'And when you had sex did you happen to use my name instead of yours?' John's face turns red. 'Yeah, sorry,' he says. 'I'm afraid I did.' 'Well,' says Jack. 'You must have been damn good. She's just died and left everything to me.'

SKYDIVING

✳ Barbara is taking her first skydiving lesson. The instructor tells her to jump out of the plane and pull her ripcord. After she's done so the instructor jumps out of the plane after her. The instructor pulls his ripcord but his parachute doesn't open. As he struggles to pull the emergency cord, he shoots downwards past Barbara. Barbara undoes the straps on her own parachute and yells, 'So you wanna race, huh?'

✳ For Sale: Parachute. Only used once, never opened, small stain.

✳ He's invented a new type of parachute. It opens on impact.

✳ If at first you don't succeed, skydiving is not for you.

✳ Skydivers: good to the last drop.

✳ What do you call it when your parachute doesn't open? Jumping to a conclusion.

✳ What's the difference between a bad golfer and a skydiver? One goes 'Whack! Awwwwghk!' The other goes, 'Awwwwghk! Whack!'

✳ Why do female skydivers wear jock straps? So they don't whistle on the way down.

SLEEP

✳ 'I hate it when my foot falls asleep during the day – it means it's going to be up all night.' *Steven Wright*

✳ 'I was once arrested for walking in someone else's sleep.' *Steven Wright*

✳ 'I went to the doctor because I'd swallowed a bottle of sleeping pills. My doctor told me to have a few drinks and get some rest.' *Rodney Dangerfield*

※ 'When I woke up this morning, my girlfriend asked if I'd slept well. I said, "No, I made a few mistakes."' *Steven Wright*

※ A woman went to the doctor to get some more sleeping pills for her husband. He'd woken up.

small towns

I come from a town so small we closed the zoo when the chicken died.

I spent a year in that town one night.

My home town is so small, the street map is actual size.

My home town is so small, when I plug in my electric razor the street lamps dim.

The town is so small and dull, they print the local paper three weeks in advance.

SPEECH IMPEDIMENTS

※ 'My wife has a slight impediment in her speech. Every now and then she stops to breathe.' *Jimmy Durante*

※ A man spots an old schoolfriend getting out of a new Rolls-Royce. 'How did you do so well?' asks the man. 'Oh,' says his stuttering friend. 'J-j-j-j-j-j-j-just by selling c-c-c-c-c-c-c-copies of the B-b-b-b-b-b-bible d-d-d-d-d-door to d-d-d-d-d-door.' 'That's amazing,' says the man. 'How do you manage to sell so many.' 'W-w-well,' says his friend. 'I j-j-just kno-o-ock on p-p-p-p-p-p-p-people's d-d-d-d-doors, show them a co-o-o-py of the B-b-b-b-b-bible and ask them if they w-w-w-w-w-w-would rather b-b-b-b-b-buy it or h-h-h-have me r-r-r-ead it to them.'

※ Teacher, to pupil, 'Jenny. What is a thimble?' Jenny, 'Is it a thort of thign?'

🍎SPEECHES AND SPEECHMAKING

✳ 'I'm going to make a long speech because I've not had time to prepare a short one.' *Winston Churchill*

✳ 'Speaking in front of a crowd is considered the number one fear of the average person. I found that amazing. Number two was death! That means, to the average person, if you have to be at a funeral, you would rather be in the casket than doing the eulogy.' *Jerry Seinfeld*

✳ 'Tonight I feel like Zsa Zsa Gabor's fifth husband. I know what to do. But how do I make it interesting?' *David Niven*

✳ A guest speaker is trying to make himself heard over the racket of a boisterous rugby club dinner. He complains to the president sitting next to him, 'It's so noisy I can't hear myself speak.' 'I wouldn't worry about it,' replies the president. 'You're not missing anything.'

✳ Advice to public speakers – if you don't strike oil within two minutes, stop boring.

✳ After that speech I feel refreshed and inspired. It's amazing what a short nap can do.

✳ As Henry VIII said to each of his wives, 'I shan't keep you long.'

✳ Harry is in the middle of a speech when someone at the back calls out, 'I can't hear you.' Someone at the front calls back, 'Could we swap places?'

✳ The secret of a good sermon is to have a good beginning and a good ending – and have the two as close together as possible.

✳ They asked me to talk about something off the top of my head. So here's a short talk about dandruff.

✳ This is like making love to Joan Collins. You know it's been done many, many times before. And much, much better.

spontaneous human combustion

My father spontaneously combusted while wearing a Barbour wax jacket. Because of the wax it took him three weeks to go out. Saved a bit on the central heating though.

🐷 SPORTS

☀ 'Hockey is a sport for white men. Basketball is a sport for black men. Golf is a sport for white men dressed like black pimps.' *Tiger Woods*

☀ 'I asked my old man if I could go ice-skating on the lake. He told me, "Wait till it gets warmer."' *Rodney Dangerfield*

☀ 'I was watching the Indy 500. I was thinking that if they left earlier they wouldn't have to go so fast.' *Steven Wright*

☀ A boxer goes to a doctor complaining of insomnia. 'Have you tried counting sheep?' asks the doctor. 'It doesn't work,' replies the boxer. 'Every time I get to nine, I stand up.'

☀ A man and wife are at a volleyball game when they notice a very affectionate couple who are running their hands over each other passionately. 'I don't know whether to watch them or the game,' says the man. 'Watch them!' says his wife. 'You already know how to play volleyball.'

☀ After seeing footage of a young Bosnian soldier throwing grenades, the coach of an American football team decides to take him on as a quarterback. This proves to be a great move and the team soon wins the Superbowl. The young man excitedly rings home to tell his mother. 'Mother, I just helped my team win the Superbowl! Aren't you happy?' 'No, I'm not!' snaps back his mother. 'Here we have the sound of gunshots all day, we are living in a slum, your sister has been molested three times, and gangsters have broken your brother's legs. Why the hell did you make us move to Detroit?'

✳ He used to be an all-round athlete. Now he's just all round.

✳ Mama Bear and Papa Bear are accused of child abuse. Baby Bear is put on the stand. The judge says, 'Do you want to live with Papa Bear?' 'No,' Baby Bear replies. 'He beats me.' The judge then asks, 'Do you want to live with Mama Bear?' 'No,' Baby Bear replies. 'She beats me too.' So the judge says, 'So who do you want to live with?' Baby Bear replies, 'I want to live with the Chicago Bears, they never beat anybody.'

✳ My dad is really annoyed, I had the TV on and he accidentally saw the entire football match – he'd just wanted to watch the results on the news.

✳ The hardest thing about prizefighting is picking up your teeth wearing a boxing glove.

✳ There was a tragic end to the water polo championships – all the horses drowned.

✳ They presented him with a cup when he was a boxer. It was to keep his teeth in.

✳ Two women are talking. 'You know,' says one. 'Eighty per cent of men think the best way to end an argument is to make love.' 'Well,' says the other. 'That will certainly revolutionise the game of hockey!'

✳ While giving a physical, a doctor notices that his patient's shins are covered in dark, savage bruises. 'Tell me,' says the doctor. 'Do you play hockey or soccer?' 'No,' said the man. 'But my wife and I play bridge.'

stress

I don't suffer from stress. I'm a carrier.

I read this article that said the typical symptoms of stress are eating too much, smoking too much, impulse buying and driving too fast. That's my idea of a perfect day.

STUPiDiTY

✳ 'Mummy, Mummy! Daddy just fell off the roof!' 'I know, I saw him go past the window.'

✳ A husband is talking to his wife, 'I'm feeling very depressed. Sometimes I think I'm nothing but a half-wit moron.' His wife replies, 'Don't worry, darling. Lots of people feel like that. In fact, most of the people we know think you're a half-wit moron.'

✳ A redneck truck driver is driving east on Route 66 when he sees another truck coming west. The CB crackles to life. 'Hey, redneck,' says a voice on the radio. 'Who are the two biggest faggots in America?' The redneck replies, 'I don't know.' The other trucker says, 'You and your brother.' The redneck is annoyed but the other driver says, 'It's just a joke. Tell it to the next truck you see.' The redneck drives for an hour and finally sees another truck. He gets on his CB and says, 'Hey, other truck, d'you know who the two biggest fags in America are?' The other trucker says, 'No. Who?' The redneck replies, 'Me and my brother.'

✳ Artificial Intelligence is no match for Natural Stupidity.

✳ Dick and Tom find three hand grenades in a field and decide to take them to the police station. 'But what if one of them blows up?' says Dick. 'Well, in that case we'll just tell them we found two,' says Tom.

✳ Don't be fooled by the fact that he looks stupid. That doesn't necessarily mean he isn't.

✳ Emily-Sue gets sick and Billy-Bob calls for an ambulance. The operator asks Billy-Bob where he lives. '1132 Eucalyptus Drive,' replies Billy-Bob. 'Can you spell that for me?' asks the operator. There's a long pause. Finally Billy-Bob says, 'How 'bout if I drag her over to Oak Street?'

✳ Even if he had two guesses he couldn't tell which way an elevator was going.

✳ Harry, to Dick, 'Add this up for me. A ton of sawdust, a ton of old newspaper and a ton of fat. Now, have you got all that in your head?' Dick, 'Yes.' Harry, 'Yeah, I thought so.'

✳ Every month Paddy would lay flowers at a lonely gravestone near his house. The name of the deceased woman was Vi Miles, from Dublin.

✳ Germs attack people where they are weakest. This explains the number of head colds.

✳ God must love stupid people; He made so many of them.

✳ Harry gets a job painting white dotted lines down the middle of roads. On his first day he does very well and paints six miles of road. On the second day he does four miles, but by the third day he's down to two. 'I don't understand it,' says his foreman. 'You were doing so well. What happened?' 'Well, it's obvious,' says Harry. 'Every day I'm getting further and further away from the can of paint.'

✳ Johnny has two brains; one is lost, the other is out looking for it.

✳ Harry left a note on his office door saying 'Back in an hour'. When he got back from lunch he saw the sign – so he sat down and waited.

✳ Tom says he's not stupid. He knows a lot but just can't think of it at the moment.

✳ How do you confuse an idiot? Forty-two.

✳ I always give people the benefit of the doubt. I never attribute to malice what can adequately be explained by crass stupidity.

✳ Ignorance can be cured. Stupid is for ever.

✳ John is showing Tom his newborn triplets. 'What d'you think, then?' asks John. Tom says, 'Well, if it was up to me, I'd keep the middle one.'

✳ Last night we discovered we'd been living with a perfect stranger for the last eight years. I thought the little old lady at our house was her mother, and she thought she was mine.

✳ Next time I want to send an idiot on some errand, I'll go myself.

✳ Nothing is foolproof to a sufficiently talented fool.

✳ My uncle isn't very bright, he painted his sundial with luminous paint so he could tell the time at night.

✳ One way to compensate for a tiny brain is to pretend to be dead.

✳ The gates are down, the lights are flashing, but the train isn't coming.

✳ What's a gross ignoramus? 144 times worse than an ordinary ignoramus.

✳ Simon goes to the funfair and takes his girlfriend through the Tunnel of Love. At the tunnel's exit a staff member sees Simon and his young lady wading through the water. 'Did your boat sink?' he asks. Simon replies, 'You mean there's a *boat*?'

✳ She's so stupid. She needed to tighten the clothes line, so she moved the house.

SUCCESS AND FAILURE

✳ 'Behind every successful man is a woman – behind her is his wife.' *Groucho Marx*

✳ 'If at first you don't succeed – you're fired.' *Lord Grade*

✳ 'I've worked myself up from nothing to a state of extreme poverty.' *Groucho Marx*

✳ 'No one is completely unhappy at the failure of their best friend.' *Groucho Marx*

✳ 'There is no sweeter sound than the crumbling of your fellow man.' *Groucho Marx*

✳ 'You tried your best and you failed miserably. The lesson is never try.' *Homer Simpson*

✳ Just when you thought he'd hit absolute rock bottom he crashed right through and found a new bottom you didn't even know was there.

✳ If at first you don't succeed, destroy all evidence that you tried.

✳ If at first you don't succeed, redefine success.

✳ If at first you don't succeed, try management.

🙂 SUICIDE

✳ How does a Russian commit suicide? He smells his armpits. How does an American commit suicide? He tells this joke to a Russian.

✳ I got home and found my wife had left a suicide note. She'd left a blank space where she wanted me to fill my name in.

✳ My psychiatrist was concerned to hear I had suicidal tendencies. He made me start to pay for sessions in advance.

✳ Patrick has ten children and swears to hang himself if his wife has another. Sure enough his wife gets pregnant and one of his friends reminds him of his suicide oath. 'I almost did hang myself,' explains Patrick. 'I made the noose and tied it to the rafter, then got on a stool. I was just about to jump, when I stopped and said to myself, "Hang on, Paddy. Perhaps we're hanging the wrong man here."'

✳ Suicidal twin kills sister by mistake!

swearing

If a mute swears, does his mother wash his hands with soap?

Little Johnny is caught swearing by his teacher. 'Johnny, you shouldn't use that kind of language,' says the teacher. 'Where on earth did you hear such talk?' 'My daddy said it,' replies Johnny. 'Well, that doesn't matter,' explains the teacher. 'You don't even know what it means.' 'I do, too!' replies Johnny. 'It means the car won't start.'

SWIMMING

✳ A woman came in last in the 100-yard breaststroke at the local swim meet. She later complained, 'The other girls were using their hands!'

✳ Tom, to Harry, 'Where did you learn to swim?' Harry, 'In the water.'

✳ I rang up my local swimming baths and said, 'Is that the local swimming baths?' They said, 'Well, that depends on where you're calling from.'

✳ My father taught me to swim the hard way – he threw me out into the middle of a lake! Learning to swim that way wasn't easy, but the really hard part was getting out of the sack!

✳ The manager of a health spa is worried by the increasingly murky water in his swimming pool. Eventually he sends a sample off for analysis. A week later he receives a report saying, 'This horse is seriously ill and should be put down immediately.'

TATTOOS

✳ 'I want to get a tattoo over my entire body of myself, but taller.' *Steven Wright*

✳ As an obstetrician, I sometimes see unusual tattoos. One patient had some type of fish tattoo on her abdomen. 'That sure is an unusual-looking whale,' I commented. With a sad smile she replied, 'It used to be a dolphin.'

TEENAGERS

✳ Advice for teenagers: leave home now while you still know everything.

✳ I'm finally 18, and now legally able to do everything I've been doing since I was 15.

✳ Two teenagers are found smoking a joint in the middle of a park. They're both arrested and taken to the town jail. The sergeant advises them they're entitled to one phone call. A while later, a man enters the station. The sergeant says, 'I assume you're the kids' lawyer.' 'Heck, no,' replies the man. 'I'm here to deliver a pizza.'

✳ Why do teenagers say they're not like anyone else and then all dress exactly alike?

🍎 TELEVISION

✳ 'I must say, I find television very educational. The minute somebody turns it on, I go to the library and read a book.' *Groucho Marx*

✳ 'Television has raised writing to a new low.' *Sam Goldwyn*

✳ 'The other day a woman came up to me and said, "Didn't I see you on television?" I said, "I don't know. You can't see out the other way."' *Emo Phillips*

✳ A TV station in the USA rings up the British ambassador and asks him what he'd like for Christmas. 'I couldn't possibly accept gifts in my position,' says the ambassador. The TV station insists and says he can have anything he wants no matter how big or small. 'Well,' says the ambassador. 'If you insist I suppose I could accept a small box of chocolates.' A month later the ambassador is watching TV when the news presenter says, 'A while back we asked a number of ambassadors what they'd like for Christmas. The French ambassador said he'd like universal peace. The German ambassador said he'd like prosperity for the world's poor. And the British ambassador said he'd like a small box of candy.'

✳ He's so stupid, his lips move when he watches TV.

✳ I love that TV show with all the different video clips of things going disastrously wrong all the time. What's it called? Oh yes, the news.

✳ Television is a device that lets people with nothing to do spend their time watching people who can't do anything.

✳ Why do you press harder on a remote control when you know the battery is dead?

temptation

Don't worry about avoiding temptations as you get older – they'll start avoiding you.

Lead me not into temptation – I can find the way myself.

TIME AND TIME KEEPING

✳ 'Men love watches that have multiple functions. My husband has one that is a combination address book, telescope and piano.' *Rita Rudner*

✳ 'Why should I care about posterity, what has posterity ever done for me?' *Groucho Marx*

✳ Time is what keeps everything from happening at once.

tortoises

Some tortoises are playing cards when they run out of beer. They pick one of their number, Billy, to go to the off-licence. Billy goes off but after waiting two days the others start getting impatient. 'Billy is really getting slow,' says one. 'He's not what he used to be,' says another. A voice shouts from behind the door, 'Oi! If you're going to talk about me behind my back I'm not going.'

Where do you find a tortoise with no legs? Exactly where you left it.

TRAMPS

✳ A tramp says to me, 'Can I have $500 for a cup of coffee?' I say, 'Coffee only costs a dollar!' He says, 'Yeah, but I want to drink it in Brazil!'

✳ A tramp says to me, 'Give me £10 till pay day.' I say, 'When's pay day?' He says, 'I don't know, you're the one who's working!'

☙ TRANSPORT, TRAVEL AND TOURISM

✳ 'A travel agent told me I could spend seven nights in Hawaii. No days, just nights.' *Rodney Dangerfield*

✳ A guide is showing a group of tourists round a ruined castle. 'Not a stone in this building has been touched in the last four hundred years,' exclaims the guide. 'Really?' says one of the visitors. 'We must have the same landlord.'

✳ A hillbilly visits his cousin in the valley and is fascinated by the railroad he finds there. He's never seen a train so he doesn't know to get out of the way when one comes whistling and steaming down the tracks towards him. Luckily the train has a cowcatcher on the front and the hillbilly is swept off the tracks without being killed. The injured hillbilly is carried back to his cousin's shack to recuperate. The cousin puts a kettle on the stove to make some tea then goes out to get some wood. He returns to find the hillbilly beating the hell out of his kettle with a hammer. 'What y'all doing to ma good kettle?' cries the cousin. 'These things is dangerous,' replies the hillbilly. 'I'm a killin' it before it gets a chance to grow up!'

✳ Barry and Michael are driving their truck down a country lane when they come to a bridge with a sign saying, 'Warning. Eleven-foot clearance'. 'Dammit,' says Barry. 'And our truck is twelve foot high.' Michael looks out of the window and checks for onlookers. 'I say we go for it,' he says. 'There's no one out here to report us.'

✳ A man goes to a travel agent to book his summer holiday. 'Last year you sold me a holiday to Bermuda and my wife got pregnant,' says the man. 'The year before it was Monte Carlo and my wife got pregnant again. And the year before that it was Hong Kong and my wife got pregnant then as well.' 'I see,' says the travel clerk. 'And what did you have in mind this year?' 'Somewhere cheaper,' replies the man. 'So she can come with me for a change.'

✳ A husband and wife rent an old country cottage for a break. The wife goes to take a bath and only emerges three hours later. 'It doesn't usually take you so long to get ready,' says the husband. 'No,' replies the wife. 'But there's no curtains. I had to get out of the tub every five minutes and breathe on the windows.'

✳ A man is having breakfast at a greasy spoon café when three bikers come in looking for trouble. The first biker spits in the man's food. The second pours coffee over the man's head, and the third pulls away his chair so he falls over. Without a word the man gets up and walks out. 'Not much of a man,' says one of the bikers to the waitress. 'Nope,' replies the waitress. 'And he's not much of a driver either, he just drove his lorry over three bikes.'

✳ A river pilot is guiding a ship up an estuary. Suddenly the ship grounds itself. The captain is furious. He yells at the pilot, 'You said you knew every sandbank in this river!' 'I do,' says the pilot. 'And that was one of them.'

✳ A passenger cruise ship passes a small desert island. Everyone watches as a tatty-looking bearded man runs out on the beach and starts shouting and waving his hands. 'Who's that?' asks one of the passengers. 'I've no idea,' replies the captain. 'But every year we sail past and he goes nuts.'

✳ A train steward calls the police after coming across a young couple having sex in a carriage. The young man is arrested for having a first-class ride with a second-class ticket.

✳ A woman rings the lost property office of the railway company and asks them if they've found a stray octopus – they ask her what colour it is.

✳ A young man asks his father, a preacher, if he can borrow the family car. 'Only if you get your hair cut,' says his father. 'Why?' asks the son, 'Moses had long hair, and so did Samson, and Jesus.' 'They did,' replies Dad. 'And they also walked everywhere.'

✳ Don't forget, when in Rome... be an awkward bastard and do as the Belgians do.

✳ Fifty men are crammed into a train carriage when one shouts, 'The next carriage is completely empty!' So they all get into that one.

'If you look like your passport photograph, in all probability you need the holiday.' *Earl Wilson*

✳ Harry is being interviewed for a job as a railway signalman. 'What would you do if two trains were approaching each other on the same line?' asks the interviewer. 'I'd switch the points in the signal box,' replies Harry. 'And what if the signal switch was broken?' asks the interviewer. 'I'd use the manual lever,' replies Harry. 'And what if that didn't work?' asks the interviewer. 'I'd use the emergency phone to call the next signal box,' says Harry. 'And what if there was no answer?' asks the interviewer. 'I'd ring my uncle and tell him to come over,' replies Harry. 'What good would that do?' asks the interviewer. 'None,' replies Harry. 'But he's never seen a train crash.'

✳ Harry went to Scotland on a sleeper train but didn't get a wink of sleep. There was a worried midget in the top bunk who spent all night pacing up and down.

✳ I got some travel sweets but they were useless. I ate the whole packet. Didn't go anywhere.

✳ If ignorance is bliss, then tourists are in a constant state of euphoria.

✳ The best time to visit Paris is between 18 and 34.

✳ The navigator of the *QEII* is steering the ship through thick fog. He turns to the captain, 'Sir, I think something is wrong with our compass.' 'Why do you say that?' asks the captain. The navigator replies, 'We've just been overtaken by a Number 8 bus.'

✳ Three passengers are on a train discussing why the train company is losing money. 'Bad management,' says one. 'Too many staff,' says another. 'Not enough investment,' says the third. Then they hear the ticket inspector coming and all run to hide in the toilets.

✳ Tom and Dick are comparing notes on their summer holiday. 'I was staying in a hotel in Poole,' says Tom. 'In Dorset?' asks Dick. 'Certainly,' says Tom. 'I'd recommend it to anyone.'

❋ Two blondes are waiting at a bus stop. A bus pulls up and one of the blondes says to the driver, 'Will this bus take me to 5th Avenue?' The bus driver says, 'No. Sorry.' The other blonde, smiles, and says, 'Will it take me?'

❋ Two women meet on a cruise ship. One says, 'This is my first cruise. My husband saved for ages to send me on this trip.' 'Oh,' says the other. 'Is this your first? I've been on twenty cruises. Mind you, my husband works for Cunard.' The first woman says, 'Well mine works hard too but there's no need to swear!'

❋ What happened to the man who locked himself in his truck? His friends had to use a coathanger to get him out.

❋ What's the best cure for sea-sickness? Sit under a tree.

twins

I used to be twins. My mother has a picture of me when I was two.

Man, to friend, 'My wife is one of a pair of twins.' Friend, 'Really? How do you tell them apart?' Man, 'Her brother has a beard.'

Why did the American conjoined twins emigrate to the UK? So the other one had a chance to drive.

UGLINESS

❋ 'I knew a girl so ugly, I took her to the top of the Empire State Building and planes started to attack her.' *Rodney Dangerfield*

❋ 'I knew a girl so ugly, she had a face like a saint – a Saint Bernard!' *Rodney Dangerfield*

❋ A doctor examines a woman and takes her husband aside. 'I don't want to alarm you,' he says, 'but I don't like the way your wife looks.' 'Me neither, doctor,' said the husband. 'But she's a great cook and real good with the kids.'

✳ 'I knew a girl so ugly, the last time I saw a mouth like hers it had a hook on the end of it.' *Rodney Dangerfield*

✳ 'I knew a girl so ugly, they use her in prisons to cure sex offenders.' *Rodney Dangerfield*

✳ 'I was so ugly when I was born the doctor slapped my mother.' *Henny Youngman*

✳ 'I'm so ugly. My father carries around the picture of the kid who came with his wallet.' *Rodney Dangerfield*

✳ 'Yes, darling, let me cover your face with kisses – on second thoughts, just let me cover your face.' *Groucho Marx*

✳ He has the sort of face only a mother could love, and apparently his mother hates it.

✳ A girl walks into a supermarket and buys a bar of soap, a toothbrush, a tube of toothpaste, a pint of milk and a single frozen dinner. The checkout guy looks at her and says, 'Single, huh?' The girl replies, 'Yes. How'd you guess?' He says, 'Because you're ugly.'

✳ A woman is sitting in the park with her baby when a man comes over and says, 'I'm sorry, lady, but that's the ugliest baby I've ever seen!' The woman bursts into tears. Another man sees this and comes over to comfort her. He hands her a tissue and says, 'Miss, I don't know what that guy said, but it's not worth crying over.' She smiles back at him as he reaches into his pocket. 'You cheer up now. Look. I've even got some peanuts for your monkey!'

✳ Don't you need a licence to be that ugly?

✳ He was an ugly baby. His mother only started to get morning sickness after he was born.

✳ I went to see my doctor. 'Doctor, every morning when I get up and look in the mirror I feel like throwing up. What's wrong with me?' He replied, 'I don't know, but your eyesight is perfect.'

'I knew a girl so ugly that she was known as a two-bagger. That's when you put a bag over your head in case the bag over her head falls off.' *Rodney Dangerfield*

※ He was so ugly, when he was a baby his mother left him on the steps of a police station – then went and handed herself in.

※ How do you know if you're really ugly? Dogs hump your leg with their eyes closed.

※ I dream of being be rich, powerful and well respected. And while I'm dreaming, I wish you weren't so damn ugly.

※ If someone tells you you're big boned and not conventionally good-looking, don't take it the wrong way. What they mean is you're fat and ugly.

※ I wouldn't say my wife is ugly, but every time she sunbathes on the lawn a pair of vultures starts circling the garden.

※ If I were as ugly as you are, I wouldn't say hello, I'd say boo!

※ If you were cast as Lady Godiva the horse would steal the show.

※ I'm not saying he's ugly, he just looks as if his hobby is stepping on rakes.

※ Moonlight becomes you, but total darkness suits you even better.

※ Oh my God! Look at you – anyone else hurt in the accident?

※ Polly wasn't a very attractive girl, all the boys used to chase her but they gave her a five-mile head start.

※ The camera always caught her worst side – her outside.

※ They broke the mould when they made him. In fact, I think they might have broken the mould before they made him.

❋ Tom, to Dick, 'Hey, have you ever gone to bed with an ugly woman?' Dick, 'No, but I've woken up with plenty.'

❋ What are you going to do for a face when the baboon wants his ass back?

❋ Wife, to husband, 'I just got back from the beauty shop.' Husband, 'What happened? Was it closed?'

❋ You have a face designed in a wind tunnel.

❋ You should have been born in the Dark Ages – you look terrible in the light.

❋ You were born ugly and built to last.
❋ You're so ugly, robbers give you their masks to wear.

❋ You've got that far-away look. The farther you get, the better you look.

❋ My wife is so ugly my friends are convinced I married her for her money.

❋ UNDERSTANDING

❋ 'Honey, just because I don't care doesn't mean I don't understand!' *Homer Simpson*

❋ 'Why, a child of four could understand this report. Run outside and get me a child of four. I can't make head or tail of it.' *Groucho Marx*

❋ If you're not confused then you don't really understand what's going on.

uniqueness

Always remember you're unique – just like everyone else.

So what if you're one in a million. That means there are more than 5,000 of you.

⚫VASECTOMY

✳ A redneck goes to his doctor to get a vasectomy but is horrified to find out how much they cost. 'I could do you a cheap one,' says the doctor. 'But it's painful.' 'I can take it,' says the redneck, so the doctor hands him a large firecracker. 'Take this home,' he says. 'Light it and hold it in your hand while counting to ten.' 'How's that going to give me a vasectomy?' asks the redneck. 'You'll find out,' says the doctor. The redneck takes the firecracker home, lights it, and holds it in his right hand while he counts to ten. When he gets to five he tucks the firecracker between his legs and holds up his left hand, '…six, seven, eight…'

✳ What's the definition of macho? Jogging home after a vasectomy.

⚫VEGETARIANISM

✳ Eating vegetables is much crueller than eating animals. At least the animals have a chance to run away.

✳ Helpful advice if you have vegetarians coming to dinner. Just serve them a nice bit of steak or veal. Since they're always going on about how tofu and Quorn taste like the real thing they shouldn't notice the difference.

✳ If we aren't supposed to eat animals, why are they made of meat?

✳ To attract a vegetarian, make a noise like a wounded vegetable.

vices

'He hasn't a single redeeming vice.' *Oscar Wilde*

waiting

If I'm not back in five minutes – just wait longer.

✹WAR AND MiLiTARY

✳ 'I was classified '4P' by the draftboard. In the event of war, I'm a hostage.' *Woody Allen*

✳ 'Military justice is to justice what military music is to music.' *Groucho Marx*

✳ 'Men are brave enough to go to war, but they are not brave enough to get a bikini wax.' *Rita Rudner*

✳ A colonel is reviewing the troops. One man he passes is sporting a huge erection. 'Sergeant Major!' the colonel shouts. 'Give this man 30 days compassionate home leave.' A few months later the same thing occurs with the same man. 'Sergeant Major! Give this man another 30 days compassionate home leave!' barks the colonel. A few months later exactly the same thing happens. The colonel is furious. 'Sergeant Major! Haven't we given this man two compassionate home leaves?' 'Yes, sir,' says the sergeant major. 'Then what's the problem? Why has he got that huge erection?' asks the colonel. The sergeant major replies, 'It's you he's fond of, sir.'

✳ A group of soldiers take a first-aid course. After they've finished they're given a test by their instructor. The instructor points to one of the solders and says, 'The sergeant major sustains a head injury during a cross-country march. What do you do about it?' The soldier replies, 'I wrap a tourniquet around his neck and tighten it until the bleeding stops.'

✳ A group of US marines are stranded on a Pacific island after the war. After a few months the sergeant decides he has to do something to boost moral. 'Good news, men,' he says. 'We're going to have a change of underwear.' It's not much but the marines are cheered up. The sergeant continues, 'Johnson you change with Kropowlski. Kropowlski you change with Peterson...'

✳ A knight and his men return to their castle after a hard day of fighting. 'How are we faring?' asks the king. 'Sire,' replies the knight. 'I have been robbing and pillaging on your behalf all day, burning the towns of your enemies in the west.' 'What?' shrieks the king. 'I don't have any enemies to the west.' 'Oh,' says the knight. 'Well, you do now.'

✻ Why is it twice as easy to train Iraqi fighter pilots as US pilots? You only have to teach Iraqi pilots to take off.

✻ A man goes into a pub and points at a beer tap. 'Do you want a pint?' asks the barman. The man nods and the barman notices that he has a huge scar across his throat. 'Where did you get that?' asks the barman. The man manages to croak, 'Falklands.' 'Blimey,' says the barman. 'Well, have this one on the house, mate. You boys did a great job over there.' The man croaks, 'Muchas gracias.'

✻ A navy psychiatrist is interviewing a potential recruit. The psychiatrist says, 'What would you do if you looked out of that window and saw a battleship coming down the street?' The recruit replies, 'I'd grab a torpedo and sink it.' 'Really? And where would you get a torpedo?' asks the psychiatrist. The recruit replies, 'The same place you got your battleship!'

✻ A sniper takes a pot-shot at a general visiting the front line. 'We know exactly where he is, sir, ' says one of soldiers. 'He's been up there for weeks.' 'Then why don't you see him off?' asks the general. The soldier replies, 'Because if we got rid of him they might replace him with someone who can actually shoot straight.'

✻ A US army platoon is on manoeuvres in the Florida swamps. The men are running low on water so the sergeant tells a private to go down to the creek and fill up their canteens. 'But, Sarge,' says the private. 'I saw an alligator in the creek.' 'Don't be such a coward,' replies the sergeant. 'That alligator is four times as frightened of you as you are of it.' 'He might be,' replies the private. 'But even if he's only twice as frightened as me that water still won't be fit to drink.'

✻ An admiral is standing on the deck of his battleship when the enemy is spotted on the horizon. 'Fetch my red shirt,' says the admiral to a nearby midshipman. 'If I'm wounded fighting this enemy ship I don't want the men to see that I'm bleeding.' 'Excuse me, sir,' says the midshipman. 'But it's not one ship, there are fifteen.' 'In that case,' replies the admiral, 'forget the shirt and pick up my brown trousers.'

✻ What should Baghdad get for its air defence system? A refund.

✻ Why did so many black GIs get killed in Vietnam? Because every time the sergeant shouted, 'Get down!' they stood up and started dancing.

'Remember, men, we're fighting for this woman's honour – which is probably more than she ever did.' *Groucho Marx*

✻ An Israeli soldier asks his commanding officer for a three-day pass. The officer says, 'Are you crazy? You have to do something spectacular to get a pass like that!' So the soldier goes off and comes back a day later in an Arab tank. The officer is impressed. 'How did you do it?' he asks. 'Well,' says the soldier. 'I jumped in a tank, went to the border, and drove along it till I saw an Arab tank. Then I shouted to the driver, "Hey! Do you want to get a three-day pass?" And we exchanged tanks.'

✻ An army fort in the Wild West is about to be attacked by renegades. The captain sends for his trustiest Indian scout. 'Use all your tracking skills to estimate the sort of war party we're up against,' orders the captain. The scout lays down and put his ear to the ground. 'Big war party,' he says. 'One hundred braves in warpaint. Two chiefs, one on a black horse, one on a white mare. Also a medicine man with a limp.' 'Good God!' exclaims the captain. 'You can tell all that just by listening to the ground?' 'No, sir,' replies the scout. 'I'm looking under the gate.'

✻ Three admirals, one in the French navy, one in the American navy, and one in the Royal Navy, are discussing bravery. 'I'll show you how brave a French sailor is,' says the French admiral, who then orders a French seaman to climb a 25-metre flagpole and jump off the top – which he does. The American admiral says his men are much braver. He calls over a US sailor and orders him to jump off a 50-metre flagpole – which he does. The Royal Navy admiral says he can do better and calls over a British seaman. 'See that 100-metre flagpole?' says the admiral. 'Climb up to the top and jump off it.' The seaman looks at the flagpole, then looks at the admiral, and says, 'What? Jump off that thing? You're out of your bloody mind, sir.' The admiral turns to his colleagues and says, 'Now that's bravery.'

✻ Three military men are introduced to each other. One steps forwards and says, 'John Collingworth, General. Married. Two sons, both doctors.' The second one steps forwards and says, 'Marcus Hill, General. Married. Two sons, both lawyers.' The third man steps forwards and says, 'Bill Marsh. Lance corporal. Not married. Two sons, both generals.'

✳ To avoid getting drafted a young man slips into a nunnery to hide from some MPs who are after him. Desperate he approaches a nun and asks her to hide him. 'Get under my robes,' says the nun. 'No one will look for you there.' The nun lifts up her robes and the man says, 'Hey, that's a fine pair of legs you've got there, sister.' 'Yeah, well if you look any higher you'll see a fine set of balls,' replies the nun. 'I didn't want to get drafted either.'

✳ A boy says to his father, 'I've decided to join the army.' 'Oh no, you're not,' says his father. 'You're not even 16. Legally you're still an infant.' 'That's all right,' replies the boy. 'Then I'll join the infantry.'

✳ A soldier receives a 'Dear John' letter from his sweetheart. Apart from breaking up with him she also asks him to return the photograph he has of her. The soldier collects a couple of dozen girlfriend pictures from his mates and sends them to his ex together with her photograph. In the package he includes a note saying, 'Sorry! Can't remember which one you are. Please pick out your picture and return the rest.'

✳ A tourist is walking through Jerusalem when he comes across the tomb of the unknown soldier, however, the inscription reads 'Solomon Goldstein. b. 1906 d.1966'. Puzzled, the tourist asks one of the guards how the solder can be 'unknown' when the tomb has his name on it. 'Well, Solomon had quite a reputation in some circles. He was very well known as a very good tailor. He was a very good tailor indeed. But as a soldier…he was terrible.'

✳ What do spooks call their navy? The ghost guard.

✪WEATHER

✳ A film crew is on location in the Arizona desert. One day an old Indian goes up to the director and says, 'Tomorrow rain.' The next day it rains. Next day the Indian goes up to the director and says, 'Tomorrow storm.' The next day there's a hailstorm. The director is impressed and hires the Indian to predict the weather. However, after several successful predictions, the old Indian doesn't show up for two weeks. Finally the director sends for him. 'I have to shoot a big scene tomorrow,' he says. 'What will the weather be like?' The Indian shrugs his shoulders and says, 'Don't know. Radio is broken.'

✻ A motorist is making his way down a flooded road after a night of torrential rain. Suddenly he sees a man's head sticking out of a large puddle. He stops his car and asks the man if he needs a lift. 'No thanks,' says the man. 'I'm on my bike.'

✻ A rambler sees an old rustic character standing in a field holding a short length of rope. 'What's the rope for?' asks the rambler. 'Tis an old country way of telling the weather,' says the rustic. 'And how does it work?' asks the rambler. 'Well,' replies the rustic. 'When it swings about, it's windy. And when it's wet, it's raining.'

✻ A ship's captain radios a lighthouse keeper, 'Radio reception is very bad. Please spell out your weather report.' The keeper replies, 'W-E-T-H-O-R R-E-P-O-R-T.' The captain says, 'My God, that's the worst spell of weather I've had in a long time.'

✻ Harry gets a job as a weatherman in the Far East; however, try as he might, he can never get a forecast right. Eventually he's sacked and has to fly home. A friend asks why he's back so soon. Harry replies, 'The climate didn't agree with me.'

✻ Harry had a fantastic country house with two wings, sadly it flew off the last time they had a big storm.

✻ I'm saving up for a rainy day. So far I've got a sou'wester, two macintoshes and a canoe.

✻ It was so cold the politicians had their hands in their own pockets.

✻ Little Johnny walks into his classroom wearing a single glove. His teacher asks him what he's doing. 'Well ma'am,' says Johnny. 'I was watching the weather programme on TV and it said it was going to be sunny, but on the other hand it could get quite cold.'

✻ People always complain about the weather, but no one ever seems to do anything about it.

✻ The drought here is terrible. The lawn's cracked, the plants have all died because of the hosepipe ban, and I can't wash my car – and do we see any famous Africans getting together to do a charity single?

✳ Tom arrives at a hotel in a Scottish village on a cold, grey, drizzly day. The weather remains the same for two weeks. Exasperated, Tom stops a little boy in the street. 'Does the weather here ever change?' he asks. 'I don't know,' replies the boy. 'I'm only six.'

✳ I wouldn't say we had wet weather in our town but even the morning dew has an undercurrent.

✳ What's a bigamist? An Italian fog.

✳ The weather in our town is incredibly wet, the buses don't have brakes they have anchors.

without one another

How can I miss you if you won't go away?

If you can't live without me – why aren't you dead already?

I'm so miserable without you, it's almost like having you around.

✪WORDS OF WISDOM

✳ 'If you can't beat them, arrange to have them beaten.' *George Carlin*

✳ 'The bigger they are, the worse they smell.' *George Carlin*

✳ 'The day after tomorrow is the third day of the rest of your life.' *George Carlin*

✳ A friend is someone you can call to help you move. A best friend is someone you can call to help you move a body.

✳ A spoken contract isn't worth the paper it's written on.

✳ A thing not worth doing isn't worth doing well.

✳ All generalisations are false.

✳ All things are possible, except skiing through a revolving door.

✳ Always keep your words soft and sweet – just in case you have to eat them.

✳ As you journey through life, take a moment every now and then to think about others – as they could well be plotting something.

✳ Better to be occasionally cheated than perpetually suspicious.

✳ Do not meddle in the affairs of dragons – because you are crunchy and taste good with ketchup.

✳ Don't become superstitious – it's bad luck.

✳ Don't hate yourself in the morning – sleep till noon.

✳ Don't kick a man when he's down unless you're absolutely certain he won't get up.

✳ Don't take life too seriously, after all no one gets out alive.

✳ Drive carefully – it's not only cars that can be recalled by their maker.

✳ Everybody lies, but it doesn't matter since nobody listens.

✳ Everyone seems normal, until you get to know them.

✳ Everywhere is walking distance if you have the time.

✳ For every action, there is an equal and opposite criticism.

✳ Good judgement comes from bad experience, and a lot of that comes from bad judgement.

✳ If a band of motorcyclists, all wearing black leather vests and covered with tattoos, cuts you off on the highway, just think the obscenities quietly to yourself.

✳ Good news is just life's way of keeping you off balance.

✳ If a thing's worth doing, it would have been done already.

✳ If flattery gets you nowhere, try bribery.

✳ If life gives you lemons, squeeze the juice into a water pistol and shoot other people in the eyes.

✳ If you can smile when things go wrong, you have someone in mind to blame.

✳ If you can tell the difference between good advice and bad advice – you don't really need advice.

✳ If you live in a glass house, you should change clothes in the basement.

✳ Intelligence has much less practical application than you'd think.

✳ If you lend someone £20 and never see that person again, it was probably worth it.

✳ It is easier to get forgiveness than permission.

✳ It's a small world. So you gotta use your elbows a lot.

✳ It's better to have someone inside the tent peeing out, than outside peeing in.

✳ It's easier to suffer in silence if you're sure someone is watching.

✳ Most of us know a good thing as soon as someone else sees it.

✳ Needing someone is like needing a parachute. If they aren't there the first time you need them, chances are you won't be needing them again.

'If you can't be a good example, then you'll just have to be a horrible warning.' *Catherine Aird*

'To do is to be.' *Descartes*, 'To be is to do.' *Voltaire*, 'Do be do be do.' *Frank Sinatra*

✳ Never entrust your life to a surgeon with more than three Band Aids on his fingers.

✳ Never get in line at the bank behind someone wearing a ski mask.

✳ Never go to a plastic surgeon whose favourite artist is Picasso.

✳ Never hit a man with glasses – use your fist.

✳ Never try to teach a pig to sing. It wastes your time and annoys the pig.

✳ Never underestimate the power of stupid people in large groups.

✳ No man is really successful until his mother-in-law admits it.

✳ Not one shred of evidence supports the notion that life is serious.

✳ One good turn usually gets most of the blanket.

✳ Opportunities always look bigger going than coming.

✳ Quitters never win, winners never quit. But those who never win and never quit are idiots.

✳ Show me a man who has both feet on the ground, and I'll show you a man who can't put on his trousers.

✳ Support bacteria. It's the only culture some people have.

✳ Talk is cheap because supply exceeds demand.

✳ The meek shall inherit the Earth but not till the rest of us are done with it.

✳ The severity of the itch is inversely proportional to the ability to reach it.

✳ The 50-50-90 rule: any time you have a 50-50 chance of getting something right, there's a 90 per cent probability you'll get it wrong.

✳ The grass is always greener on TV.

✳ The great thing about teamwork is that you never have to take all the blame yourself.

✳ The lion shall lie down with the lamb. But the lamb probably won't get much sleep.

✳ The sooner you fall behind, the more time you have to catch up.

✳ There is no substitute for genuine lack of preparation.

✳ Those who can't laugh at themselves leave the job to others.

✳ Too many people find fault as if there's a reward for it.

✳ We cannot change the direction of the wind – but we can adjust our sails.

✳ Whatever hits the fan will not be evenly distributed.

✳ When it's you against the world, I'd bet on the world.

✳ You can fool some of the people some of the time, and that is sufficient.

✳ You're never quite as stupid as when you think you know everything.

✳ A friend in need is a pest indeed.

✳ A good day is when you wake up without a chalk outline around your body.

✳ A person needs only two tools: oil and tape. If it doesn't move and it should, use oil. If it moves and it shouldn't, use tape.

✳ Being happy doesn't mean everything's perfect; it just means you've decided to see beyond the imperfections.

✳ Being miserable because of a bad former relationship just proves that the other person was right about you.

✳ Don't bite your nails, especially if you're a carpenter.

✳ If you scratch your rear, don't bite your fingernails.

✳ If you try and don't succeed, cheat. Repeat until caught. Then lie.

✳ If you woke up breathing, congratulations! You have another chance!

✳ Never do card tricks for the group you play poker with.

✳ The early bird gets the worm, so don't be an early worm.

✳ There are two types of people – some are in the swim, the others are in the soup.

✳ You can't fall off the floor.

🍎 WORK AND BUSINESS

✳ A man goes to his bank manager for advice, 'How do I set up a small business?' he asks. 'Easy,' replies the bank manager. 'Buy a big one and wait.'

✳ A businessman gets on an elevator in his office building. A woman already inside greets him saying, 'T-G-I-F.' He smiles at her and replies, 'S-H-I-T.' The woman looked at him, puzzled, and again says, 'T-G-I-F.' Again the man answers her with, 'S-H-I-T.' The woman says, 'Do you know what I'm saying? T-G-I-F means, "Thank God it's Friday."' 'I know,' replies the man. 'But S-H-I-T means, "Sorry, Honey, it's Thursday."'

✳ 'We're overpaying him but he's worth it.' *Samuel Goldwyn*

✳ A man asks a judge to let him off jury service. Judge, 'But surely your firm can manage without you for a few weeks.' The man replies, 'Certainly. They can manage without me altogether – and I don't want them to find out.'

✳ A man takes the ferry to work every day but one morning he oversleeps. He hurries to the docks and sees the ferry ten feet from the quayside. Determined not to miss it he takes a running jump and, by the skin of his teeth, just manages to grab hold of the ferry's passenger rail. One of the crew helps pull him up over the side. 'Y'know,' he says. 'If you'd waited another second or two we'd have docked.'

✳ A new employee is called into the personnel manager's office. 'What's the meaning of this?' asks the manager. 'When you applied for your job, you told us you had five years' experience. Now we discover this is the first job you've ever had.' 'Yes,' replies the young man. 'But your ad also said you wanted somebody with imagination.'

✳ A small child asks a businessman, 'What does two and two make?' The businessman replies, 'Are you buying or selling?'

✳ According to the latest statistics, there are twelve million Americans who aren't working. And there are plenty more if you count the ones with jobs.

✳ After ten years working for the same firm he was finally given the key to the executive bathrooms. Then after he'd given them a good clean, he had to give it back.

✳ Any suggestions on how to rescue the company, please put them in the suggestion box down the hall. And don't forget to flush it.

✳ An art collector is walking down the road when he notices a mangy cat in a shop doorway lapping milk from a saucer. He realises that the saucer is extremely old and valuable, so walks into the store and offers to buy the cat for two pounds. The store owner replies, 'I'm sorry, but the cat isn't for sale. The collector says, 'Please, I need a cat around the house to catch mice. I'll pay you twenty pounds for it.' The owner says 'Okay. Sold.' And hands over the cat. The collector continues, 'Hey, for the twenty pounds I wonder if you could throw in that old saucer. The cat's used to it and it'll save me from having to buy a dish.' The store owner says, 'Sorry, chum. That's my lucky saucer. So far this week I've sold sixty-eight cats.'

✳ Business is looking up. It's flat on its back.

✳ Applebottoms' Apple Pie and Associated Apple Pastry Products factory has announced very disappointing results. They've had 500 men and women working non-stop all year and only managed to produced a single triangular apple pastry. The manager admitted this represented a very small turnover.

✳ At work we now have one day a week where we just leave the phones ringing and don't answer them. Which is good because it really can get quite stressful at the Samaritans.

✳ Chairman, to his directors, 'Gentlemen. Last month we were teetering on the edge of a precipice. Today we are going to take a great step forward.'

✳ God is chatting to the Archangel Gabriel. 'Y'know I just created a 24-hour period of alternating light and darkness.' 'Wow,' replies Gabriel. 'What are you going to do now?' 'I think I'll call it a day,' replies God.

✳ Harry operates a one-day dry-cleaning service. People give him clothes on the understanding that one day they might get them back again.

✳ He made his fortune walking the streets selling batteries – every Christmas morning, just after the kids opened their presents.

✳ I work for a really good firm. They let me work from home and they gave me a company car. Of course because I work from home, they gave me a car that doesn't work.

✳ Helium was up, feathers were down. Paper was stationary. Fluorescent tubing was dimmed in light trading. Knives were up sharply. Pencils lost a few points. Elevators rose, while escalators continued their slow decline. Mining equipment hit rock bottom. Diapers remain unchanged. Balloon prices were inflated. Scott Tissue touched a new bottom.

✳ How do you get 20 vice-presidents in a mini-van? Promote one and watch the other 19 crawl up his backside.

✳ I get home so seldom that if I'm seen around the house the neighbours gossip.

✳ I'd quit my job but I need the sleep.

✳ If lawyers are disbarred and clergymen defrocked, doesn't it follow that electricians can be delighted, musicians denoted, cowboys deranged, models deposed, tree surgeons debarked, and dry cleaners depressed?

✳ If work was so good the rich would keep more of it for themselves.

✳ It was always my dream to work at home and now it's come true in a way – my wife's thrown me out so I have to sleep at the office.

✳ It's terrible the hours I have to do in my job. I'm only at home with my family six weeks in the entire year. But it's all right. The six weeks soon pass.

✳ My office has sick building syndrome. I got to work yesterday and the building wasn't there. It phoned in later saying it had a sore throat.

✳ No one could ever call me a quitter. Do you know why? I always get fired.

✳ One day the manager of a brokers' firm walks past a new employee counting put and call slips. The guy does it faster than anyone he has ever seen. 'That's amazing,' says the manager. 'Where did you learn to count like that?' 'Yale,' answers the employee. 'Yale? I don't believe it. I went to Yale too. What's your name?' 'Yimmy Yohnson,' says the employee.

✳ Things are very bad at the shop, a man bought something with a £50 note and we had to make him a partner before we could give him his change.

✳ Two business owners are comparing working practices. One says to the other, 'I make sure each of my employees takes a week off every two months.' 'Why on earth would you do that?' asks the other. The first replies, 'It's the best way of finding out which ones I can do without.'

✳ Sure I multi-task. I read in the bathroom.

'If you really want something in this life, you have to work for it. Now, quiet. They're about to announce the lottery numbers!'
Homer Simpson

✳ This isn't an office; it's Hell with fluorescent lighting.

✳ Tom is driving along in his car when his boss calls him on his mobile. 'I'm promoting you to Sales Manager,' he says. Tom is so surprised he almost loses control of the car. A few seconds later the phone rings. It's the boss again, 'Henderson has resigned, I'm promoting you to take his place as Sales Director.' Again Tom is so surprised the car swerves all over the place. Seconds later the phone rings a third time. Again it's the boss. 'Harris has had a heart attack,' he says. 'You're the new Managing Director.' Tom is so astonished he loses control completely and crashes the car into the embankment. Later a policeman asks him what caused the accident. Tom says, 'I careered off the road.'

✳ Two businessmen are fishing in a rowing boat, when a storm blows up and capsizes them. One of the men can swim but the other can't. 'Can you float alone?' shouts the swimmer to his sinking partner. The partner shouts back, 'This is no time to talk shop!'

✳ A firm advertises for a 'Problem Solver' with a salary of £100,000. Tom goes for an interview and is offered the job on the spot. 'That's great,' says Tom. 'But tell me, how can you afford to pay me such a high salary?' 'That,' says his employer, 'is your first problem.'

✳ Who was the world's greatest financier? Noah – he managed to float a company when the whole word was in liquidation.

✳ Two teams from American and Japanese corporations have a boat race. On the big day the Japanese win by a mile and the discouraged Americans hire a consulting firm to investigate the problem. The findings are that the Japanese team had eight people rowing and one person steering, while the American team had one person rowing and eight people steering. Based on these results the American team is completely reorganised to include four steering managers, three area steering managers, and a new performance review system for the person rowing the boat to provide work incentive. The following year the Japanese win again, so the Americans lay off the rower for poor performance and give the managers a bonus for discovering the problem.

✳ Wanted: Man to test for gas leaks with a lit match. Must be willing to travel.

☕WORK AND BUSINESS: INTERVIEWS AND APPLICATIONS

❋ A young man goes for a job interview and is asked what sort of employment package he expects. 'What I expect is a £30,000 a year starting salary. Six weeks holiday a year and a Jaguar for a company car.' 'Okay,' says the interviewer. 'How about this? We pay you £40,000 a year rising to £60,000 after two years. You get eight weeks annual leave. You get your own secretary and PA and we promote you to board level after four years?' 'Wow!' says the young man. 'You've got to be joking!' 'I am,' replies the interviewer. 'But you started it.'

❋ An applicant for a job with the US Federal Government is filling out the application form. He comes to the question: 'Do you favour the overthrow of the United States Government by force, subversion, or violence?' After thinking about it he ticks 'violence'.

❋ An applicant is being interviewed for admission to a prominent medical school. 'Tell me,' enquires the interviewer. 'Where do you expect to be ten years from now?' 'Well, let's see,' replies the student. 'It's Wednesday afternoon. So I guess I'll be on the golf course.'

❋ An applicant is filling out a job application. When he comes to the question, 'Have you ever been arrested?' He answers, 'No.' The next question, intended for people who had answered in the affirmative, was 'Why?' The applicant wrote, 'Never got caught.'

❋ Harry had to bend over backwards to get his job, although I believe the recruitment officer had to go before a tribunal as a result.

❋ Employer, to job applicant, 'In this job we need someone who's responsible.' Applicant, 'I'm the one you want. On my last job, every time something went wrong, they said I was responsible.'

❋ Employer, to job applicant, 'Do you think you can handle a variety of work?' Applicant, 'I ought to, I've had ten different jobs in four months.'

✳ Four job applicants are told that they have to answer a single question and the one who gives the best answer will get the job. The question is 'What's the fastest thing in the world?' The first applicant comes in and gives his answer, 'Thought is the fastest thing,' he says. 'It's instantaneous.' The second applicant comes in and says, 'A blink is the fastest thing. It's a reflex that you don't even have to think about.' The third applicant comes in and says, 'It must be electricity. You can throw a switch and 20 miles away a light will come on.' Finally the fourth applicant shuffles in looking very ill. 'I guess the fastest thing in the world must be diarrhoea,' he says. 'Last night in bed I had terrible cramps in my guts and before I could think, blink, or put on the light...'

✳ Harry goes for a job interview. Sitting next to him is a well-spoken applicant wearing a Cambridge University tie. After a moment the applicant notices Harry's apparel. 'I say,' says the well-spoken man. 'I see you're wearing a Cambridge tie as well.' 'Yup,' replies Harry. 'I hope you don't mind me saying,' observes the applicant. 'But you don't look like the sort of chap who'd have gone to Cambridge.' 'Nope,' says Harry. 'Tell me,' asks the applicant, 'when you were at Cambridge, what did you do there?' 'I bought a tie,' says Harry.

✳ 'Why do you want to be a joiner?' 'Because I'm the sociable type.'

✳ King Kong applies for a job as a lifeguard. 'Can you swim?' asks the interviewer. 'No,' he replies. 'But I can wade out for miles.'

✪ WORK AND BUSINESS: OFFICE LORE

✳ 'If it ain't broke, break it.' *George Carlin*

✳ A clean desk is a sign of a cluttered desk drawer.

✳ According to my calculations the problem doesn't exist.

✳ Don't be irreplaceable. If you can't be replaced, you can't be promoted.

✳ Don't piss me off. I'm running out of places to hide the bodies.

✳ Avoid employing unlucky people – throw half the CVs in the bin without reading them.

✳ Doing a job *right* the first time gets the job done. Doing the job *wrong* fourteen times gives you job security.

✳ Go ahead and take risks. Just be sure that everything will turn out okay.

✳ How do I set a laser printer to stun?

✳ I can only please one person per day. Today is not your day. Tomorrow is not looking good either.

✳ I don't work here. I'm a consultant.

✳ I love deadlines. I especially like the 'Whooshing' sound as they go flying by.

✳ I must be a proctologist – I work with assholes!

✳ I thought at one point I could see the light at the end of the tunnel – turned out to be some bastard with a torch bringing me more work.

✳ I thought I wanted a career. It turns out I just wanted a pay cheque.

✳ If everything's going much better than expected it can only mean one thing – you've overlooked something.

✳ If it wasn't for the last minute, nothing would ever get done.

✳ If you've got to work for an idiot you may as well work for yourself.

✳ In an office the authority of a person is inversely proportional to the number of pens they are carrying.

✳ Monday is an awful way to spend $\frac{1}{7}$th of your life.

✳ Never be afraid to try something new. Remember, amateurs built the Ark. Professionals built the *Titanic*.

❋ Never put off until tomorrow what you can avoid altogether.

❋ Never do today that which will become someone else's responsibility tomorrow.

❋ Of course I don't look busy. I did it right the first time.

❋ Process and procedure are the last hiding place of people without the wit and wisdom to do their job properly.

❋ Sarcasm is just one more service we offer.

❋ Success always occurs in private, and failure in full view.

❋ Talk is cheap – supply exceeds demand.

❋ Teamwork – means never having to take all the blame.

❋ Tell me what you need, and I'll tell you how to get along without it.

❋ The screw-up fairy has visited us again.

❋ The world is full of willing people. Half willing to work, the other half willing to let them.

❋ There is always one more imbecile than you counted on.

❋ Too much ambition results in promotion to a job you can't do.

❋ Warning: dates in calendar are closer than they appear.

❋ Who is General Failure and why is he reading my hard disk?

❋ Work harder. People on state benefits depend on you.

❋ A cubicle is just a padded cell without a door.

❋ A pat on the back is only a few inches from a kick in the butt.

✳ You have to get 100 per cent behind your boss. It really is the only way to stab him in the back.

✳ You should give 100 per cent at work: 12 per cent Monday; 23 per cent Tuesday; 40 per cent Wednesday; 20 per cent Thursday; 5 per cent Friday.

✳ You will always get the greatest recognition for the job you least like.

✳ A bus station is where a bus stops. A train station is where a train stops. On my desk, I have a workstation…

✳ A.S.A.P. means Always Say A Prayer.

✳ Ambition is a poor excuse for not having enough sense to be lazy.

✳ Can I trade my job for what's behind door number one?

✳ He who hesitates is probably right.

✳ I haven't lost my mind. It's backed up on disk somewhere.

✳ If I worked as much as others, I would do as little as they.

✳ Many people quit looking for work when they find a job.

✳ Mental backup in progress – Do Not Disturb!

✳ No one is listening until you make a mistake.

✳ On the keyboard of life, always keep one finger on the escape key.

✳ Once you've climbed the ladder of success, you're over the hill.

✳ The more crap you put up with, the more crap you're going to get.

✳ To err is human. To forgive is not company policy.

✳ Today's mighty oak is just yesterday's acorn that held its ground.

work and business: redundancy

A boss approaches his four employees and tells them he has to fire one of them. The black employee replies, 'I'm a protected minority.' The female employee replies, 'And I'm a woman.' The oldest employee says, 'Fire me, buster, and I'll hit you with an age discrimination suit.' Everyone turns to look at the young white guy. He thinks for a moment then says, 'I think I might be gay...'

My father came home and told us he'd been fired. His company had replaced him with a machine that was able to do everything he could, but do it much, much better. The tragic thing was my mother went out and bought one too.

❦ WORK AND BUSINESS: SECRETARIES

❋ 'I had two secretaries, one to answer my letters, the other to send locks of hair to my admirers. I have had to let them both go, poor fellows: one is in hospital with writer's cramp, and the other is quite bald.' *Oscar Wilde*

❋ A secretary in an office runs out of typing paper and asks what she should do. Her colleagues tell her to use copier machine paper instead. So she takes her last remaining blank piece of paper, puts it on the photocopier, and starts running out blank copies.

❋ Did you hear about the secretary who hung her dress behind the office door, then took her boss to the cleaner's?

❋ Sherry the secretary walks into her boss's office and says, 'I'm afraid I've got some bad news for you.' 'Sherry,' says her boss. 'Why do you always have to give me bad news? Try to be more positive.' 'Okay,' replies Sherry. 'The good news is you're not sterile...'

✳ Did you hear about the typist who lost all her fingers in an accident? She was rehired as a shorthand writer.

✳ Film producer Samuel Goldwyn's secretary told him their files had become so crowded they'd have to destroy all correspondence more than six years old. 'Okay,' said Goldwyn. 'But be sure to make copies.'

✳ There's an important meeting at the corporation and one by one each of the directors and executives are summoned for an interview with the managing director. Finally only the most junior executive is left. He enters the MD's office and sits down. 'Young man,' says the MD. 'Have you had sexual relations with Miss Jones, my secretary?' 'No, sir,' says the executive. 'Not even a quick fling at an office party?' queries the MD. 'No, sir. Never,' replies the executive. 'So you've never laid a finger on her?' says the MD. 'Not once,' replies the executive. 'Excellent,' replies the MD. 'In that case you can be the one who tells her she's fired.'

✳ Two secretaries are talking about their work. 'I hate filing,' says one. 'No matter how careful I am, I can never find the papers I'm looking for. I forget where I've put them.' 'I used to have that problem too,' replies her friend. 'Now I make 26 copies of everything I type and file one under each letter of the alphabet.'

worms

How can you tell which end of a worm is which? Tickle it in the middle and see which end laughs.

Why don't worms have balls? They can't dance.

☻YOU KNOW IT'S GOING TO BE A BAD DAY WHEN...

✳ ...you wake up, discover your waterbed has sprung a leak... and then remember you don't have a waterbed.

✳ ...you find your son's Action Man doll dressed in drag.

✳ ...you put your bra on backwards and it fits better.

✳ ...you start to pick up the clothes you wore home from the party last night – and can't find any.

✳ ...you turn on the news and they are showing escape routes out of the city.

✳ ...the bird singing outside your window is a vulture.

✳ ...you call the Samaritans and they put you on hold.

✳ ...you discover that your child's idea of humour is putting super glue in your haemorrhoid lotion.

✳ ...your horn sticks on the motorway behind 32 Hell's Angels.

✳ ...you realise that the phone number written on the wall of the public lavatory is for your wife's mobile.

✳ ...you compliment the boss's wife on her unusual perfume and she isn't wearing any.

✳ ...your four-year-old tells you that it's almost impossible to flush a grapefruit down the toilet.

zebras

What did the idiot call his pet zebra? Spot!

🐛zoos

✳ A zookeeper sees a visitor throwing five-pound notes into the monkey enclosure. 'What are you doing that for?' asks the keeper. 'The sign says it is okay,' replies the visitor. 'No, it doesn't,' says the keeper. 'Yes, it does,' replies the visitor. 'It says, "Do not feed. £5 fine."'

※ Two old ladies visit a zoo. They go to the giraffe enclosure and see a male standing by the fence. 'Look at the size of its balls,' says one old lady. 'Y'know, I think I could squeeze them from here.' So saying she reaches through the bars of the enclosure, grabs the giraffe's balls and clenches her fist. The giraffe's eyes open wide, it lets out a bellow, leaps out of the enclosure, and dashes off. A zoo-keeper runs over. 'What's happened?' he says. 'What did you do?' The old ladies tell him they squeezed the giraffe's balls. The keeper says, 'Well, you'd better squeeze mine too. I'm going to have to catch the bastard.'

※ What's the difference between a zoo in England, and a zoo in Ethiopia? In an English zoo there's an information board outside each enclosure telling you about the animals inside. In an Ethiopian zoo they do the same – but include a recipe.

ZZZEEE LAST JOKES

※ 'Go and never darken my towels again!' *Groucho Marx*

※ 'In summing up, I wish I had some kind of affirmative message to leave you with, I don't. Would you take two negative messages? My mother used to say to me when I was younger, "If a strange man comes up to you, and offers you candy, and wants you to get into the back of his car with him…GO!"' *Woody Allen*